A Guide to
Graphic
Organizers
second edition

*To my wife and friend, Gerry, for the many years of
support and quiet when I am locked away in my
office preparing a manuscript, sometimes grumpy with writer's block
but always ready for another great meal to reinvigorate my thoughts.*

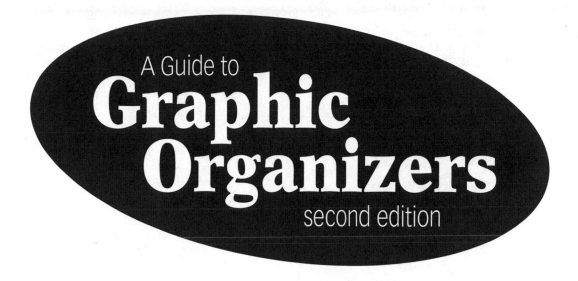

A Guide to
Graphic
Organizers
second edition

**Helping Students Organize and
Process Content for Deeper Learning**

Second Edition of
The Cooperative Think Tank
and
The Cooperative Think Tank II

James Bellanca

CORWIN PRESS
A SAGE Publications Company
Thousand Oaks, CA 91320

For information:

Corwin Press
A Sage Publications Company
2455 Teller Road
Thousand Oaks, California 91320
www.corwinpress.com

Sage Publications Ltd.
1 Oliver's Yard
55 City Road
London, EC1Y 1SP
United Kingdom

Sage Publications India Pvt. Ltd.
B 1/I 1 Mohan Cooperative
 Industrial Area
Mathura Road, New Delhi 110 044
India

Sage Publications Asia-Pacific Pte. Ltd.
33 Pekin Street #02-01
Far East Square
Singapore 048763

Printed in the United States of America.

Library of Congress Cataloging-in-Publication Data

Bellanca, James A., 1937-
A guide to graphic organizers: helping students organize and process content for deeper learning / James Bellanca.—2nd ed.
    p. cm.
Includes bibliographical references and index.
ISBN 978-1-4129-5299-6 (cloth)
ISBN 978-1-4129-5300-9 (pbk.)
  1. Graphic organizers. I. Title.

LB1044.88.B45 2007
371.39—dc22

2006103448

This book is printed on acid-free paper.

07 08 09 10 11 10 9 8 7 6 5 4 3 2 1

Acquisitions Editor:	Cathy Hernandez
Editorial Assistant:	Megan Bedell
Production Editor:	Veronica Stapleton
Copy Editor:	Dorothy Hoffman
Typesetter:	C&M Digitals (P) Ltd.
Proofreader:	Carole Quandt
Indexer:	Michael Ferreira
Cover Designer:	Scott Van Atta
Graphic Designer:	Karine Hovsepian

Contents

Preface

During my author's break (trying to undo writer's block) I walked downstairs into the basement room. Carpenters Garcia and Ian were readying studs for the divider wall. Ian was using the portable power saw while Garcia turned up the pressure on the power drill. Around the perimeter of the ceiling, I noticed a red beam of light.

"Wow," I exclaimed. "Lots of power. What's the red light?"

Garcia looked up. "That's a laser level. It makes sure we have the top of the new walls even all around."

"Yep," added Ian. "My grandfather sure could have used that in our house."

"Do these tools really make a difference?" I asked.

Garcia nodded. "Cuts our work time in half and we are a lot more accurate."

"Power." "Accuracy." "Speed." "The right tools." These words resonated with me. The parallels between the carpenters' up-to-date power tools, their increased efficiency, precision and accuracy seemed apt descriptors for some of the points I wanted to make about graphic organizers. What better way to describe what happens when teachers provide students with tools that make learning easier, thinking sharper and more precise, and results more powerful?

A LITTLE HISTORY

Way back when, actually in the mid-1970s, I met my first graphic organizer. I was participating in a values clarification workshop with Merrill Harmin, Sidney Simon, and Howie Kirschenbaum. Among the many practical strategies they taught, I latched on to the "Sunburst," a visual for brainstorming created (as far as I know) by Robert Hawley. With my Senior English students at New Trier High School (Illinois), the sunburst was an instant success.

Through my years of teaching, creating and directing two alternative schools, leading a regional education service center, and founding SkyLight Professional Development, I developed my interest in best instructional practices. Long before research validated my intuitions about the power of strategic teaching, I had collected an array of graphic organizers. In 1990, I combined graphic organizers with cooperative learning to publish *Cooperative Think Tank I*, soon followed by *Cooperative Think Tank II*.

Since those publications, much has happened in the field of strategic instruction. Robert Marzano and his associates at the Mid-continent Research for Education and Learning Education Laboratory concluded a meta-analysis to identify those research-supported best practices that

Sunburst

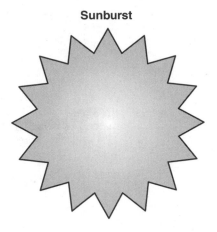

produced the largest effect sizes for student achievement. Included among these top-notch strategies were nonlinguistic representations, cooperative learning, questioning and cueing, and hypothesizing. In the strategy labeled "nonlinguistic representations," graphic organizers stand out as one of the most highly effective achievement-producing tactics.

Beyond the achievement research, brain research has validated the value of graphic organizers as a tool that enhances learning, especially among those students who are classified in Howard Gardener's *Theory of Multiple Intelligences* as "visual-spatial learners."

THE CURRENT STATE

Today, most textbook publishers, many professional development consultants, and even some software developers advocate the use of graphic organizers in daily instruction. Teachers from kindergarten to college have listened and learned. For the most part, their use of these tools is well thought out. In some others, misconceptions and inappropriate use foil their benefits.

THE PURPOSES FOR THIS REVISED EDITION

First, the time is right! It is time to update information about the many new and useful organizers that have emerged since 1990. It is time to identify the strong and consistent research behind this very sensible, practical, and easy-to-use teaching tool. It is time to put this tool into the context of those other high-effects instructional strategies that truly make a difference in student learning, promote teacher wisdom, and communicate the joy in learning. Like carpenters, surgeons, and others who have benefited from new tools that increase the quality of their work, so too can teachers.

Second, the needs are great. What are these needs? Novice teachers and seasoned veterans need to have ready at hand a single source that they can rely on as they make instructional choices for their daily power lessons. Such lessons will provide teachers with the best means to promote improvements in how and what students learn.

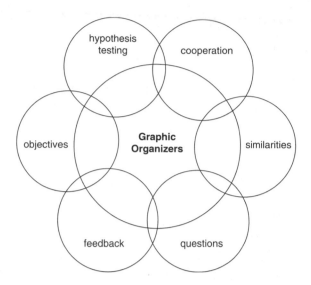

There is also a need to provide teachers with the research, the theory base, and sensible advice that have emerged in the last decade that allow them to use their new tools well. Such advice indicates which strategies and tactics have the most impact on student achievement as well as the "how to." These are the supports teachers need when they are challenged by narrow interpretations of *No Child Left Behind,* low expectations of teaching ability by those who wish to reduce all teachers into script readers, and increased pressure to "cover" more material more quickly as the preface to the next standardized test.

In a time when funding is short for elaborate professional development, new programs, and text materials, no-frills instruction is needed. No-frills tools anchor no-frills instruction with tools that are easy to use but that provide power-packed results. Graphic organizers, usable on many levels, meet these criteria. There is no need for reams of paper to make multiple student copies, elaborate projection technology, or other tools that sap limited funds. At the very least, teachers can draw the organizer on the board and ask students to replicate it in their notes or copy it onto a large sheet of newsprint for group work. Once the students hear the simple procedures, they can use their textbooks to gather and make sense of the concepts they are studying. Not fancy. Not frilly.

THE VARIED USES OF GRAPHIC ORGANIZERS

Graphic Organizers are tools with many uses. They work in many situations.

In the Classroom

1. Used by teachers to organize classroom discussions. (e.g., As students talk, teachers collect the information in an organized pattern such as the Web or Sunburst.)

2. Used by students to complete a task within a single lesson. (e.g., Students use a comparison Venn to understand the relationships between two characters in a story.)

3. Used by students as a learning tool. (e.g., Students learn to use the organizer with homework and in multiple classroom tasks throughout the school year.)

4. Used by students as a cooperative learning tool that promotes "positive interdependence." (e.g., In each group, students create a PMI to assess a completed math assignment. They make a single chart that captures each student's ideas and feelings.)

5. Used by students to develop their thinking, problem solving, and metacognition. (e.g., Students work in cooperative groups with the Fishbone organizer and a variety of cause-effect problems. They reflect on ways to improve their causal thinking via this graphic organizer.)

In Professional Development

1. Teacher trainers "walk the talk." They include graphic organizers in their workshop designs to model and encourage active engagement. (e.g., Math teachers work in subject groups with a Tri-Pie to identify applications of new research on best math instruction practices.)

2. Teacher study groups review prior knowledge and update applications of graphic organizers. (e.g., Teacher grade-level teams select one organizer to add to students' repertoires of "learning-to-learn" tools.)

3. Teachers update their use of graphic organizers for studying in classes that are information based. (e.g., Mrs. Gonzalez is completing her certification on special education law, which is presented in lecture fashion. She reorganizes her notes using different organizers.)

In School Meetings

1. Principals present key information via a PowerPoint slide organized with a graphic. (e.g., To show the year's priorities, the principal uses a Ranking Ladder.)

2. Principals use organizers to foster a learning community. (e.g., The principal facilitates learning groups that use a Decision Maker's flow chart to promote agreement on new discipline rules.)

THIS BOOK'S STRUCTURE

This book is divided into two major sections. The first section combines a selection of those graphic organizers from *The Cooperative Think Tank I* and *The Cooperative Think Tank II* plus others developed since the last edition of these books. Feedback from teachers, professional developers, and teacher educators helped with this selection. The second section provides context for the learning theory, the research, NCLB, and other instructional strategies that deepen and extend students' learning. These include suggestions for best use of graphic organizers with cooperative learning, thinking processes, and assessment tactics.

SECTION I (CHAPTERS 1–24)

Each chapter in the first section is organized in a consistent pattern to illuminate the best use of the highlighted graphic organizer.

Title

Name of the organizer.

Learning Phase

This refers to the three stages of learning postulated by cognitive psychologist Reuven Feuerstein. Graphic organizers are especially important in the first two stages: gathering information and making sense of information (see Chapter 27). The most appropriate stage is provided, although some organizers may serve well in a second stage. Some uses of organizers' stages overlap.

Level of Difficulty

Three levels, based on feedback from teachers, are identified: Easy, Moderate, and Challenging. Use these markers as suggested guides. Save the challenging strategies for very able middle-grade students, or for high school students.

Purpose

What is the reason or benefit gained?

Thinking Process

What is the thinking process that is most facilitated by this organizer?

Organizer

This is a blank sample of the organizer. Frequently, numbers that appear in specific areas of the organizer align with the procedural use instructions that follow.

Appropriate Uses

This is a list of suggestions on specific ways teachers might use this organizer. These instructions apply to individual uses or learning group uses.

Key Vocabulary

These are words associated with the learning of the organizer. These words introduce students to the language of thinking. Teachers may select and adapt these words to the cognitive age of the students. Teachers also may add the words from the content topics they are teaching.

Lesson Design

This design incorporates other instructional tactics shown by research to impact student achievement. The design targets individual instruction. Teachers can add to the lesson's impact by adapting the design for use by learning groups (see Chapter 30) and by teaching for thinking and transfer (see Chapter 26).

Organizer Examples

Three sample organizers are presented: elementary, middle, and secondary. These present a visual picture of what a student-completed organizer might look like.

More Ideas

In this part, teachers can see ideas for using the organizer with topics and concepts in literacy, mathematics, science, social studies, and other areas. Although teachers may select any of these, the primary purpose of these lists is to stimulate teachers' thinking about like ideas from their own curricula.

Make Your Own

This blank provides a space to lay out the components of this organizer with material directly from the curriculum.

Your Ideas

This space allows teachers to select ideas from the above lists that may be best for their students, or to write in their own ideas for the content they can enrich with this organizer.

Graphic Organizer (Blank Master)

This provides teachers with a master to copy and distribute. It is preferable that teachers make an overhead copy to show students on the board or screen. This enables students to hand draw the pattern and sear it into their memory with habitual, independent use. When learning groups are using the pattern, assign a recorder to draw the pattern on a large sheet of newsprint (see Chapter 30). This encourages positive inter-dependence among group members, a necessary ingredient for building the team spirit in classrooms as learning communities.

SECTION II (CHAPTERS 25–32)

This section provides a discussion on specific elements and classroom uses of graphic organizers. Its intent is to help teachers enrich student learning by amplifying other research-supported concepts and practices that enhance instruction via graphic organizers. Each chapter discusses the theoretical constructs, the research, and the relationship of the practice to instruction by graphic organizers. In this context, each chapter also provides brief descriptions of these best practices.

Chapter 25: Invent Your Own Graphic Organizer

This chapter from the original *Cooperative Think Tank* encourages teachers to construct new organizers that may fit their curriculum more tightly.

Chapter 26: Graphic Organizers: Tools for Lifelong Thinking and Learning

This chapter discusses the importance of teaching students how to transfer use of graphic organizers across the curriculum and into non-school learning opportunities.

Chapter 27: Skillful Thinking Is Not an Accident

This chapter introduces the instructional framework for using graphic organizers as a tool to promote higher achievement through sharper think-ing. It introduces the three phases of learning outlined by cognitive psy-chologist Reuven Feuerstein and shows how graphic organizers can create more efficient learners in each phase.

Chapter 28: Promoting Students' Thinking About Their Thinking

For advocates of constructivism, metacognition is the *sine qua non* of learning. This chapter outlines the rationale and suggested approaches for making student reflection about their thinking a central element in every lesson that incorporates a graphic organizer.

Chapter 29: Developing the Quality of Student Thinking

This chapter introduces the role of cognitive functions as the quality indicators of highly efficient thinking. The chapter shows how teachers can identify student thinking with graphic organizers that is inhibited by undeveloped functions and suggests tactics to make the thinking more efficient.

Chapter 30: Using Graphic Organizers With Learning Groups

Building on the original model for using graphic organizers in cooperative learning groups, this chapter presents practical suggestions for imbedding graphic organizers in every lesson.

Chapter 31: The Multiple Uses of Graphic Organizers in Assessment

This chapter presents a matrix model of assessment. It demonstrates how teachers can incorporate graphic organizers into their assessment of content, cooperation, and cognition.

Chapter 32: No Child Left Behind and Research

Myths abound about use of graphic organizers in the context of the No Child Left Behind (NCLB) legislation. This chapter illustrates how and why graphic organizers are an essential component in any classroom lesson with the purpose of increasing student achievement with scientifically researched tools.

APPENDIX

The Appendix provides a list of URLs, directing readers to Web sites with helpful information on graphic organizers, thinking, and brain research.

WHAT'S NEW? A SUMMARY

This new edition combines two books into one and expands the discussion of key components that will enrich the instructional use of graphic organizers. In addition to modifications in the presentation of every organizer, this edition includes five new organizers with full exposition (made possible by "selective abandonment" of five organizers used less often in classrooms). It also provides up-to-date and content-centered suggestions for uses of each graphic organizer in key areas of the curriculum.

Most notable is the addition of the second section. From a brief discussion of cooperative learning in the early editions, this section has grown to include deeper discussions of the cognitive connection, achievement and brain research, NCLB, and assessment. In the first editions, the research on graphic organizers was just emerging. That was also true of sound studies on other instructional strategies that have since become staples of the best practice literature.

ACKNOWLEDGMENTS

The foundation for this book is built on Reuven Feuerstein's important Theory of Structural Cognitive Modifiability. That theory is the alpha and omega for empowering students to use graphic organizers. From the time that I met Reuven in the mid-1990s, he has proven to be a gracious mentor and dear friend, helping me to understand the "why" that underpins the "what" and "how" of cognitive development.

I must also recall other mentors and friends who have mediated my thinking about thinking over the years. Teaching the value of rigorous knowledge and student-centered instruction to a young English teacher, Bob and Peg Pink, Mary Ida McGuire, Rose Morrow, Arline Paul, and Bob Applebaum helped form my beliefs. Howie Kirschenbaum, Barbara Glaser, Joel and Margie Goodman, Eliot Masie, Sid Simon and Merrill Harmin supported the early steps on my pathway as a professional developer and author. In the ensuing years, Roger and David Johnson, Richard Foster, Howard Gardener, Madeline Hunter, Art Costa, Ron Brandt, and Bernice McCarthy all shared insights that deepened my understanding of teaching and learning practices.

Each time I work with this material, I have to think of colleague and friend Robin Fogarty. Her devotion to thinking and espousal of professional development that empowers teachers to "seek out the skylight" prompted her to encourage the writing of the first editions of this book.

Next, I must thank those who have helped most with this revised edition, beginning with my editor, Cathy Hernandez, whose succinct guidance of the feedback process started with her own sharp-eyed assessment. Close behind came her selection of a reviewers' panel marked most by their in-depth knowledge of instruction and professional development. Their reviews were thorough, precise, and most helpful in guiding the changes for this revision. And they were gentle on my ego!

On the practical side, I must thank Mary Jane Bloethner and Donna Ramirez for their usual attention to detail and their computer skills in preparing the sample organizers for text. In this same category, I thank my youngest, Kate, who polished the form of my citations and bibliography.

Finally, accolades go to the many teachers, colleagues, and friends who have discussed instruction, provided new organizers, and challenged my thinking with their very constructive feedback.

—Jim Bellanca

PUBLISHER'S ACKNOWLEDGMENTS

Corwin Press gratefully acknowledges the contributions of the following reviewers:

Yolanda Abel, Instructor of Teacher Preparation
Johns Hopkins University, Baltimore, MD

Kathryn Abels, Exceptional Children Resource Teacher
Bishop Spaugh Community Academy, Charlotte, NC

Sherry L. Annee, Biotechnology and Biology Teacher
Brebeuf Jesuit Preparatory School, Indianapolis, IN

Robbie Burke, Social Science Teacher
Taylor Street Middle School, Griffin, GA

Randy Cook, Physics and Chemistry Teacher
Tri County High School, Howard City, MI

Debbie Fowler, English Teacher
Hart County High School, Munfordville, KY

Leslie Hughes, Seventh and Eighth Grade English Teacher
Saint Joseph School, Crescent Springs, KY

Roger T. Johnson, Professor of Science Education Curriculum and
    Instruction
University of Minnesota, Minneapolis, MN

Michelle Kocar, Principal
Avon Heritage South Elementary School, Avon, OH

T. Lee, Sixth Grade Gifted ELL Social Studies, Civics, and English
    Teacher
Belvedere Middle School, Los Angeles, CA

Honorine D. Nocon, Assistant Professor of Education
University of Colorado, Denver, CO

Mara Sapon-Shevin, Professor of Inclusive Education—Teaching and
    Leadership Programs
Syracuse University, Syracuse, NY

About the Author

James Bellanca founded SkyLight Professional Development in 1982. As its president, he mentored more than a dozen author/consultants as he led SkyLight in pioneering the use of strategic teaching and comprehensive professional development. Prior to meta-analyses that marked the effectiveness of cooperative learning, graphic organizers, and other cognitive strategies on student achievement, he coauthored more than a dozen textbooks that advocated the application of these tools across the curriculum with the theme "Not just for the test but for a lifetime of learning." Currently, he is building on the theories of cognitive psychologist Reuven Feuerstein to develop more effective responses to the learning needs of those low-performing students whose academic achievement continues to lag behind those who have greater learning advantages.

Topic: _____		
K	W	L

1

KWL

APPROPRIATE USES

1. At the start of a lesson or unit, to help students recall what they think they already know or what they learned in a prior lesson. Prior knowledge collection can focus on any one of the following:

- Use learning tool (e.g., the Web, a Word program).
- Use a thinking process (e.g., analyzing, predicting).
- Use content (mathematics, literacy, science, music).
- Use a cooperative learning strategy (think-pair-share).
- Use a cognitive function (reflection) or deficiency (impulsivity).
- Use an instructional tactic (think-pair-share).

2. At the end of a unit to help students capture what they learned about the focus point.

Key Vocabulary

Prior, gather, brainstorm

Attribution

Donna Ogle introduced the KWL into classrooms in 1986. Others have added additional letters such as "H" for "How we will learn."

LESSON DESIGN

Check Prior Knowledge of the KWL Organizer

1. Show the KWL for all to see. Ask how many have used the KWL. (If none, go on to explain its purpose.)

2. Ask for volunteers to tell how they used the KWL and how it helped them learn the material.

Explain the KWL's Purpose

1. The KWL is an organizer to help students check their prior knowledge of a topic, concept, or process before learning about it. With this prior knowledge, the brains of the students will recall what they already know (the K of KWL) about the topic. When they get new information, students will use their brains to join the old knowledge with the new.

2. The second benefit of the KWL is to stir interest in what students also want (the W of KWL) to know additionally about the topic. The best students are those who ask questions!

3. The third benefit is to provide a chance for students at the end of a lesson to look back and assess what they learned in the lesson.

Clarify and Model the Task

1. Introduce the topic of the day's and/or week's lesson. Teachers may use the title of the next textbook chapter or ask a "launch question" about the topic.

2. Show the organizer for all to see. Explain the parts (K column, W column, and L column). Start with K column (what we think we know about the topic).

3. Group students into trios. Starting with the shortest person in each trio and working to the tallest, assign the roles of presenter, recorder, and manager. Review responsibilities of each (pp. 216–217) and the DOVE guidelines (p. 216).

4. Provide each recorder with a large sheet of newsprint (or butcher paper) and markers. Instruct the recorder to make a large KWL similar to the model.

5. Invite each trio to brainstorm all they think they know about the topic or the launch question. Take just two or three responses. Repeat the process with the "What do we want to know about this topic?" in the W column.

Complete the Task

1. Instruct each trio to continue brainstorming in each of these columns.

2. When several of the learning groups have completed the tasks, stop the work and invite one group from the back of the classroom to come to the front. Two will hold the completed chart and the recorder will read the K and the W lists.

3. Invite other students to add different items to the learning group's lists. Likewise, they can add all items on their own list.

4. Instruct the recorder to keep the list for the group. The groups will return to these lists at the end of the lesson.

5. During the lesson, highlight any material that relates to the questions posed.

6. At the end of the lesson, instruct each group to rotate its three roles so that each student has a different job.

7. Invite the trios to brainstorm what they learned in this lesson (the L of KWL). They should check to see that they learned all the items under "W" and add anything else not on the original lists.

Guide Reflection

1. **Focus on Content.** Match trios together into learning groups of six. Invite each trio to share its "learned list" telling what was important about each item in relation to the topic of the lesson (e.g., "The Continental Congress was important because . . . ," "Harriet Tubman played a key role in American history because . . .").

2. **Focus on Process.** In the learning groups of six, the group will select one member who was not yet the recorder during this lesson for that role. In turn, each member (starting with the person sitting to the right of the recorder) will complete the sentence, "When using the KWL, I learned that. . . ." (The recorder will list these responses on a new sheet of newsprint.)

3. If time allows, do a round robin of the recorders. Each will select two items from the list to share with the class.

KWL ORGANIZER EXAMPLES

Elementary Grade Example

Topic: <u>Mathematics: Addition</u>

K	W	L
numbers, plus, and side by side, columns, two digits	how to add nickels, how to add decimals, how to add dimes	how to add money (pennies to quarters), how to add decimals, how multiplication is additional

Middle Grade Example

Topic: <u>Technology: PowerPoint</u>

K	W	L
slides, motion, sound, flow, images, charts	photographs, less words, rehearsal, sending by mail, auto-content wizard	templates, photographs, practicing, sending by mail, outlines, wizards, spell check, text boxes, designs

Secondary Grade Example

Topic: <u>The Underground Railroad</u>

K	W	L
Harriet Tubman, safe houses, abolitionists, Canada	dangers, accomplishments, states, other people involved, effect on Lincoln	Frederick Douglass, Susan B. Anthony, Emancipation Proclamation, routes, places

MORE IDEAS

Elementary Grade Examples

Mathematics: Mixed numbers, sets, diagrams

Language Arts: Aesop's Fables, Chitty Chitty Bang Bang, Winnie the Pooh

Science: Solids, liquids and gases, thermometer, sources of energy

Social Studies: Maps, tables, graphs, geographic features of our state

Other: Nations of the world in our classroom (e.g., Nigeria, Croatia, Italy, Tibet), where I have lived (e.g., New York, Danville, Indianapolis, San Jose, Mexico City), where I have visited (Disney World, Gettysburg, my grandmother's house)

Middle Grade Examples

Mathematics: Measuring temperature, finding the mean, plane shapes

Language Arts: Wind in the Willows, writing a story, comparing two characters in a story

Science: Healthy food, life in a river, NASA

Social Studies: Cliff dwellers, early explorers of America, the Boston Tea Party

Other: Melodic notation, two-part harmony, Hispanic influences on American sculpture

Secondary Grade Examples

Mathematics: Limits of values of functions, proof of the chain rule, conditional probability

Language Arts: Figurative language, soliloquy, Nathaniel Hawthorne

Science: Nuclear fusion, asteroids, Newton's Second Law

Social Studies: The fall of the Roman Empire, apartheid, Machu Picchu

Other: American jazz, George Balanchine, Bob Fosse

Make Your Own

Topic: _____

K	W	L

Your Ideas

_____

_____

_____

_____

_____

_____

_____

_____

_____

KWL Graphic Organizer

Topic: _____		
K	W	L

2
Web

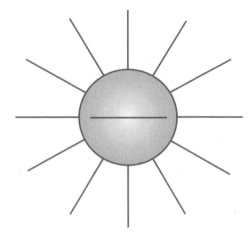

APPROPRIATE USES

1. Use a web as an advance organizer to gather prior knowledge for a new unit via student brainstorming or think-pair-share.

2. Use in learning groups of three to gather information from print or video materials in response to a specific, but open-ended declaration such as "find as many examples as you can of words with the root 'struct'" or "Identify the character's traits that appear in this chapter."

3. Use it to gather responses from a think-pair-share question. Show the web on the board or projection screen for all to see and copy in their notebooks.

4. Use a web to collect brainstormed advantages or disadvantages of a way of doing a task or accomplishing a goal.

5. Invite each student to make a web of key ideas or events from a lesson. Use the gathered ideas to prepare a summary of the day's learning.

6. Use as an assessment tool for the class to brainstorm what they learned or did well in completing a task.

Key Vocabulary

Traits, characteristics, attributes, summary, brainstorm, prior

Attribution

Introduced by Robert Hawley as the "sunburst" in Simon, Kirschenbaum, and Howe's *Values Clarification: A Handbook of Practical Strategies for Teachers and Students* (Dodd-Mead, 1978).

LESSON DESIGN

Check Prior Knowledge of the Web Organizer

Show a sample for all to see. Call for a show of hands to each question.

a. Ask how many have used a web in other classes.

b. Ask how many use the web on their own as a study or learning tool.

c. Ask for volunteers to explain the purpose and benefits of using a web. Enter the answers on the displayed web.

Explain the Web's Purpose

The web is used best for gathering information from prior knowledge through brainstorming or from printed materials. In this lesson, explain how you will address both purposes.

Clarify and Model the Task

1. Divide the class into pairs with a minimal amount of movement. As you explain the task step by step, model use of the web on the board.

2. Instruct students to draw a web in their notebooks. In the center of the webs, students will write the "key word" or topic that you assign for this lesson. You may assign the same word for all or a different word for each pair.

3. Instruct students to find examples of the key word or topic in the reading material you have selected (e.g., from a book, duplicated handout, or magazines). Check for understanding by soliciting examples from the first few paragraphs of the material you selected.

4. Allow time for students to read the first three paragraphs and then ask for examples.

Complete the Task

1. Walk among the pairs and coach as needed. Focus feedback on the quantity of ideas generated in each pair.

2. After the allotted time, invite randomly selected representatives of the pairs to contribute to your master web that all can see. Take one idea per pair for an unduplicated organizer. If important details or concepts are missing, add them after the students have exhausted their contributions.

Guide Reflection

1. **Focus on Content.** Ask "What do you think is the most important information that you have gathered?" and "Why do you think so?" Use wait-time and provide the opportunity for each student to respond (see p. 207).

2. **Focus on Thinking.** Ask "What did you do well in the gathering step?" and "How could you improve your information gathering?" Focus on those students who did not have a chance to respond to the content questions.

WEB ORGANIZER EXAMPLES

Elementary Grade Example

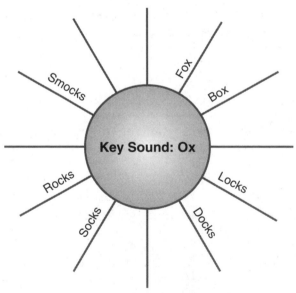

Reading: A Rhyming Web

Middle Grade Example

Language Arts: Elements in a Sentence

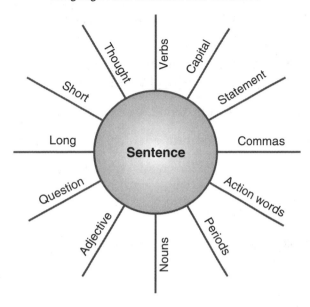

Secondary Grade Example

Social Studies: Hispanic-American Heroes

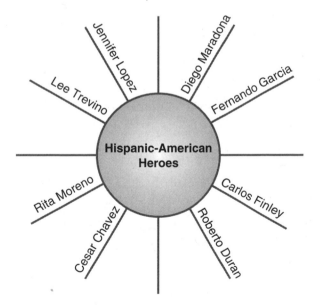

MORE IDEAS

Elementary Grade Examples

Mathematics: Operations with numbers, geometric shapes, types of word problems

Language Arts: Parts of speech, characteristics of the three Billy Goats Gruff, words to describe "my best school work"

Science: Mountains, healthy food, dinosaurs

Social Studies: Our neighborhood, our state, my culture

Other: Safety rules, books I've read, study skills

Middle Grade Examples

Mathematics: Algebraic symbols, factoring strategies, scientific applications of math

Language Arts: Public speaking skills, topics for journal writing, events in "The Most Dangerous Game"

Science: Tsunamis, chemical compounds, electricity

Social Studies: Rosa Parks, the Trail of Tears, Pearl Harbor

Other: Reasons to go to college, ways to win friends

Secondary Grade Examples

Mathematics: Algebraic functions, ways to represent data, ratio and proportion

Language Arts: The novels of James Baldwin, Carson McCullers's short story "Like That"

Science: Rocks, winter weather in our town, bacteria

Social Studies: Mexican culture, politics in our state, values of democracy

Other: Advantages of service learning, service projects, standards for a project

Make Your Own

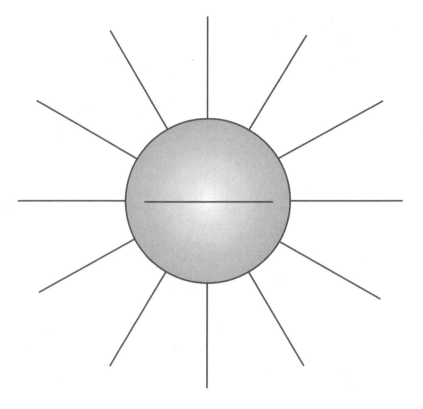

Your Ideas

_____

_____

_____

_____

_____

_____

_____

_____

Web Graphic Organizer

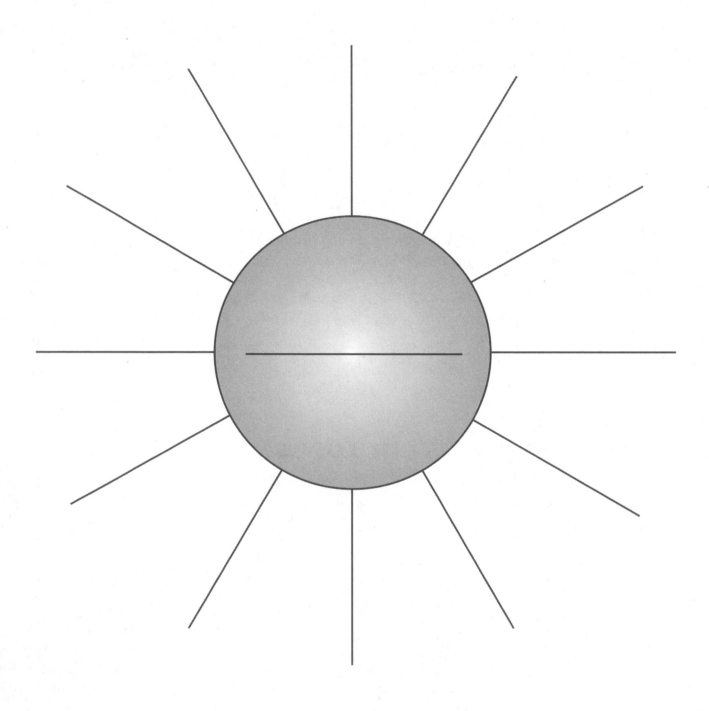

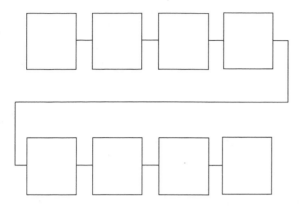

Sequence Chart

3

APPROPRIATE USES

1. Use as an advance organizer to check and organize known information about a topic in the curriculum.

2. As students are reading nonfiction or fiction passages, teach students to use the sequence chart
   - To place events from literature or history in order of time
   - To place science or math procedures in order of performance
   - To place writing procedures in order of performance
   - To make predictions about next events in a story
   - To form an hypothesis about the outcome of a scientific experiment, an historic event or a story plot.

3. Use completed sequence charts as tool to initiate a written summary of events.

Learning Phase: Gathering information

Level of Difficulty: Easy

Purpose: To enable students to place events or procedures into a sequential order

Thinking Process: Sequencing

Key Vocabulary

Sequence, chronological, problem

Attribution

Developed by the author

LESSON DESIGN

Check Prior Knowledge of the Sequence Chart Organizer

1. Show the blank sequence chart for all to see.

2. Ask how many have used this organizer. Check to estimate skill level of its users.

On the blackboard or overhead, list the following dates: 1492, 2003, 1941, 1776, 1865. Ask the students to put the dates in chronological order from the earliest to the present. Ask a volunteer to come to the board and make the order. Ask the students to identify a major event associated with each event.

1492: Columbus lands in the Americas.

1776: The Declaration of Independence is signed.

1865: Lee Surrenders, ending Civil War.

1941: Pearl Harbor is attacked; United States enters World War II.

2001: 9/11 Attack on World Trade Center occurs.

Explain the Sequence Chart's Purpose

1. Explain how each event that occurs in time sets up an order called a sequence of events. It is important to learn how to sequence events or tasks in time order (chronological) when studying and working in almost any field.

2. Using the list of historic events above as an example, fill in the sequence chart.

Clarify and Model the Task

1. Select an age-appropriate story (e.g., Elementary: "The Lion and the Mouse"; Upper Grades: *The Discovery of Radium* by Madame Curie). Ask a student to tell you the problem or challenge the main character faces.

- **The Problem:** Madame Curie was looking for the source of uranium rays.
- **The Events:** Ask the class to make a list or use a web to identify as many events in the story as they can recall. Record these events for

all to see in whatever order they emerge, but not in chronological order.

o Studied different compounds.
o Measured with electrometer.
o Searched for lab space.
o Examined different materials.
o Discovered amount of material was different.
o Hypothesized that combination of elements made for rays.
o Found a closet for a lab.

The Sequence Chart: Invite the class to place the items on the chart (no more than one item suggested by one student and only one item per box).

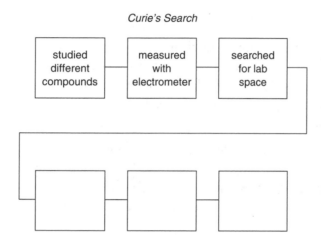

Curie's Search

2. Check for understanding of the process used by asking several students to explain the procedure in order (e.g., problem, events list, order by number, chart to see).

Complete the Task

1. After all agree that the items are in the correct order or sequence, divide the class into groups of three. Assign a recorder, reader, and checker/encourager in each group. (Make the student with the smallest shoe size the recorder and work to the largest as the checker/encourager. Allow students to have some good-natured fun by comparing shoe sizes in each group. After they have identified who has the largest shoe size, the smallest, and so on, assign a role to each "size.")

2. Assign the short story (literature) or historic events (social studies chapter).

3. Distribute three blank sheets of 8.5 × 11 paper and a pencil to each group with spaces for date and student names. On the board, show the order of steps they are to follow. Use the labelers: First, Second, Third, plus a key word (e.g., "read") for each.

- *First:* Read the assigned material. The reader will read softly aloud as the others follow along.
- *Second:* Identify the problem, conflict, or challenge around which the events are built. The recorder may sketch a picture of the problem on one blank sheet and label it "#1: The Problem."
- *Third:* Select the six to eight most important events that lead to the solution of the problem.
- *Fourth:* On the second sheet, labeled "#2: The Events," fill in a sequence chart with mini-sketches of the events chosen.
- *Last:* Use two or three words as a label for each box.

4. Ask the group checkers to make sure that each member of the group can explain the chart.

Guide Reflection

1. **Reflect on Content.** Match groups of three to make groups of six. Ask each checker to explain the problem's sketch. Ask each recorder to explain the events. Ask the reader to check for understanding by the other group. If time allows after both groups have shared, they may discuss any differences noted.

2. **Reflect on Process.** Return the students to the groups of three. On the third sheet, labeled #3: "We learned," ask each member to write one thing learned about using the sequence chart. Give each group a paper clip to hold all three sheets assembled in numerical order.

SEQUENCE CHART ORGANIZER EXAMPLES

Elementary Grade Example

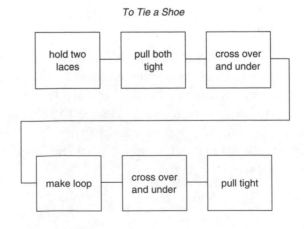

To Tie a Shoe

Middle Grade Example

To Find Information on the World Wide Web

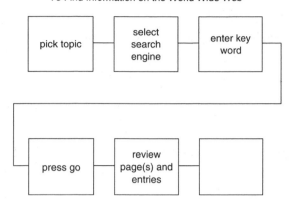

Secondary Grade Example

Life of Langston Hughes

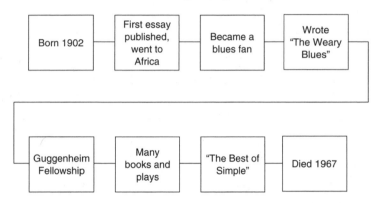

MORE IDEAS

Elementary Grade Examples

Mathematics: Doing a math operation, counting in sets of 10, counting in cardinal or ordinal sequence

Language Arts: Retelling events from a story; writing sequential summary of bus line up procedures, writing a recipe for a favorite food

Science: Putting step name on index card for experiments: floating objects, boiling water to cook an egg, catching butterflies, digestive system

Social Studies: Order the events as Washington crosses the Delaware, Lincoln frees the slaves, the life of Francisco Rojas

Other: Order procedures for boarding the school bus, hanging up winter coats, playing scrabble; drawing and/or sketching a friend's portrait

Middle Grade Examples

Mathematics: Solving an algebra problem, translating relationship words into math expressions (e.g., "5 less than x" to "x–5").

Language Arts: Writing a three-paragraph essay, plot line in a TV show (e.g., *Roots*) or movie (e.g., *West Side Story*), or plot line in a short story (e.g., "The Rocking Horse Winner")

Science: Procedures in a lab experiment for measuring weights, the life of astronaut Ellen Ochoa, the invention of the striking clock

Social Studies: Lives of famous Americans who broke racial barriers (e.g., Jesse Owens, Jackie Robinson, Rosa Parks, Cesar Chavez, Rita Moreno); "My Life's History," a video essay; "Labor Movement" in American timeline

Other: Preparing to play a competitive game (e.g. hockey championship, figure skating championship), cleaning a bedroom, cooking tacos

Secondary Grade Examples

Mathematics: Preparing an income tax statement, making a budget, measuring for a distance problem

Language Arts: Writing a research paper, the plot line of Julia Alvarez's *How the Garcia Girls Lost Their Accents*, the timeline of Edgar Allen Poe's short stories

Science: Invention of ground control radar, lab procedures for microscope use, life of Nobel Prize chemist Mario Molina

Social Studies: Battle of Waterloo, life of Chief Pontiac, California Gold Rush

Other: Maya Lin and the Vietnam War Memorial, the life and death of Selena, selecting a college

Make Your Own

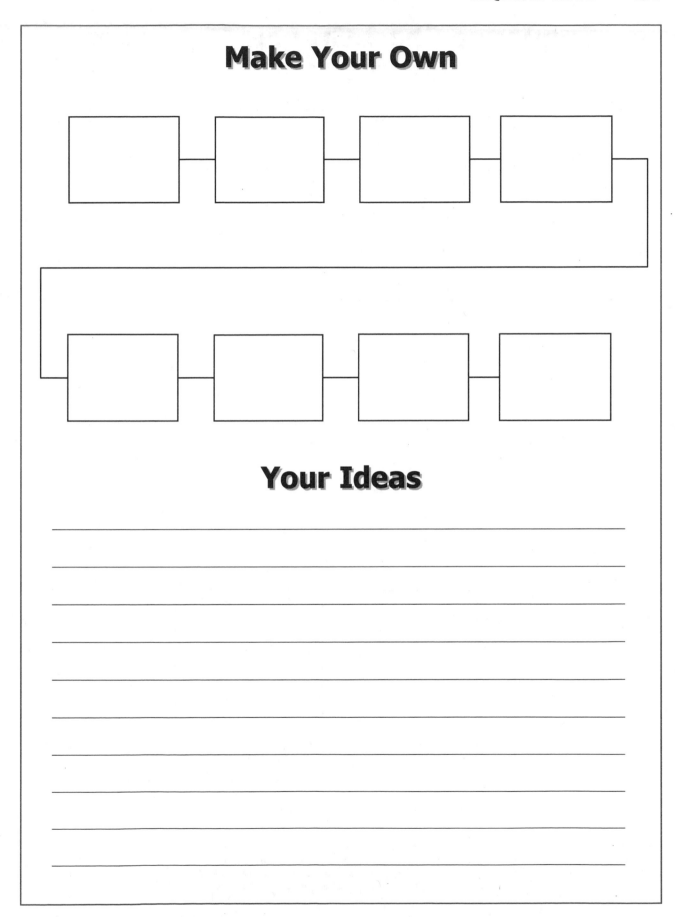

Your Ideas

_____

_____

_____

_____

_____

_____

_____

_____

_____

Sequence Chart Graphic Organizer

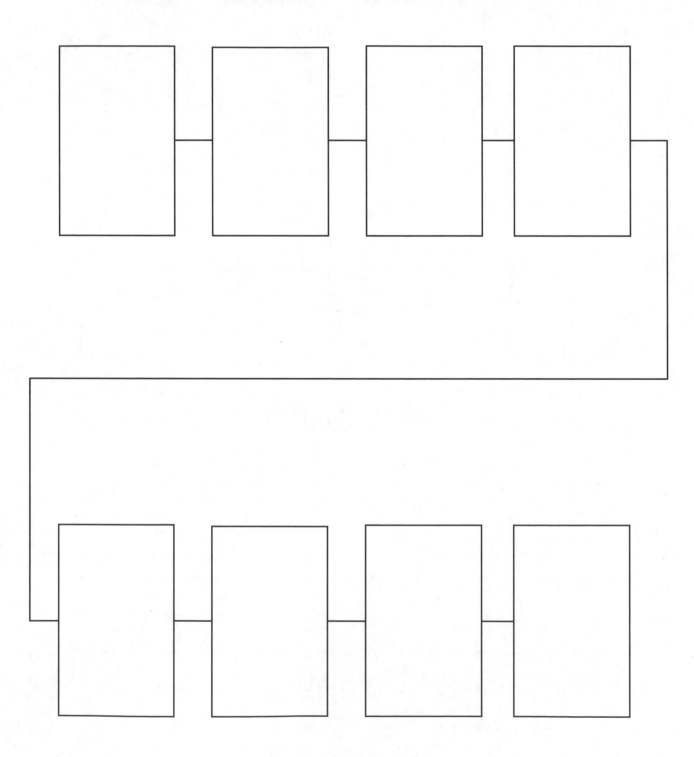

4

Starburst

APPROPRIATE USES

1. Use as an advance organizer for students to brainstorm prior knowledge by category.

2. Use as follow-up to the web organizer, after students have brainstormed possible categories and selected five. Use with ranking ladder to help students rank order top five group headings from ideas brainstormed on the web.

3. Use as prior knowledge follow-up to KWL using items ranked as most important to learn from W column.

4. Use as a prior knowledge check to classify information that students already know about subtopics in a new unit of study.

5. Use in middle of a lesson when students are having difficulty connecting facts or concepts to a central idea.

6. Use when you want students to gather information from class discussions or lectures. Post categories on the star, and then brainstorm ideas heard under the appropriate header.

7. Use to create a study guide for student notebooks.

Learning Phase:
Gathering information

Level of Difficulty:
Moderate

Purpose: To guide students' collection of data regarding different points of view, values, attributes, or themes

Thinking Process:
Classifying

8. Use as an advance organizer to prepare students to write a paragraph summary of the topic or seven-paragraph essay with five subheadings, beginning paragraph, and an ending paragraph.

9. Use to classify feedback during the assessment of a project or task.

Key Vocabulary

Attributes, differentiate, classify, prior, categories

Attribution

This organizer was developed by Robin Fogarty, *Brain Compatible Classrooms* (1997). Thousand Oaks, CA: Corwin Press.

LESSON DESIGN

Check Prior Knowledge of the Starburst Organizer

Show a blank starburst on the overhead or board. Ask students what they see and how it might be used to help them gather information about a topic.

Explain the Starburst's Purpose

To guide the collection of information for a topic or lesson by helping students differentiate subtopics and/or supportive facts.

Clarify and Model the Task

1. Write in the central topic. If using the organizer to gather information from a textbook chapter, enter the chapter title (#1). You may also ask students to footnote the author, source, and source data underneath the starburst. "Information taken from. . . ."

2. Using subtopics selected from the prior knowledge check or taken from your textbook's subheadings, show students where they will fill in the five subtopical blanks (#2–6).

3. If using pairs or threes in cooperative groups, review the DOVE guidelines. Distribute newsprint and markers and assign roles.

4. Allow sufficient time for all students to read no more than one-fifth of the reading material you have selected.

5. Ask students to give you specifics from the finished material that fit under the subheadings on the organizer. Use wait-time and distribution of opportunity to increase participation. When you receive a response, ask the student to put it under one heading. Check for agreement from the other students. If disagreement occurs, discuss the best placement.

6. After you have placed five or six sub-items, review the classifying process: What items go where on the starburst? Check for understanding of the classifying process (set up class or group name as the headings (#2–6), find details that fit under each header, explain reasons for placement with a key characteristic).

Complete the Task

1. Invite the students to continue reading the assigned material. As they read, they are to continue entering data on the appropriate "burst" of the star.

2. Walk among the students, monitor, coach, and encourage completion of the starburst.

Guide Reflection

1. Review the completed organizer. Return to the overhead or board with the model organizer you started. Invite random students to use their organizers to fill in the model. Check for agreement and understanding as needed. Encourage quotes from the printed material used and reasons for placements of details in a group.

2. If you intend for students to add this organizer to their repertoire of learning strategies and become skillful in using it as an information-gathering tool or to help them develop their classifying ability, review the targeted vocabulary (see preceding list), and prompt them "to think about their thinking" with a think-pair-share or a write-pair-share (see p. 209). "What did this organizer teach you about collecting and classifying data?"

STARBURST ORGANIZER EXAMPLES

Elementary Grade Example

Parents:
at home,
no uniform,
work hard,
friend, rules
about strangers,
bus stop

Teachers:
in school, books, smile,
work hard, no uniform,
friend, grade homework,
make us smart

Police Officers:
obey law, fight crime,
patrol traffic, friend,
badges, uniforms,
police car

Social Studies:
Safety Friends

Firefighters:
fires, helmets
and coats, fire
engine, water
hoses, danger,
inspect
schools,
alarm
bells

Paramedics:
when sick or hurt,
ambulance,
uniform,
badge,
on sleeve,
medicine

Middle Grade Example

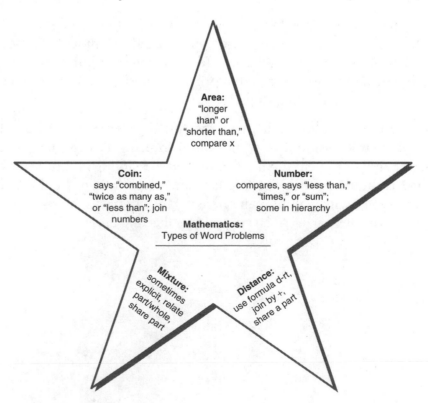

Area:
"longer
than" or
"shorter than,"
compare x

Coin:
says "combined,"
"twice as many as,"
or "less than"; join
numbers

Number:
compares, says "less than,"
"times," or "sum";
some in hierarchy

Mathematics:
Types of Word Problems

Mixture:
sometimes
explicit, relate
part/whole,
share part

Distance:
use formula d-rt,
join by +,
share a part

Secondary Grade Example

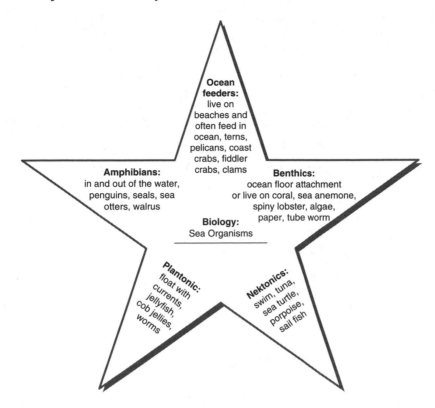

Ocean feeders: live on beaches and often feed in ocean, terns, pelicans, coast crabs, fiddler crabs, clams

Amphibians: in and out of the water, penguins, seals, sea otters, walrus

Benthics: ocean floor attachment or live on coral, sea anemone, spiny lobster, algae, paper, tube worm

Biology: Sea Organisms

Plantonic: float with currents, jellyfish, cob jellies, worms

Nektonics: swim, tuna, sea turtle, porpoise, sail fish

MORE IDEAS

Elementary Grade Examples

Mathematics: Spatial patterns, size patterns, money

Language Arts: Parts of a story, parts of speech, word families

Science: Food groups, dinosaurs, rockets

Social Studies: Good neighbors, safety rules, friends

Other: Art projects, healthy foods, favorite hobbies

Middle Grade Examples

Mathematics: Integers, polyhedrons, five laws of number operations, algebraic symbols

Language Arts: Expository writing guidelines with examples, short story characters, African American poets

Science: Body systems, human organs, storm forces

Social Studies: Cultures in America, maps and charts, periods of U.S. immigration

Other: Avoiding gangs, characteristics of good friends, body language effects

Secondary Grade Examples

Mathematics: Postulates, frequency tables, sampling techniques

Language Arts: Modern American women poets, characters in a play, Shakespearean heroes

Science: Geological faults, causes of global warming, laws of physics

Social Studies: Current economic theories, postwar recoveries, South Pacific migration patterns

Other: College choices, art movements, modern symphonies

Make Your Own

Your Ideas

_____

_____

_____

_____

_____

_____

_____

_____

Starburst Graphic Organizer

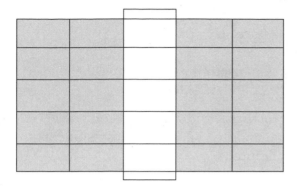

Gathering Grid

APPROPRIATE USES

1. Use as an advance organizer to capture prior knowledge on three or more similar items or concepts.

2. Use when reading textbook or other expository material to find similarities among three or more persons.

3. Use when collecting data about three or more physical objects.

4. Use when reading fiction to find similarities among three or more characters, events, places, or themes.

Key Vocabulary

Similar, distinguish, differentiate, infer, subtle, sort, traits

Attribution

Created by the author.

Learning Phase:
Gathering information

Level of Difficulty:
Medium

Purpose: To enable students to identify similarities among like persons, places, objects, events, or ideas by sorting attributes

Thinking Process: Sorting, identifying similarities

LESSON DESIGN

Check Prior Knowledge of the Gathering Grid Organizer

1. Show the grid. Name it and use a sample of a completed grid to show what goes in each part:
   - The shared attributes, qualities (state, party)
   - The item title (presidents)
   - The names or items for comparison (Bush, Reagan, etc.)
   - The specific descriptors (CIA, movies, etc.)

2. Ask for a show of hands: Who has seen or used this organizer? (If no hands go up, proceed. If some hands go up, invite those students to help with the explanation and procedures.)

Explain the Gathering Grid's Purpose

The grid is a tool for identifying and sorting similarities among like items (e.g., persons, places, events, concepts).

Clarify and Model the Task

1. Guide students through the information on the sample grid. Introduce the vocabulary words.

BUSH	REAGAN	PRESIDENTS	LINCOLN	WASHINGTON
50	50	states	kept as is	13 colonies
Republican	Republican	party	Republican	
Iraq	Grenada	war(s)	Civil	Revolutionary
CIA	movies	known for	Gettysburg Address	cherry tree

2. Put students into pairs. Instruct each pair to select a completed chapter in the textbook. Ask them to agree on the topic for sorting, the items for the top, and the attributes for the center column. Allow 5 minutes.

3. Invite several pairs to share their samples to check for understanding of the correct use of the gathering grid.

Complete the Task

1. Give each student a blank copy of the organizer (p. 38).

Assign the next chapter to read either as homework or as an in-class task. Before reading, provide students with the headers. Instruct them to read purposefully so they can select items to complete the blank spaces in the center column. If appropriate to the material they must read, add additional rows.

2. When the grids are complete, pair the students. Instruct them to compare grids and agree on any corrections they can. Allow 3 minutes.

3. Show the incomplete organizer on the board or overhead for all to see.

4. Ask students to identify the items of disagreement. Use a class discussion with equitable distribution of opportunity to resolve the conflicts. Complete the grid. Invite students to replicate the final grid.

Guide Reflection

1. **Focus on Content.** Invite students to participate in analyzing the grid to prepare for an essay that identifies the similarities among the items on the grid. Use the President's Grid (previous page) to illustrate how they should organize for this task. Column 1 in the figure on page 34 provides a sample. Column 2 provides an alternative sequence with paragraphs identified.

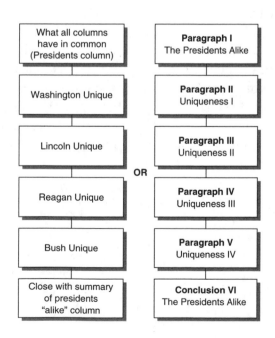

What all columns have in common (Presidents column)	**Paragraph I** The Presidents Alike
Washington Unique	**Paragraph II** Uniqueness I
Lincoln Unique	**Paragraph III** Uniqueness II
Reagan Unique	**Paragraph IV** Uniqueness III
Bush Unique	**Paragraph V** Uniqueness IV
Close with summary of presidents "alike" column	**Conclusion VI** The Presidents Alike

OR

- Divide the class into trios. Assign and review roles and responsibilities for cooperative learning groups (e.g., recorder, materials manager, reporter) and the DOVE guidelines (p. 216) for working together to achieve a common goal.
- Instruct the recorder to obtain newsprint, markers, and tape from the materials table. Show recorders how to transcribe the grid onto a large sheet of newsprint using the master sample (p. 38).
- Group members will agree on the sequence for this chart and fill in the items. Monitor their progress.
- After the groups are finished, ask for any two groups to show their chart and explain their sequence. Ask "why did you do _____?" Prompt clarity in their reasoning.
- Instruct each student to write a short essay using charts and the sequences. Invite each to prepare and outline for you to check. Do outlines in class, but assign the final essay as homework.
- Put students who have more difficulty preparing to write the essay into a single group and show them how to break apart the grid for use in the essay. Encourage them to delay editing (spell check, punctuation) until they have organized their ideas.

2. **Focus on Process.** Place students in new pairs. Ask each pair to write a set of procedures instructing a friend on how to set up a gathering grid.

Invite students, in pairs, to explain to each other how to prepare a grid. Alternate explanations of the four ingredients.

Write these instructions in a journal or on a sheet of 8.5 × 11 paper.

Assemble the pairs in groups of six. Each pair will read its list. The other pairs will add "missing" items to their lists. Each group of six will brainstorm a list of the benefits of the gathering grid as a tool for connecting ideas and showing similarities. Invite the group that has done the least sharing in this lesson to start. Identify as the reader for the group a student who is not the strongest reader in the group. Be encouraging and celebratory. Ask the other groups to add items that they have on their lists but not on the read list.

GATHERING GRID ORGANIZER EXAMPLES

Elementary Grade Example

My Friends

AMY	TONYA	COMMON CHARACTERISTICS	CRUZ	SUSAN
8	8	ages	9	8
Irish	Nigerian	cultural background	Guatamalan	German
TV games	her goldfish	hobby	none	dolls
soccer	brothers: 1, 0, 3, 1	shared interest	sisters: 0, 2, 1, 2	

Middle Grade Example

Sports

BASEBALL	BASKETBALL	ELEMENTS	FOOTBALL	HOCKEY
9	5	number of players	11	6
4 bases	basketball court	field/court	100-yard field	ice rink
bat, glove, ball	basketball	equipment	football/helmet	stick, puck
runs	baskets 2/1/3	scoring	3 points/7 points	goals
9 innings	4/15 min.	periods	4/15 min.	3/20 min.

Secondary Grade Example

Notable Chicanos

OSCAR ACOSTA	RODOLFO GONZALEZ	NAMES	DOLORES HUERTA	CESAR CHAVEZ
El Paso	Colorado	city/state born	New Mexico	Yuma, Arizona
Catolicas Por La Raza	War on Poverty	organization	United Farm Workers	NFWA
anti-poverty	civil rights	mission	civil rights	workers' rights
legal system	Vietnam War	issue	grape industry	pesticides

MORE IDEAS

Elementary Grade Examples

Mathematics: Numbers, coins, word problems

Language Arts: "The Three Little Pigs," *Madeline,* favorite author's books

Science: Rocks, dinosaurs, butterflies

Social Studies: Community helpers, famous presidents, bike rules

Other: Favorite games, favorite TV character, trips taken

Middle Grade Examples

Mathematics: Geometric shapes, word problems, operations with numbers

Language Arts: Favorite book, topics for writing, types of sentences

Science: Floatable objects, the planets, volcanoes, simple machines

Social Studies: Illegal substances, safety laws, cultures in this class

Other: Types of popular music, current clothes styles, pro sports teams

Secondary Grade Examples

Mathematics: Number operations review, equations, trigonometric functions

Language Arts: Types of poems, August Wilson's plays, local news reports

Science: causes of global warming, tectonic plates, properties of atoms

Social Studies: World wars, Native American tribes, Egyptian pharaohs

Other: College to choose, twenty-first-century composers, artists of Central America

Make Your Own

<table>
<tr><td></td><td></td><td></td><td></td><td></td></tr>
<tr><td></td><td></td><td></td><td></td><td></td></tr>
<tr><td></td><td></td><td></td><td></td><td></td></tr>
<tr><td></td><td></td><td></td><td></td><td></td></tr>
<tr><td></td><td></td><td></td><td></td><td></td></tr>
</table>

Your Ideas

_____

_____

_____

_____

_____

_____

_____

_____

_____

Gathering Grid Graphic Organizer

Who	What	Where	When	How	Why

Summary:

6

5+1 Newspaper

APPROPRIATE USES

1. Use to advance students' precision in gathering factual details from print materials.

2. Use to enable students to gather details from group and classroom discussions.

3. Use as an advance organizer for gathering factual prior knowledge from students' prior experiences.

4. Use to prepare students for constructing accurate summaries of events witnessed.

5. Use to help students separate fact from opinion in a magazine article.

6. Use as a note-taking organizer for interviewing a person for a news article or essay.

7. Use as a note-taking organizer when reading documents for a research report or speech.

Learning Phase:
Gathering information, making sense

Level of Difficulty:
Moderate

Purpose: To enable students to identify and summarize information systematically

Thinking Process:
Summarizing

Key Vocabulary

Summary, fact, opinion, noun, clause, topic, sentence

LESSON DESIGN

Check Prior Knowledge of the 5+1 Newspaper Organizer

1. Show the students a newspaper and a news magazine (e.g., *Time*, *Newsweek*). Ask volunteers what they have in common and what are the differences between them. If students are familiar with the Venn diagram (p. 85), show a model for all to see. Write in the similarities and differences as identified by the students. Allow the opportunity for many to respond to this higher-level question (finding similarities).

2. If students have not identified that the news is about events (what), people (who), places (where), and times (when), use questions to draw these out.

3. Project or draw a newspaper organizer for all to see. Highlight the key words. Ask, "How many have seen this organizer?" "Used it?" Ask them to speculate on its purpose and why it may have the name "5 + 1." Reinforce correct notions.

Explain the 5+1 Newspaper's Purpose

1. Bridge to the purpose: To gather accurate and precise information in order to separate fact from opinion.

2. Point out the six questions that go into a news article: who, what, when, where, how, and why (#1) and the summary statement (#2).

Who	What	Where	When	How	Why

Summary:

3. You may wish to make this a paired task with one person being the reader and the other the recorder.

Clarify and Model the Task

1. Distribute to each student copies of a current news article and a copy of this organizer. Distribute copies of a short article from a news magazine or newspaper. Select an article of interest to the students in the class.

2. Ask students to read the article. For struggling readers, read the article aloud so all can follow.

3. Distribute copies of the organizer, one per student.

4. Invite them to re-read the article and fill in each of the columns with nouns, clauses in each of the five fact columns, and reasons given in each of the why columns.

5. Review "noun" and "clause" vocabulary.

6. Ask them to place an asterisk (*) by any item in the why column that is not a fact, but someone's opinion, including their own inferred reasons.

7. Before they begin with the organizer, you may ask for volunteers to give you suggestions for placement in the column. If the suggestion is okay, ask all to put the answer in the suggested column. Do this also on the master organizer for all to see.

8. Check for understanding of the task by calling for "thumbs up" (I know what to do) and "thumbs down" (I am not sure). Re-coach the unsure students.

Complete the Task

1. Walk among the students as they work on their columns. Monitor and coach.

2. When most are finished listing the nouns and phrases, go to the display of the organizer. Call on students to give you responses. Fill these in on the master. Allow the opportunity for responding by starting with students in the back row. Take only one answer from each student. Continue until all unduplicated responses are showing on the display organizer.

3. Let students disagree with any placements. Facilitate the discussion and ensure all placements are in the correct columns.

4. Instruct the students for making each column into a statement. Use the what column for your model. Monitor and coach their sentence construction before calling for answers to show in your display organizer.

5. Show them how to construct a topic sentence that captures the main idea connecting the sentences. Use a different story so that they can construct sentences from their own (e.g., "In the news story about the California fires, I learned about damage that was done to the many homes last week by a careless smoker.").

6. Ask for three to four sample sentences. Give constructive feedback.

Guide Reflection

1. **Focus on Process.** Do a "think-pair-share" (p. 209) with the question "What I learned about using the 5 + 1 graphic organizer to gather information was . . ." After pairs talk, do a wraparound (p. 209) starting in the middle of the room. Let each person share in turn. Allow duplicates, but no discussion. Remind students of the DOVE guidelines (p. 216).

2. **Focus on Transfer.** Keep the same partners. Do a second think-pair-share with the sentence, "This graphic organizer will help me when I _____" (e.g., "read my textbook," "do my homework," "read the newspaper," "watch TV," "listen in a discussion") "because . . .". Start the wraparound where you left off with the first one (above) and follow the same procedure. You may wish to change the "when" phrase for every fifth or sixth student to generate different ideas.

5+1 NEWSPAPER ORGANIZER EXAMPLES

Elementary Grade Example

Language Arts: "Whistle for Willie"

Who	What	Where	When	How	Why
Peter, Willie, mother, father,	carton, sidewalk, chalk, father's hat, shadow	home, street, grocery store	daytime	whistle	so Willie could follow him

Summary:

Willy learned to whistle for his dog. His dog was named Willie. He tried all sorts of tricks. He put on his father's hat. He did learn to whistle. Willy followed home. (Based on a short story by Ezra Jack Keats in *Keats's Neighborhood*, Viking Press.)

Middle Grade Example

Social Studies: Jockey Takes Cue

Who	What	Where	When	How	Why
Jockey Paul O'Neil, City Affair, Horseracing Regulation Authority, Zinedine Zidane	head-butting horse, deciding to suspend	Stratford Race Course, London	July 24	Horse threw jockey off	Bad sportsmanship

Summary:

The Horseracing Authority was voting to suspend the jockey of City Affair. Paul O'Neil head butted the horse just like the French soccer player Zidane butted his opponent in the World Cup. The Authority thinks this is bad sportsmanship. (Based on news article "Whoa! Jockey Takes Cue from Ill-Mannered Zidane," *Chicago Tribune*, July 25, 2006.)

Secondary Grade Example

Biology: Extending the Robot's Reach

Who	What	Where	When	How	Why
surgeons, urologists, cardiologists	myomectomies, cervical cancers, hysterectomies, pyeloplasties,kidney procedures, spleen removal, mitral valve repairs	major hospitals	in near future	using robots	very delicate touch, tight spaces, hard-to-reach places

Summary:

In the near future, medical specialists will use robots to help with operations that need a very delicate touch or are in hard-to-reach places of the patient's body. Cervical cancers, spleen removals, kidney procedures, and mitral valve repairs show the range of operations that could use the robots. Right now, they are too expensive. (Based on article "New Surgical Breakthroughs Using Robots," *U.S. News and World Report*, July 31, 2006.)

MORE IDEAS

Elementary Grade Examples

Mathematics: Counting butterflies, measuring pyramids, the dollar

Language Arts: Interview parents about family history, read *Paper Bag Princess* or other stories by Robert Munsch, watch favorite TV cartoon, *Lettuce, the Dancing Rabbit*

Social Studies: Our mayor, our town library, meet the major

Science: Types of dinosaurs, robins, dragonflies

Other: The ballet *Peter and the Wolf,* an adventure with my family

Middle Grade Examples

Mathematics: Fractions in the kitchen, using tangent ratios, numbers in the stock market

Language Arts: Read weekly news magazine articles, read a story by a favorite author

Science: Watch Animal Planet or Discovery Channel documentary, read science textbook chapter, read article in a science magazine on current curriculum topic or chapter (library)

Social Studies: Watch History Channel documentary, interview neighbors about city services, read social studies textbook chapter

Other: Plan articles for classroom newsletter, write daily "I learned" summaries, write summaries of the highlights of the month in your school, or about Hall of Fame athletes in students' favorite sports

Secondary Grade Examples

Mathematics: Biography of famous mathematician, explanation of math used in a rocket launch, instructional summary for applying algebraic formulas in physics

Language Arts: Read a play by August Wilson, read a novel by Jane Austen or Charlotte Brontë, read a nonfiction book from the current best-seller list

Science: Read an article on a current science-related issue or topic (e.g., global warming, the UN's Millennium Development Goals), chapter in science textbook, biography of Nobel Prize winners in science (e.g., Michelson, Merrifield)

Social Studies: Commentary from TV news magazine (e.g., *60 Minutes, The NewsHour with Jim Lehrer, 20/20)*, the roles and responsibilities of the three branches of the U.S. government, a president's contribution to world peace

Other: A book on my favorite hobby, the life and times of an American composer (e.g., Bernstein, Marsalis, Blades), the contributions of Hispanic and African American artists (e.g., William Johnson, Henry Tanner, Rupert Garcia, Sam Saenz)

Make Your Own

Who	What	Where	When	How	Why

Summary:

Your Ideas

_____

_____

_____

_____

_____

_____

_____

_____

_____

_____

5 + 1 Newspaper Organizer

Who	What	Where	When	How	Why

Summary:

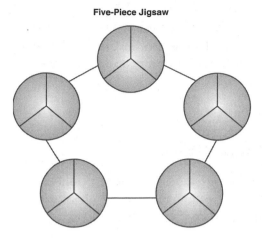

Five-Piece Jigsaw

7

Jigsaw

APPROPRIATE USES

1. Use as the core activity in a lesson to help students gather information from multiple sources.

2. Use as a reading guide for fiction so that students can gather information on a single theme or character from multiple points of view.

3. Use as an interview tool that encourages students to take notes by category.

4. Use as a discussion note-taking guide so that students can differentiate the information they are hearing by predetermined categories.

5. Use with younger children to enhance fluency. With younger children, keep it simple. Display the organizer with the category words already identified. After reading the material, use an all class discussion to obtain details for each category. Read in short bursts and return to the classifying task for a short time each day.

Learning Phase: Gathering information, making sense

Level of Difficulty: Challenging

Purpose: To provide students with a tool to gather information in categories

Thinking Processes: Differentiating, classifying

Key Vocabulary

Jigsaw, differentiate, analyze, category

Attribution

The Jigsaw Classroom was developed by Eliott Aronson at the University of Texas in 1970. The method was developed as a popular cooperative learning tactic used to reduce school violence and racial conflict. Robin Fogarty (1997) adapted the jigsaw model into a graphic organizer.

LESSON DESIGN

Check Prior Knowledge of the Jigsaw Organizer

1. On the overhead, show a picture or sketch of a jigsaw puzzle. Ask students to speculate why they think the term jigsaw is used. (The type of saw used to cut the original wood puzzle pieces was called a jigsaw.)

2. On the overhead or board, show the blank jigsaw organizer.

Jigsaw Organizer

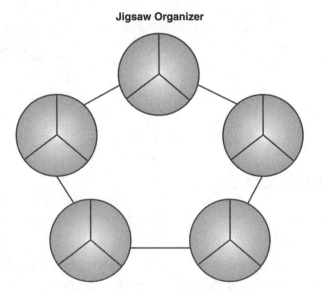

3. Complete this advance organizer by asking students the following "higher-order" questions. Use wait-time and a technique such as "names from a hat" or "numbered lotto draw" to ensure maximum distribution of expectation to answer. Seek several responses to each question:

- How is a jigsaw similar to getting ready for a final exam?
- Explain why you think an organizer in the shape of a jigsaw will help you gather information about (topic of your choice).
- What do you think might happen to your thinking if you use a jigsaw organizer to gather information from (text, article, etc.)?

Explain the Jigsaw's Purpose

1. Draw on the responses to the previous question set.

2. Bridge to the jigsaw as an organizer with the purpose of grouping pieces of information about an idea so that you can study how each piece contributes to the whole.

Clarify and Model the Task

1. Return attention to the jigsaw organizer that you have displayed.

2. In the space provided on the top, write in the topic.

3. Invite students to take their textbooks and open to the chapter they are going to study. Invite them to scan the chapter. (If they are unfamiliar with the term *scan*, explain it to them: "to look through the chapter at the headings".) The largest type size indicates the chapter title. Use three to six level-1 subheads. To double check that they have all the main ideas that the chapter will address, ask the students to read the chapter's opening paragraph. If the chapter has a summary, they may also check that. From these three sources, the students should identify the principal sub-ideas.

4. Check for understanding of the term *scan*. Invite students to complete the scan.

Complete the Task

1. When students are ready with their ideas for subtopics, select a volunteer to write responses on the board next to the displayed jigsaw.

2. Solicit nominations for the headers to be placed in each of four to seven pieces. After the class has provided an unduplicated list, explain that these headers will guide their classification of the details they collect from reading the chapter. Through discussion, identify the six most important subheaders.

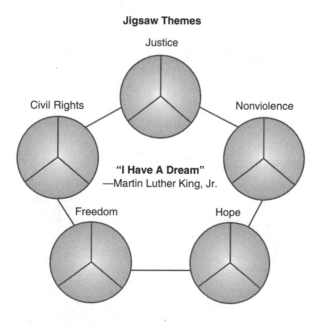

3. Form groups of three. Assign roles (recorder, checker, encourager). Review the DOVE guidelines (p. 216) and give each group a large sheet of newsprint, several colored markers, and a highlighter for each member.

4. Instruct the students to read the assigned material. Jigsaw the sections. Each will have one of the sections headed by the subtopic selected. As the students read their assigned sections, they will highlight the information that supports or explains the subtopic.

5. After students have completed reading in the first round of subtopics, they will read the second section and mark the information.

6. After completing the second round, the students will fill in the jigsaw organizer. Each will take a turn sharing with the full group of three as they complete the entire jigsaw.

7. Monitor and coach the students as they place the details in the categories.

Guide Reflection

1. **Focus on Content.** Match groups of three into groups of six. The groups of three will share the information found in each category and explain to the other group how that information is related to the main idea of the chapter.

2. **Focus on Process.** The groups of three will review the steps of the process: (a) identify the main idea or key concept of the chapter, (b) scan for sub-ideas, (c) subdivide the reading and gathering tasks according to sub-ideas, and (d) complete the jigsaw.

After this review, the group will make a list including (a) which steps in this process they did well, (b) which steps they could improve, and (c) questions for discussion about this process.

JIGSAW ORGANIZER EXAMPLES

Elementary Grade Example

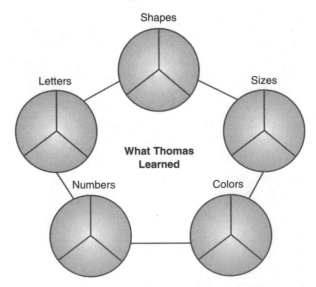

Middle Grade Example

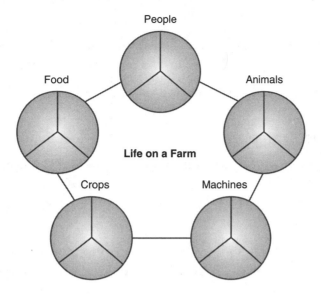

Secondary Grade Example

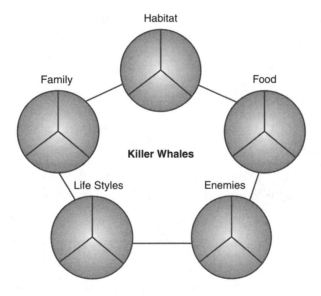

MORE IDEAS

Elementary Grade Examples

Mathematics: Number connections to people, places, holidays, family vacations

Language Arts: Keats's Neighborhood by Ezra Jack Keats: people, animal friends, mysteries, adventures; "Papa's Mark" (Gwendolyn Battle-Lavert): Who? What? When? Where?

Science: Butterflies: colors, shapes, favorite flowers, size; *Songs of the Water Boatman and Other Pond Poems* (Joyce Sidman): animals, plants, seasons, events

Social Studies: Rosa (Nikki Giovanni): courage, persistence, pride, fear; *Hot Air* (Marjorie Priceman): adventure, history, fun, high jinks

Other: The Rescuers (Disney): animals, adventures, people, machines

Middle Grade Examples

Mathematics: Key words: addition, subtraction, multiplication, division, relations; 8th-grade math concepts: what I am learning about properties of rational numbers, inequalities, irrational numbers, polynomials

Language Arts: All about writing: description, narration, persuasion, exposition. *The Lottery* (Shirley Jackson): Mr. Summers, the black box, Mrs. Hutchinson, the town

Science: Acids and bases: properties of each, examples of each; waves: nature, properties, behavior, standing

Social Studies: Immigration history: entry ports, nationalities, jobs, relocations. Native American tribes: history, leadership, tragedies, current state

Secondary Grade Examples

Mathematics: Data representations: format, purpose, uses, benefits; statistical measures: types of data, definitions, advantages, disadvantages

Language Arts: The English Romantic poets: names, style, beliefs, great works; Toni Morrison: influences, themes, style, characters, locals

Science: Careers in botany: reasons, current issues, opportunities, requirements, preparation; lasers: theory, applications, difficulties, language

Social Studies: The Great Depression: causes, short-term effects, politics, long-term effects; the slave trade: origins, economics, human effects, today

Other: Visions in Native American art: First Nation, Navajo, Hopi, Aboriginal; Asian influences in modern music: animal sounds, melodies, rhythms, instruments

Make Your Own

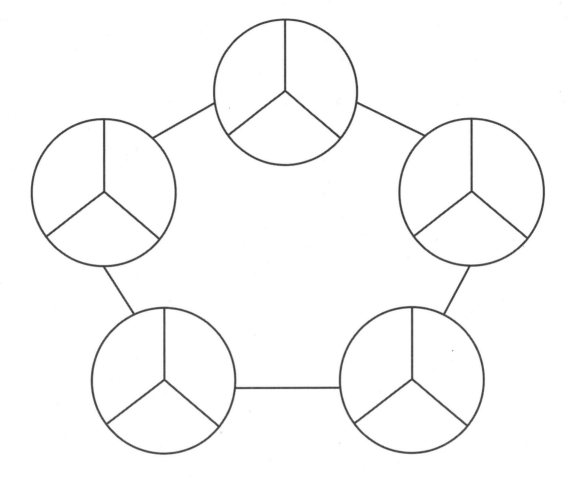

Your Ideas

_____

_____

_____

_____

_____

_____

_____

_____

Jigsaw Graphic Organizer

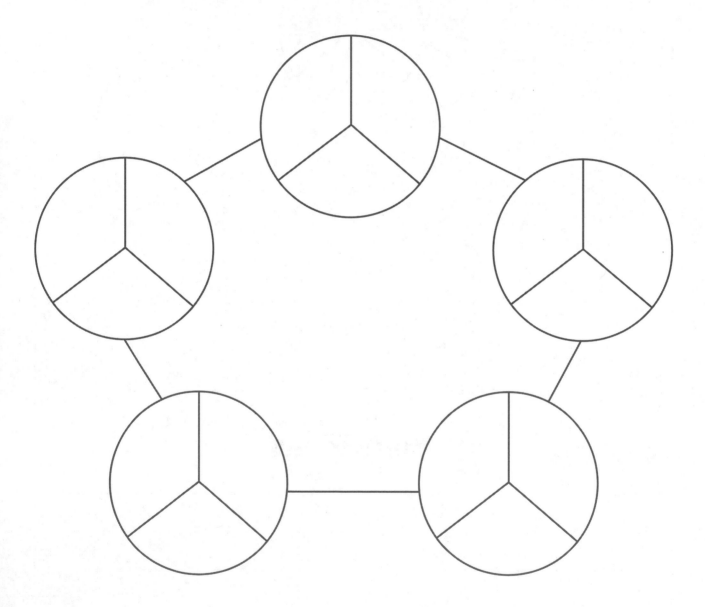

8

Ranking Ladder

APPROPRIATE USES

1. Use as an advance organizer to introduce concepts in a new lesson.

2. Use in a lesson to secure students' opinions of the relative importance of key concepts, characters in a story, or events.

3. Use at the end of a lesson to generate discussion by asking students to rank the value or importance of what they learned.

4. Use at end of a unit, a quarter, or semester to review important people, places, events, or concepts.

5. Use to probe for reasons: "Why do you think that?"; "What evidence do you have for your rankings?"

6. Use to stir debate by asking for disagreements with a ranking of reasons given.

Learning Phase: Making sense

Level of Difficulty: Easy

Purpose: To help students rate the order of importance or value of people, objects, events, or concepts

Thinking Processes: Differentiating and proving

Key Vocabulary

Rank order, criteria, relative

Attribution

Developed by the author.

LESSON DESIGN

Check Prior Knowledge of the Ranking Ladder Organizer

1. Draw a ladder on the board or overhead. Ask students to give examples of why ladders are used. List at least three answers (e.g., climb, put out fire, elope).

2. Ask a volunteer to come up to the board and "rank order" the answers from bottom to top. (Place the most important item at the top.)

3. Ask this student to defend the order made. Then ask if other students have different orders and why.

Explain the Ranking Ladder's Purpose

1. Tell the students that the rungs on the ladder make a visual tool that depicts the order of importance they apply to three or more objects or ideas. Explain the three vocabulary terms: *rank order, criteria,* and *relative* as each applies to this organizer's use.

2. Explain or ask students about examples of where else they might use a ranking ladder to see the importance of items in relation to each other (e.g., their favorite subjects in school, characters they most like or dislike in a story, helpful assignments).

3. Explain or discuss why it is helpful to give the reasons for the rank orders (e.g., clarifying, thinking about thinking).

4. Summarize the purpose for using the ranking ladder.

Clarify and Model the Task

1. Instruct each student to duplicate the ranking ladder in his or her journal.

2. Give students three characters from a story the class has read or three items from a chapter in the textbook from the last chapter studied.

3. Ask all to rank the items from "most important to you" to "least important" with "most important" on the highest rung.

4. Pair students and instruct them to show and explain their rankings.

5. After both have shared, select random students to share the rankings and the explanations of both partners. Put one of the third set paired on the blank to model the process one more time.

6. Check for understanding of the procedures for ranking on the ladder.

Complete the Task

1. Invite students to sketch a second ladder in their journals.

2. Give them the words to rank that you have selected from the material in the current unit (e.g., rank the characters in a story according to importance in the plot; rank historic figures according to their contributions to history; rank order the impact of types of fuel on global warming).

3. Repeat the think-pair-share tactic with the new words. Monitor the paired discussions to ensure each partner gets an equal chance to speak.

Guide Reflection

1. Review the thinking that they must do to make a ranking. Brainstorm the list of elements in the process before ranking them in order using a ladder that you have drawn on the board or overhead.

Ranking Ladder

2. Solicit reasons for any differences in the proposed rank orders.

RANKING LADDERS ORGANIZER EXAMPLES

Elementary Grade Example

What Does a Best Friend Do?

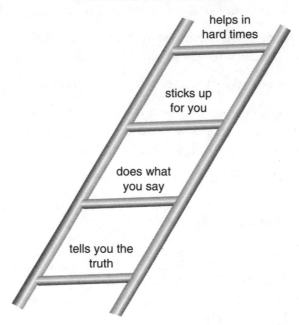

helps in
hard times

sticks up
for you

does what
you say

tells you the
truth

Middle Grade Example

What Is the Best News Medium?

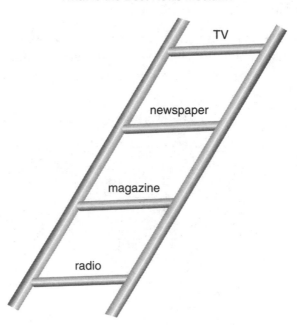

TV

newspaper

magazine

radio

Secondary Grade Example

What is Most Important for School Success?

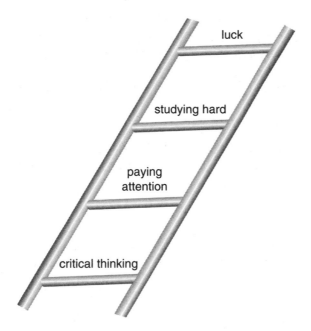

luck

studying hard

paying
attention

critical thinking

MORE IDEAS

Elementary Grade Examples

Mathematics: Most important: correct numbers?, correct operation sign?, correct answer?; most fun: addition?, multiplication?, subtraction?, division?

Literacy: Smartest: Three Billy Goats Gruff?, Madeline?, Little Red Riding Hood?, Ariel?, Three Little Pigs?; most important: prefixes?, suffixes?, roots?

Science: Favorite animal: dog?, cat?, hamster?, elephant?, giraffe?, lion?; favorite season: winter?, summer?, autumn?, spring?

Social Studies: Most important: police?, firefighters?, paramedics?, nurses?, crossing guards?; favorite holiday: New Year's Day?, Presidents' Day?, Fourth of July?, Valentine's Day?, St. Patrick's Day?, M. L. King Jr.'s Birthday?, Mother's Day?, Father's Day?

Other: Most important: a good friend?, a good lunch?, a good family?, study hard?, get good grades?, enjoy what you are learning?, be smart?, obey the teacher?

Middle Grade Examples

Mathematics: Easiest to learn: algebra?, arithmetic?, geometry?; most difficult word problems: number?, coin?, time?, distance?, age?, mixture?, area?, percentage?, rate?

Language Arts: Prefer to read: poetry?, short story?, essay?, novel?; most important in a story: characters?, author's style?, setting?, plot?, theme?

Science: Hurts the environment most: gasoline fumes?, fireplace smoke?, diesel fumes?, forest fires?; most helpful for good health: no smoking?, no drugs?, daily exercise?, healthy food?

Social Studies: Bravest: Rosa Parks?, Martin Luther King, Jr.?, Muhammad Ali?, Jesse Owens?; best citizen: votes?, pays taxes?, obeys laws?, defends country?

Other: Favorite music: jazz?, hip-hop?, rock and roll?, country?; most important to school success: study hard?, be smart?, have friends?, play sports?, join clubs?

Secondary Grade Examples

Mathematics: Most important to understand for factoring polynomials: combining polynomials?, factoring by guessing?, completing the square?, factoring by quadratic formula?; most important thinking when solving word problems: understanding the problem? (e.g., understand what is given and what is expected), using key words precisely? (e.g., a factor of, quotient of), making a plan?, making a generalization?

English: Best novel read this year?; most important criterion for writing an essay: style?, punctuation?, grammar?, ideas?, details?, organization?

Science: Global issue needing most immediate attention of world leaders: global warming?, nuclear proliferation?, deforestation?, chemical waste deposits?, genocide?, endangered species?; diseases needing most immediate research: mumps?, HIV/AIDS?, multiple sclerosis?, depression?

Social Science: Greatest president: Washington?, Lincoln?, Teddy Roosevelt?, Franklin Roosevelt?, John F. Kennedy?; most history-changing event: fall of Roman Empire?, Battle of Waterloo?, Pearl Harbor?, atomic bomb?, 9/11 attack?

Other: Best choice for college: large state university?, in-state university?, small liberal arts college?, community college?, prestigious private university?; most important job preparation: grades?, clothes?, recommendations?, experience?, portfolio?

Make Your Own

Your Ideas

_____

_____

_____

_____

_____

_____

_____

_____

_____

_____

_____

Ranking Ladder Graphic Organizer

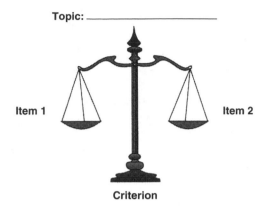

Topic: _____

Item 1

Item 2

Criterion

Scale

APPROPRIATE USES

1. Use to weigh prior knowledge about a new topic or unit. Survey the class to identify the most important information they know.

2. Use to weigh points of view held by various historic figures (Washington and Hamilton), authors from a period (Bronte and Keats), literary characters (Macbeth and McDuff), scientific views (creationism and evolution), political beliefs on current issues (Democrats and Republicans). Use authentic material from their time or instigate a debate on a current issue (e.g., global warming).

3. Use to weigh costs and benefits for solving a classroom problem.

4. Use to evaluate a character's decisions in a play or novel.

5. Use to weigh a student's personal decision about schoolwork.

Key Vocabulary

Weigh, concept, value, standard, pro, con

Learning Phase: Making sense.

Level of Difficulty: Easy

Purpose: To provide students with a visual tool to show value of ideas or objects that they are evaluating

Thinking Processes: Assessing and judging

Attribution

Created by the author.

LESSON DESIGN

Check Prior Knowledge of the Scale Organizer

1. Show a picture of the scale organizer. Ask students to give a thumbs up if they have seen a scale like this or used the graphic as an organizer.

2. Present students with a current political or social issue with which they are likely to be familiar. (For primary students, use a school- or community-based issue or an example from a familiar story.)

3. Ask for a show of hands from those who support the issue (the pro side). Count these and record the number on one side of the scale.

4. Ask for a show of hands from those who are against the issue (the con side). Count and record the number.

5. Ask the students what they think would happen to a real scale with the number differences from this vote.

Explain the Scale's Purpose

1. Inform the students that this organizer gives them a visual tool for showing the weight or value of contrasting ideas.

2. Share some age-appropriate examples of contrasting ideas in which different numbers of people may support each or one may be more serious than the other.

Clarify and Model the Task

1. Form learning groups of three. Review the DOVE guidelines and roles (p. 216).

2. Provide each trio with a large sheet of newsprint and markers. Ask the recorder to divide the newsprint in half with a line. On the top section, the recorders will copy the scale organizer displayed on the board or overhead, as shown on p. 63.

3. Show a second scale. This one will be out of balance. Tell the recorders *not* to draw this one until the learning group has finished its discussion and voting. Later they will sketch it on the bottom half of the newsprint.

4. Select the issue or topic for the scale from a just completed unit of study (see sample ideas).

5. Set up a mock situation that presents two sides of an argument about an idea in the unit (e.g., President Lincoln should not have freed the slaves). Ask for a pro and con vote. Record the vote and show the change in the scale.

6. Ask the learning groups to come up with statements for a vote. Invite several to state the case and count the vote.

7. Check for understanding of this basic process.

Complete the Task

1. Show the scale for all to see. Inform the students that they will be using the graphic to help them with a more complex weighing task.
   - Assign the topic.
   - Present a "criterion" by which they will make their judgment.
   - Invite the students to brainstorm all the possible ways that each side of the argument meets the criterion.

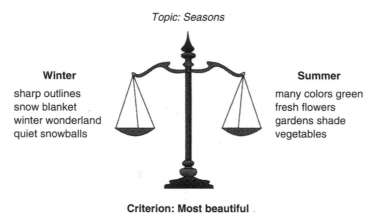

Topic: Seasons

Winter
sharp outlines
snow blanket
winter wonderland
quiet snowballs

Summer
many colors green
fresh flowers
gardens shade
vegetables

Criterion: Most beautiful

   - Use a vote for the weight of each item on the list according to the criterion. Total the "weight" to determine the tipping of the scale.
   - Draw the tipped scale to show the comparative balance.

2. Provide each learning group with reading material for the current unit. Use either supplementary materials or material from the textbook. Instruct each group to select one key concept and to make a statement that will allow a pro and a con argument. Post these on the newsprint. Review the statements and the criterion.

3. After reviewing the statements, instruct students to find at least five other persons (students, teachers, parents, neighbors) not in this class to read and vote. Record the votes and create the second scale showing the new balance.

4. Students may interview those who vote and record reasons for the vote on the newsprint.

Guide Reflection

1. **Focus on Process.** Ask each learning group to review the vocabulary and the steps in making the scale "tip."

Ask each student to make a journal entry from the stem, "Using the scale, I noticed that. . . ." If time allows, invite as many volunteers as possible to share the stem completions.

2. **Focus on Content.** Ask students to explain "why" one side better met the criterion given. Place students whose votes favored the "pro" on one side of the room; place those whose votes favored the "con" side on the other side. Taking turns by side, allow each side to try to convince the other of its point of view. Students may switch sides if persuaded.

SCALE ORGANIZER EXAMPLES

Elementary Grade Example

Topic: Pets

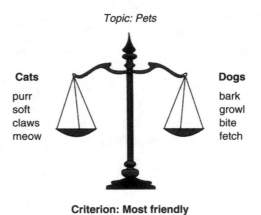

Cats
purr
soft
claws
meow

Dogs
bark
growl
bite
fetch

Criterion: Most friendly

Middle Grade Example

Topic: Media

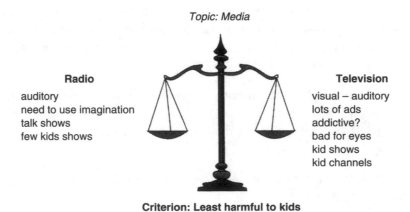

Radio
auditory
need to use imagination
talk shows
few kids shows

Television
visual – auditory
lots of ads
addictive?
bad for eyes
kid shows
kid channels

Criterion: Least harmful to kids

Secondary Grade Example

Topic: The Iraq War

Yes
end of Saddam Hussein
new democratic government
voting

No
civil strife
religious sects
insurgent magnet
cost in lives
cost in money

Criterion: Established democracy

MORE IDEAS

Elementary Grade Examples

Mathematics: Favorite number operation, favorite coin, favorite word problem type

Language Arts: Favorite book, favorite story character

Science: Zoos, yes or no; junk food, yes or no

Social Studies: Historic places to visit (fun), good manners (importance), good citizens or hard workers? (most important)

Other: More school holidays, yes or no?; favorite vacation places, best TV shows

Middle Grade Examples

Mathematics: Geometry or algebra (easiest), fractions or decimals (most difficult), problem solving or measurement (most important to learn)

Language Arts: Science fiction (like or don't like), expository writing (easy or hard), poetry (like or don't like)

Science: Brain or heart (more important), lever or gears (most helpful), DNA or RNA (most valuable)

Social Studies: Global warming (fact or fiction), space exploration (necessity), whale hunting bans (beneficial)

Other: Hip-hop music (good or bad), myspace.com (safe or sorry), smoking (healthy?)

Secondary Grade Examples

Mathematics: More or less math required, number operations or problem solving

Language Arts: Read a book or write a paper, *Native Son or Black Boy*, by Richard Wright; Robert Frost or Edgar Allan Poe

Science: Cloning (allow or forbid?), food irradiation (help or harm?), water control (boon or bust?)

Social Studies: Campaign finance laws (strict or loose?), War Powers Act (control or freedom?), presidential power (greater or lesser?)

Other: Abstract (expressionists or photo realists?), TV (wasteland or wealth?), family planning (private or public?)

Make Your Own

Topic: _____

Item 1

Item 2

Your Ideas

_____
_____
_____
_____
_____
_____
_____
_____
_____
_____
_____

Scale Graphic Organizer

Topic: _____

Item 1 **Item 2**

P (+)	
M (−)	
I (?)	

10
PMI

APPROPRIATE USES

1. Use to help individual students assess understanding of concepts in a unit of study.

2. Use to help individual students assess contributions to a learning group.

3. Use to help individual students assess use of graphic organizer.

4. Use to help learning groups assess their collaborations.

5. Use to help teachers provide feedback to students alone or in groups regarding content knowledge, cooperative team's work together, use of a graphic organizer, or improvement of a cognitive function.

Learning Phase: Making sense

Level of Difficulty: Easy

Purpose: To provide a framework for assessment of learning by individuals and learning teams

Thinking Process: Assessing

Key Vocabulary

Assess, evaluate, judge, determine, criterion, standard, indicator

Attribution

The PMI was developed by Edward DeBono (1983).

LESSON DESIGN

Check Prior Knowledge of the PMI Organizer

1. Show the PMI for all to see. Beside it, post a KWL (p. 1).

PMI

P (+)	
M (–)	
I (?)	

KWL

K	W	L

2. Explain the PMI organizer (pluses, minuses, interesting questions).

3. Match students into pairs. Ask pairs to talk together about the organizer and identify what they know or have done with it. After a minute, ask for volunteers from each pair who have prior experience to share their experiences. Write these under the K column of the KWL.

4. After recording students' contributions, add your own.

5. Invite the pairs to complete this question: "I wonder how this organizer will help me?" Record responses in the W column.

Explain the PMI's Purpose

1. Using the completed K and W columns, focus the students' attention on the PMI as an assessment tool for use by individuals and groups in evaluating content understanding, cooperative teamwork, and thinking functions.

2. Check for understanding by asking the pairs to identify what they have learned so far about the PMI. Record responses under the L column of the KWL.

Clarify and Model the Task

1. Design your next lesson in the curriculum around a graphic organizer familiar to the students.

2. After guiding reflection on the lesson, invite the cooperative groups of three to assess their thinking during that lesson.

- Show the PMI. Give each group an additional sheet of newsprint. Ask them to rotate the learning group's roles.
- Remind them of the thinking focus used in the lesson.
- Guided by the recorder, the group will complete each column on a fresh sheet of newsprint. Starting with the P (pluses) column, they will assess what were the pluses of using the graphic organizer in the lesson. When finished, they will ask, "What were the minuses for using that organizer?" Last, they will generate questions about the organizer's use and place these in the I column.

3. Invite up to three teams to come to the front of the classroom. With two holding the sheet, the reporter will review the learning group's responses.

Complete the Task

1. Invite the groups to repeat the PMI process, focusing on (a) how well they worked together and (b) the content learned.

2. Provide additional newsprint and instruct the learning students to make a page entry into their journals. On each journal page, they will record the group-generated PMI.

Guide Reflection

1. **Focus on Content.** In their journals, students will complete an "I learned . . ." stem about the core ideas of the lesson. If time allows, call on students from different parts of the room to share their statements.

2. **Focus on Process.** In their journals, students will complete a PMI on the graphic organizer's use in this lesson. If time allows, call on students to share from one of the columns.

PMI ORGANIZER EXAMPLES

Elementary Grade Example

Learning My Multiplication Tables

P (+)	Do good (sic) in math Help with division Do problems faster
M (−)	Hard work 7×8 and 6×9 The tens mix me up
I (?)	Will this help in science? How fast can I go?

Middle Grade Example

Solving Discount Problems

P (+)	Save $ Use math skills Choose what to buy
M (−)	Takes time
I (?)	What will I do with the money I save? Is cheaper better?

Secondary Grade Example

Buying a Term Paper on the Internet

P (+)	Get done faster. Somebody else does the work. Don't have to read the books.
M (−)	Getting caught = F. Cost $ Papers not always good. Need to proofread.
I (?)	What would happen if two people bought the same paper?

MORE IDEAS

Select an assessment tool for each lesson in which you imbed a graphic organizer. Use the PMI at the end of the lesson as one means for assessing student performance. The following samples show a variety of usable assessment tools with the PMI.

An Elementary Rubric

Content: *Louie's Search* (Ezra Jack Keats)

Graphic Organizer: Sequence Chart

Cooperative Social Skill: Encouragement

Cognitive Function: Accuracy

To what degree did this student . . .

Pick out key events? /_____/ _____/ _____/
                            None   Some   All

Construct the
sequence chart
with events in order? /_____/ _____/ _____/
                            None   Some   All

Use encouraging
words in the
learning group? /_____/ _____/ _____/
                            None   Some   All

Make accurate
descriptions of
events? /_____/ _____/ _____/
                            None   Some   All

A Middle Grade Checklist

Content: *West Side Story*
Graphic Organizer: The Prediction Tree
Cooperative Social Skill: Doing Role
Cognitive Function: Using Relevant Clues
A Checklist

	Teacher	Student
Content:		
Student collected character details	_____	_____
Student collected event details	_____	_____
Student collected setting details	_____	_____
Student collected time details	_____	_____
Student used details to make predictions	_____	_____
Student predictions were accurate	_____	_____
Graphic:		
Student used tree to chart predictions	_____	_____
Student labeled tree parts	_____	_____
Student made precise placements	_____	_____
Student defended placements	_____	_____
Function:		
Student found relevant clues	_____	_____
Student placed clues in appropriate category	_____	_____
Student made valid predictions	_____	_____
Cooperative Social Skill:		
Student knew responsibilities	_____	_____
Student performed responsibilities	_____	_____

Student Summary Using PMI. Teachers complete the checklist and give to students. Students complete checklist and then prepare PMI chart.

Secondary Grade Rubric

Content: Laws of Energy Conservation
Graphic: Fishbone
Cognitive Function: Use of logical evidence
To what degree does the student know

How to calculate
kinetic energy? /_____/ _____/ _____/
Not yet   Satisfactory   Superbly

How to calculate
changes in
gravitational energy? /_____/ _____/ _____/
Not yet   Satisfactory   Superbly

How to solve
problems with
falling objects? /_____/ _____/ _____/
Not yet   Satisfactory   Superbly

How to calculate
momentum? /_____/ _____/ _____/
Not yet   Satisfactory   Superbly

The effect of
unbalanced forces? /_____/ _____/ _____/
Not yet   Satisfactory   Superbly

How to label a
fishbone chart? /_____/ _____/ _____/
Not yet   Satisfactory   Superbly

How to place
supporting details? /_____/ _____/ _____/
Not yet   Satisfactory   Superbly

How to check logic
of concepts
and details? /_____/ _____/ _____/
Not yet   Satisfactory   Superbly

Student's PMI Summary. Using the rubric results from the teacher, the
student prepares a PMI chart and writes a summary of the major points
from each column.

Make Your Own

P (+)	
M (−)	
I (?)	

Your Ideas

_____

_____

_____

_____

_____

_____

_____

PMI Graphic Organizer

P (+)	
M (–)	
I (?)	

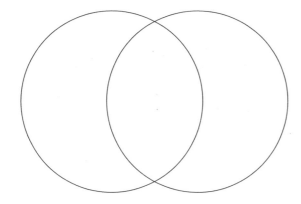

11

Venn Diagram

APPROPRIATE USES

1. Use as an advance organizer by comparing content of current lesson with content of previous lessons. Show on board or overhead for all to see. Elicit information and its placement on the Venn from students.

2. Use as an advanced interdisciplinary organizer. Compare what students know about the topic or theme from other courses.

3. Within a lesson or unit, use to compare the key concepts or themes.

4. Within a lesson or unit, use to show similarities between key people, places, events, or objects.

> **Learning Phase:** Making sense
>
> **Level of Difficulty:** Easy to moderate
>
> **Purpose:** To enable students to identify similarities and differences
>
> **Thinking Process:** Finding similarities

5. At the end of a lesson or unit, use to help students summarize the similarities that bind events, people, or places together.

Key Vocabulary

Similar, different, compare, contrast, traits, characteristics, attributes

Attribution

Created by nineteenth-century mathematician Thomas Venn.

LESSON DESIGN

Check Prior Knowledge of the Venn Diagram Organizer

1. Show an Olympic medallion on the board or overhead or show a picture of the Olympic flag. Point out the five overlapping circles and explain its symbolic value.

Olympic Symbol

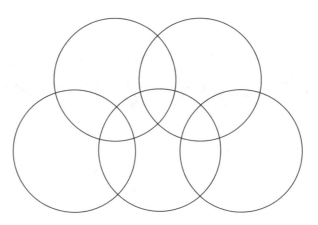

2. Show a two-circle Venn diagram. Point out how it is similar to the Olympic symbol (overlapping) and different (2 versus 5 circles). Ask how many are familiar with the Venn diagram. If none, move to the next step. If any are familiar, ask them to explain what they know. At the side of the displayed Venn, write key words that the students contribute. Try to call on every student who has an idea. Take one idea from each until you have a full list of "what they know."

Explain the Organizer's Purpose

1. Tell the students that this organizer, the Venn, was invented by a German mathematician to show how number sets overlapped.

2. Explain that they are going to learn how to use the Venn to show how ideas or objects are similar. (At this point be specific about what ideas or objects you have selected.) Refer back to the key vocabulary list and discuss the meaning of the words "similar" and "different."

3. Ask for examples of each word from what they see in the classroom or from materials currently under study. Interject synonyms for these two key words.

Clarify and Model the Task

1. Display the blank Venn for all to see. Label each part as you use an example that students can see (e.g., the teacher's desk, a student's desk). Label each circle with one object's name.

2. Show the students how to put what is unique or different about each object in the outer spaces (#1) and what they note is common to both (similar) in the overlapped space (#2). After entering the first sample words, solicit other words that show other similarities and differences. Enter these on the displayed Venn.

Venn Diagram

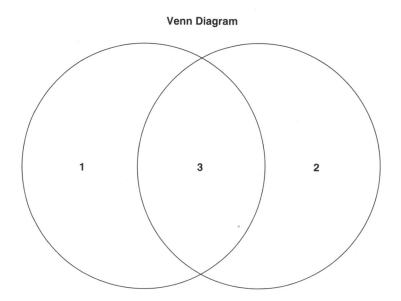

3. Check for understanding about the location the objects have in common and how they differ from each other by asking several different students to use the Venn with other objects in the room.

Complete the Task

1. For elementary students: Instruct them to copy the Venn on a full sheet in their journals or on an 8.5 × 11 sheet of paper given to each. Select another object that they can see in the room. Ask for a "starter" word for each #1 space (differences) and the #2 space (sameness).

For middle and upper grade students: Provide them with two objects or concepts from the current unit of study (see the sample organizers below to help you select the ideas from your curriculum).

2. Walk about the classroom and coach students as they fill in the Venns.

Guide Reflection

1. **Focus on Content Learned.** Invite students to complete an "In this comparison, what I learned about the similarity between _____ and _____ was . . ." in a journal entry.

2. **Focus on Thinking Element.** Invite students to make a journal entry describing what was easy and/or difficult in finding the similarities.

VENN DIAGRAM ORGANIZER EXAMPLES

Elementary Grade Example

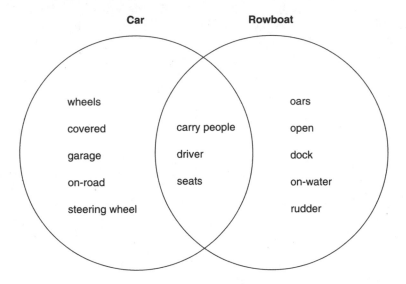

Middle Grade Example

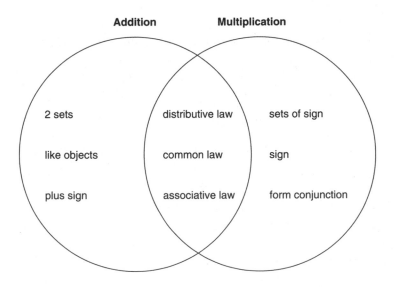

Secondary Grade Example

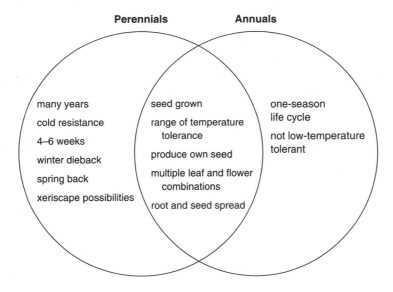

Perennials   **Annuals**

many years	seed grown	one-season life cycle
cold resistance	range of temperature tolerance	not low-temperature tolerant
4–6 weeks	produce own seed	
winter dieback	multiple leaf and flower combinations	
spring back	root and seed spread	
xeriscape possibilities		

MORE IDEAS

Elementary Grade Examples

Mathematics: Number sets, positive and negative numbers, rational and irrational numbers

Language Arts: Phoneme blending and phoneme segmenting, two characters in a story, two favorite authors

Science: Butterflies and dragonflies, stars and planets, frogs and salamanders

Social Studies: Good and bad neighbors, Memorial Day and Labor Day, Central America and South America

Other: Baseball and softball, jazz and hip-hop, ballet and ballroom

Middle Grade Examples

Mathematics: Qualitative comparison and numerical comparison problems, squares and circles, ratio and proportion

Language Arts: Fiction and nonfiction, point of view and bias, Scout and Boo (*To Kill a Mockingbird*)

Science: Killer whales and great white sharks, planets and moons, Marie Curie and Thomas Edison

Social Studies: Supply and demand, Tanzania and Kenya, Chief Crazy Horse and Geronimo

Other: Alcohol and marijuana, charcoal and pastels, working alone and working in a cooperative group

Secondary Grade Examples

Mathematics: Undergeneralization versus overgeneralization, sufficient information versus relevant information, percent problems versus area problems

Language Arts: *Autobiography of Malcolm X* versus *Benjamin Franklin's Autobiography,* poetry of Gwendolyn Brooks versus poetry of Langston Hughes, *Masque of the Red Death* versus *The Pit and the Pendulum*

Science: Energy and mass, atoms and quarks, cell parts and human parts

Social Studies: Aztec and Inca civilizations, Battle of Gettysburg and the Battle of Antietam, England's House of Commons and America's House of Representatives

Other: The styles of Dave Brubeck and Wynton Marsalis, aerobic versus anaerobic exercises, love and affection

Make Your Own

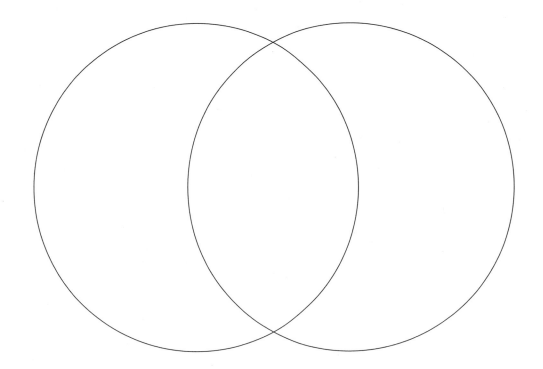

Your Ideas

_____

_____

_____

_____

_____

_____

_____

_____

_____

Venn Diagram Graphic Organizer

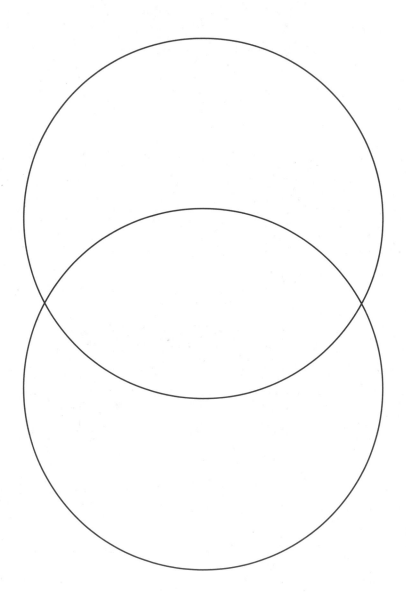

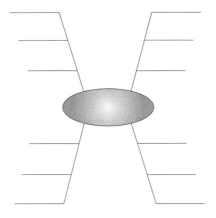

12

Spider Map

APPROPRIATE USES

1. Use to connect details in a story to the theme.

2. Use to connect details in nonfiction material to a core concept.

3. Use to connect details to main ideas in a class or group discussion.

4. Use to connect details to various characters in a story (book, video, play).

Key Vocabulary

Relationships, connections, analysis

LESSON DESIGN

Check Prior Knowledge of the Spider Map Organizer

1. Show the sample map to the class with the overhead.

2. Name it and ask how many have used the spider map in a previous lesson. With fiction? With nonfiction?

3. Invite volunteers who have prior experience to label the parts of the map and indicate an example of what they might enter on each part.

4. Use wait-time and distribute the opportunity to respond among the various volunteers.

Labeled Spider Map

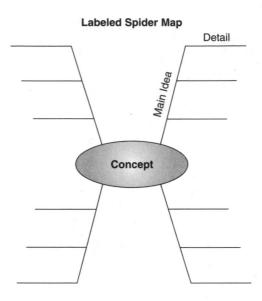

Explain the Spider Map's Purpose

1. Ask students to speculate on how they might use the spider map with a story they are reading.

2. Ask students to speculate on the value of using the spider map when reading a story or a nonfiction article. Distribute the opportunity for many to contribute by drawing names from a hat or box.

3. Summarize their contributions to the value of the spider map and highlight that value in the purpose statement.

Clarify and Model the Task

1. Provide each student with a five- to seven-paragraph news article taken from the daily paper or a news magazine. (For younger children, read the article as they follow.) Invite all to read the article.

2. Invite students to help you fill in the labeled spider map with the topic, main ideas, and details. Allow all students an opportunity to respond.

3. When the map is completed, check for understanding of the process.

Complete the Task

1. Match students in pairs. (For younger children, pair a strong reader with a less strong reader. The strong reader will read the material as the other follows along.)

2. Assign a short story to read.

3. After students complete the reading task, instruct them to draw a spider map on a sheet of 8.5 × 11 paper. Check for understanding of the procedures for completing the map. Working together, the students will complete the map.

4. Walk among the pairs and coach as needed.

Guide Reflection

1. Form groups of six from three pairs. Assign an order for this sharing.

2. **Focus on Content.** Each group will focus on one main idea and its details.

After this sharing, the other groups may add details. All should record added details on their maps.

Instruct each student to compose a summary of a main idea the group selected from the map. When these summaries are completed, allow each student the chance to read them to the group of six.

3. **Focus on the Process.** In the group of six, each student may tell how the spider map helped with the understanding of the story.

SPIDER MAP ORGANIZER EXAMPLES

Elementary Grade Example

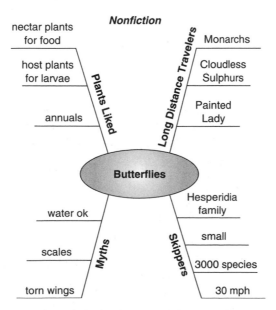

Middle Grade Example

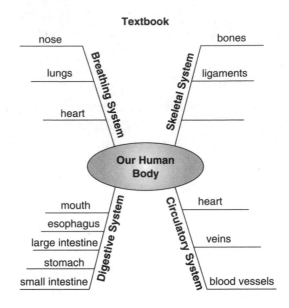

Textbook

Our Human Body

Breathing System: nose, lungs, heart

Skeletal System: bones, ligaments

Digestive System: mouth, esophagus, large intestine, stomach, small intestine

Circulatory System: heart, veins, blood vessels

Secondary Grade Example

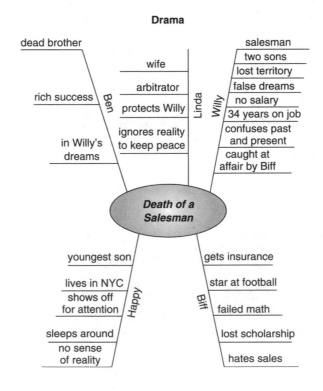

Drama

Death of a Salesman

Ben: dead brother, rich success, in Willy's dreams

Linda: wife, arbitrator, protects Willy, ignores reality to keep peace

Willy: salesman, two sons, lost territory, false dreams, no salary, 34 years on job, confuses past and present, caught at affair by Biff

Happy: youngest son, lives in NYC, shows off for attention, sleeps around, no sense of reality

Biff: gets insurance, star at football, failed math, lost scholarship, hates sales

MORE IDEAS

Elementary Grade Examples

Mathematics: Geometric shapes, patterns, graphs

Language Arts: Grimm's fairy tales, *The Snow Princess, The Wild Swans*

Science: Meteors, levers, weather instruments

Social Studies: The pilgrims, the Alamo, the Washington Monument

Other: School rules, my neighbors, *Sesame Street*

Middle Grade Examples

Mathematics: Tesselations, numbers in our lives, rules of place value

Language Arts: *To Kill a Mockingbird, A Raisin in the Sun, The Children's Hour*

Science: Shooting stars, bacteria structure, invertebrates

Social Studies: The Navajo Nation, the early explorers, Ellis Island

Other: My family's heritage, Chicago, 9/11

Secondary Grade Examples

Mathematics: Sampling, scale statistics, representing data

Language Arts: "Letter from Birmingham Jail," *Medea, Jane Eyre*

Science: Laser applications, force fields, acids

Social Studies: Global warming, nuclear proliferation, women's rights

Other: Urban crime, R. C. Gorman, Gordon Parks

Make Your Own

Your Ideas

_____

_____

_____

_____

_____

_____

_____

_____

_____

_____

Spider Map Graphic Organizer

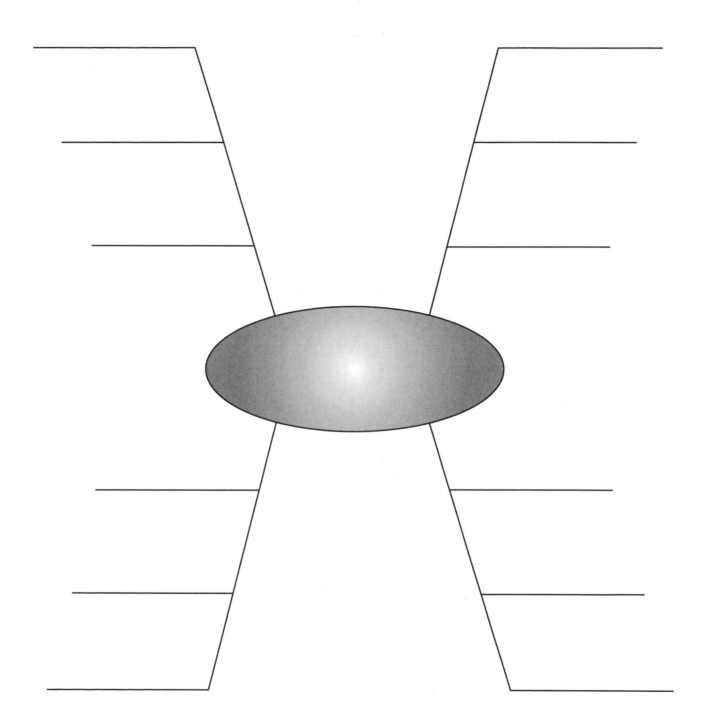

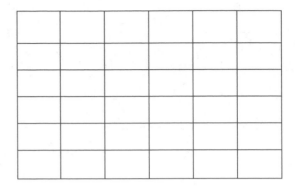

13

Classification Grid

APPROPRIATE USES

1. Use to generate ideas according to shared attributes in a genre, topic, or family group of ideas.

2. Use to organize ideas generated according to specific headings.

3. Use to encourage students to think "outside the box" to create a new topic, object, event, or idea by changing specific characteristics, traits, or attributes held in common among several existing topics, objects, events, or ideas.

4. Use to facilitate classification by noting similarities and differences between two or more similar objects, persons, or places.

Key Vocabulary

Classify, similarity, difference

LESSON DESIGN

Check Prior Knowledge of the Classification Grid Organizer

1. Draw a grid on the board for all to see or show a grid with the overhead.

2. Ask students to tell you about grids that they know (e.g., gridiron, software grids). Ask what they have in common.

3. Tell the class about the creator of *The Lone Ranger*, an old-time radio show. Each week the writers had to write a new story about the same characters with a slight plot variation. The Lone Ranger had a horse named Silver and used silver bullets as he and his faithful companion, Tonto, brought law and order to the Old West. This show was the forerunner of modern TV soap operas such as *Days of Our Lives* or *Desperate Housewives*.

To help the writers come up with a fresh story each week, this show invented the word grid (show the word grid below).

Lone Ranger **Word Grid**

Good guy	Sidekick	Bad guy	Gal	Conflict	Setting	Ending
doctor	Indian	city slicker	floosie	man vs. nature	1800s	cliff hanger
lawyer	bum	land baron	dance hall girl	robbery	closet	everyone happy
Indian chief	deputy	bully	school teacher	town vs. stranger	Montana	serial
marshal	relative	ex-con	widow	large bank deposit lost	town	tragic
stranger	friend	gambler	miner's daughter	man vs.self	desert	butler did it
bartender	foreigner	politician	eastern cousin	good vs.evil	saloon	boy marries girl
shop owner	town drunk	lawyer	wife	family wins a million dollars	mountain	bad guy is transformed
preacher	little kid	bank clerk	old sweetheart	train stuck on cliff	town hall	everyone dies
uncle	a bear	little kid	tomboy	ranchers vs. disease	livery stable	bad guy wins
wife	ex-con	gang member	little sister	cowboys vs. Indians	main street	stranger becomes sheriff

4. Ask students to discuss what they think the value of the word grid was to the show.

Explain the Classification Grid's Purpose

1. Using the model from *The Lone Ranger* show, illustrate the parts of a grid that classify or separate words, objects, or concepts into a common group in which all the single items are alike in one important way.

2. Ask the students to think of a favorite weekly TV show. How would they fill in this grid with its characters and events?

3. Reaffirm the purpose of the grid as a visual classification tool that can be used to generate ideas for a story (as above) or to make sense out of information they collect from reading or doing an experiment.

Clarify and Model the Task

1. Divide the class into learning groups of three. Review the DOVE guidelines, roles and responsibilities, and procedures for a cooperative task that has a shared, common goal.

2. Provide a duplicated copy of the grid (see Master, p. 100) to each member of the group. Each recorder will have a second copy printed on a transparency for the learning group's "official" copy to be submitted for the class discussion.

3. On the board or overhead, display the grid figure with the labeled columns that you select (see examples on pages 97–98).

4. Assign the students the reading material they will use. If fiction, use story elements such as main character, plot, setting; if nonfiction provide up to six appropriate headers. Instruct the students to take notes and fill in the grid as they read or wait until all have finished so they can fill in the grid as a team.

5. Check for understanding by asking the groups to read the first five paragraphs of the print material assigned and start filling in the grid.

Complete the Task

1. Allow the learning groups sufficient time to complete the grids.

2. Assign each learning group a number. Draw a number from a hat or box to select the group that will display its grid for the class.

3. Instruct the selected group to walk through its grid. The other groups will review their own grids and search for items that they can add to the first group's. If any group suggests any change, they must be prepared to explain why.

Guide Reflection

1. **Reflect on Content.** Ask each individual to complete an "I learned . . ." stem about the topic or concept placed on the grid.

Use a small-group round robin that allows each member to share the completed statement with the learning group.

If time allows, use a "wraparound" that allows each student to share the completed stem statement with the class.

2. **Reflect on Process.** Ask each student to write down the steps taken for completing the grid.

Check for a full list of sequenced procedures. Write it on the board or overhead for all to see.

Make a master copy for all to include in a notebook or journal. Review this list prior to additional assignments with the grid.

CLASSIFICATION GRID ORGANIZER EXAMPLES

Elementary Grade Example

Math Grid					
Quantity	Operation	Quantity	Operation	Quantity	= < >
8	+	5	×	2	=
4	–	7	%	4	<

Middle Grade Example

Grammar Grid					
Adverbs	Verbs	Adjectives	Nouns	Prepositions	Conjunctions
Happily	Running	White	Window	Over	But
Very	Buying	Unique	Cow	From	However

Secondary Grade Example

Sewing Grid					
Fabric	Nackline	Sleeve	Fasteners	Color	Hemline
Cotton	Jewel	Long	Zipper	Red	Short
Nylon	V-neck	Cuff	Buttons	Yellow	Mid-calf

MORE IDEAS

Elementary Grade Examples

Mathematics: Geometric shapes, decimals, units of assessment

Language Arts: Story elements: Madeline, Samantha, Peter Pan

Science: Liquids, solids, gases

Social Studies: Explorers, astronauts, pioneers

Other: Community characteristics, team games

Middle Grade Examples

Mathematics: Linear functions, values of integers, multidimensional patterns

Language Arts: Character traits: *The Hobbit, Harry Potter, Wind in the Willows*

Science: Earth's layers, ecosystems, topographic signatures

Social Studies: Powers of the federal government, fundamental liberties, functions of a free press

Other: Drugs, school sports teams, friends

Secondary Grade Examples

Mathematics: Newton's laws, the chain rule, continuity

Language Arts: Author's style: Faulkner, Wright, Joyce

Science: Cells, infections, muscles

Social Studies: Impact of technologies, continental population patterns, nation building trends

Other: College choices, career choices, religions of the world

Make Your Own

Your Ideas

_____

_____

_____

_____

_____

_____

_____

_____

_____

Classification Grid Graphic Organizer

	Before		After	
	Agree	*Disagree*	*Agree*	*Disagree*
1.				
2.				
3.				

14

Agree-Disagree Chart

APPROPRIATE USES

1. Use to stimulate debate on a current event or an issue under study.

2. Use to distinguish differing points of view in an argument.

3. Use to investigate two sides of a disagreement.

4. Use to evaluate biased information.

Key Vocabulary

Debate, disagree, point of view, position

Learning Phase: Making sense

Level of Difficulty: Moderate

Purpose: To help students chart different points of view in a debate, disagreement, or argument

Thinking Process: Evaluating

LESSON DESIGN

Check Prior Knowledge of the Agree-Disagree Organizer

1. Show the chart on an overhead or the board for all to see. Include the words *agree* and *disagree*, *before* and *after*. Name the chart.

2. Identify how many students (a) know the meaning of each term, (b) have used the chart previously, and (c) have a question to ask about how the chart works when two or more points of view are made about a topic or issue.

3. Make a list of the questions. Post the list throughout the lesson.

Explain the Agree-Disagree Chart's Purpose

1. On the overhead or board, write an age- and content-appropriate "controversial" statement such as "George Washington should not have crossed the Delaware" or "Hamlet should have made a prompt decision."

2. Ask for volunteers to agree and disagree with their reasons. Chart these on the board under "before" on the organizer.

3. After several responses, divide the class. All students who disagree stand against the right wall; all who agree stand against the left wall. Ask each group to come up with additional reasons for its choice.

4. Sit the students and ask for the additional reasons. Chart these on the graphic model under "after."

5. After completing the entries, ask the students to explain how the chart helps when there are different points of view.

6. Summarize the responses into the purpose statement.

Clarify and Model the Task

1. Select an age-appropriate story for the students to read. (*Aesop's Fables* provides a multi-age option.)

2. Post the chart with a list of statements. Here is a sample from E. B. White's *Charlotte's Web*.

	Before		After	
Charlotte's Web	Agree	Disagree	Agree	Disagree
1. Spiders are a nuisance.				
2. Spiders are scary.				
3. Spiders have no feelings.				

3. For each of the questions, ask each student who agrees to give a thumbs up. Count and record in the "before" column. Repeat this with the disagree vote.

4. Ask students to read the story. (For young students, read it to them.)

5. After the story, repeat the voting and record results in the "after" column.

6. Check for understanding of the chart's use.

Complete the Task

1. Assign students to cooperative learning groups of three. Review the DOVE guidelines and the roles of recorder, vote counter, and question asker (p. 216). Give each group a chart to tally its responses.

2. Give each group a copy of a short article, a textbook chapter, or a short story to read. The news articles should describe a current conflict or disagreement in the news that relates to the curriculum. All groups may have the same material or you may differentiate the material by group.

3. Post the master chart for all to see with the agree-disagree statements. Give each group its own blank chart for recording its results.

4. After students have read the assigned material, walk among the groups as they discuss and record their votes.

Guide Reflection

1. **Focus on Content.** Ask a sample number of recorders to report on the changes in agree-disagree status after reading the article.

Ask each learning group to discuss its reasons for any changes. After 3–5 minutes, sample the question askers for some of their best reasons for any changes. Use a web (p. 8) so that all can see the recorded, unduplicated reasons.

2. **Focus on Process.** Ask each learning group to complete a PMI chart assessing the pluses, the minuses, and the interesting questions about using the agree-disagree chart with the reading material.

Ask the vote counter in each group to share the points made with the PMI. (Start with the pluses. After several are made, go to the minuses and then to the questions. Make an unduplicated list on the overhead or board for all to see.)

AGREE-DISAGREE CHART ORGANIZER EXAMPLES

Elementary Grade Example

Animal Licenses/ Animal Warden	Before		After	
	Agree	Disagree	Agree	Disagree
1. All outside cats should wear a tag.				
2. Outside dogs should wear a tag.				
3. Other pets should wear a tag.				
4. Inside pets should wear a tag.				

Middle Grade Example

The Most Dangerous Game	Before		After	
	Agree	Disagree	Agree	Disagree
1. It is okay to hunt humans.				
2. The "good guy" always wins.				
3. The lion is the most dangerous game.				

Secondary Grade Example

Alcohol	Before		After	
	Agree	Disagree	Agree	Disagree
1. Black coffee will sober you up.				
2. There is an equal amount of alcohol in a glass of wine and a glass of beer.				
3. Alcoholism is a disease.				

MORE IDEAS

Elementary Grade Examples

Mathematics: Decimals, money, measuring worms

Language Arts: Aladdin, The City Mouse and The Country Mouse, "King Frost"

Science: Properties of matter, prisms, chemical experiments

Social Studies: Our neighborhood, Statue of Liberty, good citizens

Other: Fire safety rules, my favorite sports team, the school bus

Middle Grade Examples

Mathematics: Cross multiplication, distributive properties, circumference

Language Arts: Short stories: "The Red One" (London), "The Inconsiderate Waiter" (Barrie), "My Red Cap" (Alcott)

Science: Continental plates, chloroplasts, genetic variation

Social Studies: Fall of the Roman Empire, Islamic cultures, causes of the Vietnam War

Other: Gangs, pop music, cell phones in school

Secondary Grade Examples

Mathematics: Normal distribution, scatterplots, trigonometric functions

Language Arts: The Fire Next Time (James Baldwin), *Maud Martha* (Gwendolyn Brooks), *Miracle Hill: The Story of a Navajo Boy* (E. Blackfoot Mitchell)

Science: Antibiotic use, offshore oil drilling, NASA

Social Studies: Hybrid engines, AIDS research, United Nations

Other: Rock concerts, being popular, crash diets

Make Your Own

	Before		After	
	Agree	Disagree	Agree	Disagree
1.				
2.				
3.				

Your Ideas

_____

_____

_____

_____

_____

_____

_____

_____

Agree-Disagree Chart
Graphic Organizer

	Before		After	
	Agree	Disagree	Agree	Disagree
1.				
2.				
3.				
4.				
5.				
6.				
7.				
8.				

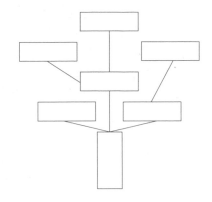

15

Prediction Tree

APPROPRIATE USES

1. Use as an advance organizer for predicting the contents of the next lesson, unit, or book to be read.

2. Use within a story, novel, or drama to predict action or character behavior in the next chapter.

3. Use for predicting the outcomes of a story, event, or decision by a character in a story.

4. Use for predicting the outcomes of a policy, a value system, or way of conceiving an issue.

5. Use for predicting the outcome of a mathematical or scientific procedure.

6. Use for conjecturing when forming a hypothesis.

Key Vocabulary

Infer, predict, estimate, guess, probable, possible, synonym

Attribution

Prediction trees are medical software tools used to analyze brain injuries. Gwendolyn Battle-Lavert (2000) developed this image of the prediction tree for use in the classroom.

LESSON DESIGN

Check Prior Knowledge of Prediction Tree Organizer

1. Show the blank organizer for all to see.

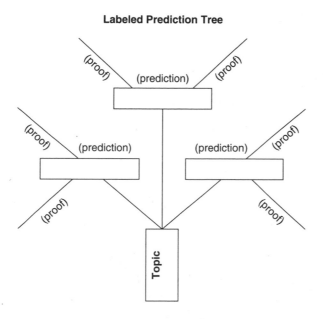

Labeled Prediction Tree

2. Ask students to raise their hands to signal "yes" (hand up), "maybe or not sure" (hand partially up), or "no" (hand down) to the following sequence of open-ended questions:
   - How many have seen the prediction tree as an organizer?
   - How many have used it for making predictions?
   - How many can explain the word *prediction*?
   - How many can provide a synonym for prediction?

3. After asking the questions, go back to ask those students who had "yes" responses to amplify or explain their answers (e.g., "How did you use the tree to make predictions?"; "What are some of the synonyms?").

4. Bridge the student responses or add your own to list reasons for students to develop the ability to make on-target predictions in and out of the classroom.

> **Sample List of Reasons**
>
> 1. In the Classroom
>   - reading interest: What will happen next?
>   - reading comprehension
>   - ability to infer from reading clues
>   - ability to refine reading and other data clues as leading to possible or probable outcomes
>   - limit guessing and random trial and error
>   - delay impulsivity
>
> 2. Outside the Classroom
>   - predict outcomes and consequences of money decisions
>   - draw inferences about news stories
>   - make predictions about safety
>   - make decisions about friends' promises

Explain the Prediction Tree's Purpose

1. Summarize the list of reasons generated to provide the purpose.

2. Write the purpose statement for the lesson for all to see.

Clarify and Model the Task

1. Select a short story. See the "more ideas" subheader below. Top elementary stories for working with the prediction tree are Robert Munsch's *Pigs* or *The Paper Bag Princess* or Gwendolyn Battle-Lavert's *The Shaking Bag*. For middle grades, *The Collected Stories of Chester Himes* and *Billy* by Alfred French provide powerful texts from African American literature that work well with prediction. For the upper grades, Hemingway's "Big Two Hearted River" and Robert Kennedy's *Thirteen Days* fit well.

2. Show the blank organizer.

Labeled Prediction Tree

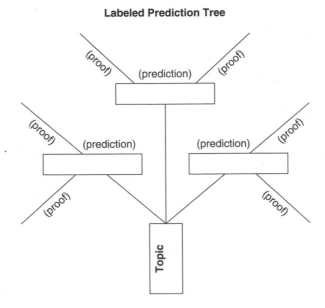

3. Use a familiar children's story (e.g., *Little Engine That Could, Three Billy Goats Gruff*) to model what goes in which space:
- Topic: story title
- Prediction: The second billy goat will go across the bridge and troll will catch him.
- Proof: ("Why I think so") That happened to the first one.
- Result: It happens (mark with a plus "+").

4. Check for understanding of the procedures:
- Put title on trunk of tree.
- Read one page.
- Ask "What do I think will happen next."
- Read to see result.
- Mark result.
- Continue procedures for each page.

5. Allow students to read the selected story alone or group into trios for a "Readers' Theater." For the latter, assign the strongest reader to the reader role; assign the second member as recorder, and the third as a materials manager. Solo readers will need a duplicated copy of this organizer and a pencil. Trios will need markers and a large sheet of newsprint plus a copy of the story per student.

6. Students read the story (in the trio, two follow along).

Complete the Task

1. Monitor and coach students who are hesitant to predict or who are struggling with the proof. Encourage them to give a number rank ("There is very little evidence. This is a guess." = 1; "There is good evidence. This is a possibility." = 2; "This is highly likely to happen. It is a probability." = 3).

The Prediction Rating Scale

1. **A wild guess:** Not likely to happen!

2. **A possibility:** It might happen.

3. **A probability:** No doubt that this is going to happen.

---

2. To coach the students who are hesitant or struggling, invite them to make more frequent stops. Ask them to return to the previous page to check what clues they can find to build their case for the prediction. Do they have sufficient proof (number of clues for the prediction)? If not, have they modified the prediction?

3. If many students are missing the clues, stop the reading and do an all-class guided practice. Take them through the reading and point out the clues for what happens on the following page.

4. If only a few are struggling, form an ad hoc group for the coaching. As the others work independently or in the trios, work with struggling group to identify clues.

5. When students have completed the trees, place a master organizer on the board or overhead for all to see.

6. Present higher-order questions with wait-time. Distribute the opportunity to respond among all the students, being extra careful to call on the struggling students as well.
- What goes on the tree's trunk?
- What is the first prediction?
- How strong is the prediction?
- What clues did you use for proof?

7. Fill in the master chart with the student responses until all predictions and proof are gathered and each individual or learning group tree matches the master tree.

Guide Reflection

1. **Focus on Content.** Ask each student to use the completed tree to write an evaluative summary about the story. The lead question is "How well did the author provide clues leading us to the story's conclusion?"
- Main sentence: Rephrase the question.
- Following sentences: What is the proof that backs up the main idea?

2. **Focus on Thinking Process.** Ask students to respond to these questions. Use wait-time and distribute the opportunity to respond to all students.
- What was a strong, successful prediction you made with this story?
- Why did the prediction "work"?
- When making predictions, what are some helpful guidelines to follow?
- When else in this class could you use the tree to help your predicting?
- In what other classes would the tree help?
- When, outside of school, would using the tree help?
- Why do you think so?

PREDICTION TREE ORGANIZER EXAMPLES

Elementary Grade Example

Language Arts: *The Velveteen Rabbit*

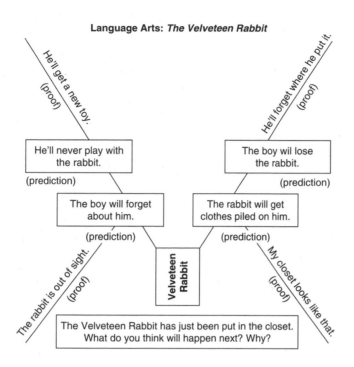

He'll get a new toy. (proof)

He'll forget where he put it. (proof)

He'll never play with the rabbit. (prediction)

The boy wil lose the rabbit. (prediction)

The boy will forget about him. (prediction)

The rabbit will get clothes piled on him. (prediction)

The rabbit is out of sight. (proof)

My closet looks like that. (proof)

Velveteen Rabbit

The Velveteen Rabbit has just been put in the closet. What do you think will happen next? Why?

Middle Grade Example

Science: *Tomato Experiment*

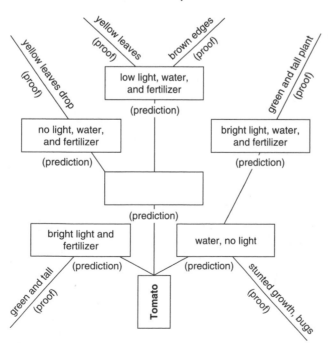

yellow leaves (proof)

brown edges (proof)

yellow leaves drop (proof)

green and tall plant (proof)

low light, water, and fertilizer (prediction)

no light, water, and fertilizer (prediction)

bright light, water, and fertilizer (prediction)

(prediction)

bright light and fertilizer (prediction)

water, no light (prediction)

green and tall (proof)

stunted growth, bugs (proof)

Tomato

Secondary Grade Example

Language Arts: *The Old Man and the Sea*

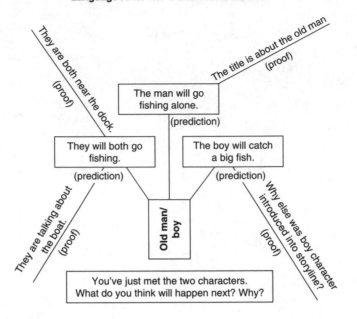

MORE IDEAS

Elementary Grade Examples

Mathematics: Car speed, time to complete a simple task estimate place 10

Language Arts: *Akiak: A Tale From the Iditarod, Kira-Kira, Joseph Had a Little Overcoat*

Science: Slinky stretch experiment, pipe length sounds, rooftop plant experiments

Social Studies: Solar energy results, What happens when a citizen . . . ?

Other: Water color combinations, do not litter campaign

Middle Grade Examples

Mathematics: Estimate mean, median, and mode in a data set; estimate reasonableness of calculated results; predict validity

Language Arts: *A Tale of Two Cities* (Dickens), *A Nervous Breakdown* (Chekhov), *To Build a Fire* (London), *Desiree's Baby* (Chopin)

Science: Earthquake prediction, heat flow, solar light

Social Studies: *The Man Without a Country* (Hale), immigration laws, drug abuse

Other: Future of hip-hop music, rising energy costs, United Nations' future

Secondary Grade Examples

Mathematics: Experimental error, deforestation effects, motion problems

Language Arts: *Invisible Man* (Ellison), *Three Years* (Chehkov), *Tar Baby* (Morrison), *Romeo and Juliet* (Shakespeare), *Spider Boy* (Oates)

Science: Nuclear proliferation, West Coast tsunami, temperature inversions

Social Studies: Technology impact on Third World cultures, terror cells, genocide

Other: Teen pregnancy, a bachelor's degree, service learning

Make Your Own

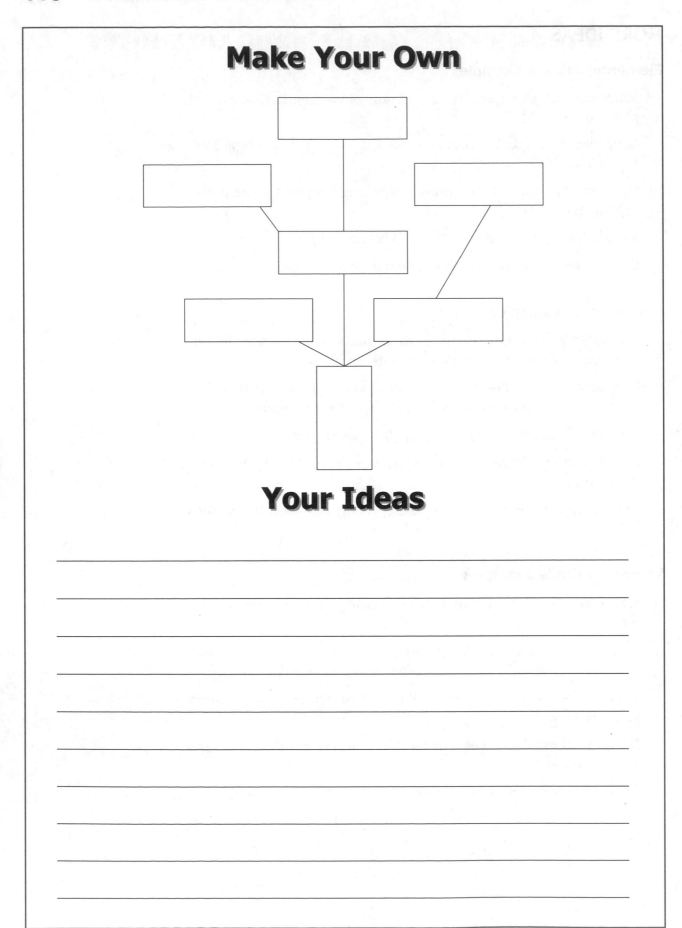

Your Ideas

Predicition Tree Graphic Organizer

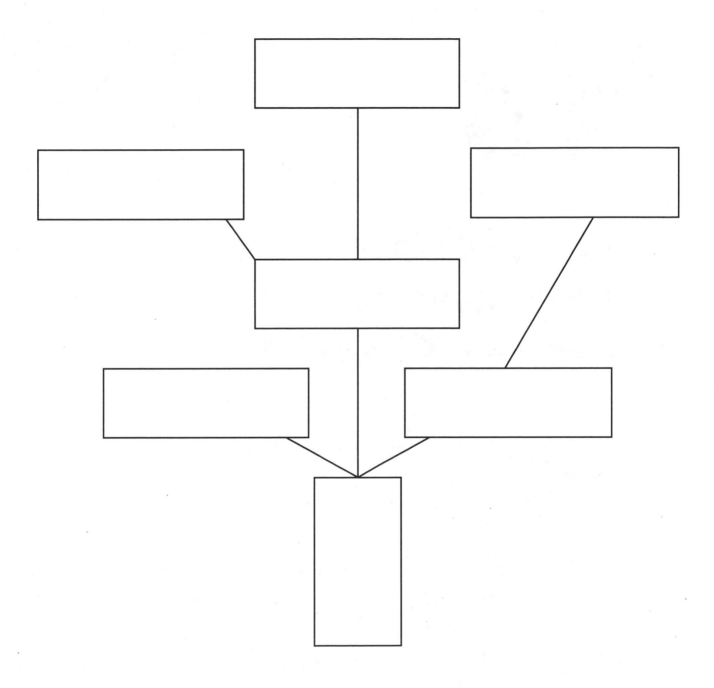

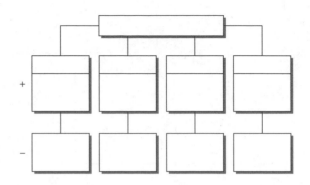

16

Decision Maker's Flow Chart

APPROPRIATE USES

1. Use when students are faced with critical issues in their daily lives inside school, during free time, on a job, at home, or in the community. These may include conflicts with friends, issues of drug use, gang pressures, and so on.

2. Use to help students make career and college choices.

3. Use to help students resolve study versus have fun decisions.

4. Use to role play decisions by key characters in novels, history, current events, science, and the arts.

5. Use to provide students with a framework for resolving family decisions.

Key Vocabulary

Need, consequence, alternative, decision, flow chart, cause, effect

Attribution

Adapted from James Bellanca and Robin Fogarty, *Patterns for Thinking* (1991). IRI/SkyLight.

LESSON DESIGN

Check Prior Knowledge of Decision Maker's Flow Chart Organizer

1. Match students in pairs. Ask them to think of a recent decision they resolved successfully in school or in their out-of-school experiences. What did it take to get that success?

2. Ask pairs to share with each other what each decided. What helped make the choice a success?

3. Call on volunteers to share the stories. Put names in a hat and draw out seven or eight to ensure random opportunity. On the board draw a web and enter key words on the web. Note duplications, but accept all answers.

Web

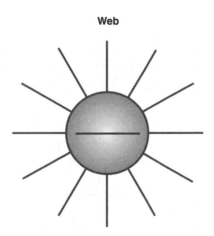

4. Ask the students to suggest the key attributes from the web organizer that help facilitate a good decision. Probe for reasons ("Why do you think that?").

5. Note the good reasons that the students provide. If known, discuss the value of having a graphic organizer to help, add it to the list, and show how it will further enrich their other processes for good decision making.

Explain the Decision Maker's Flow Chart's Purpose

1. Project a chart for all to see.

Decision Maker's Flow Chart

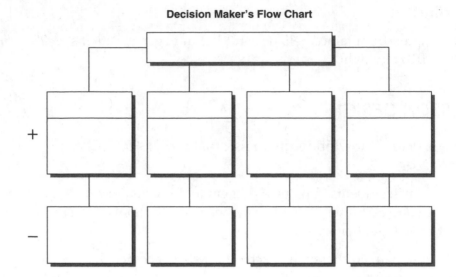

2. Explain that this chart will add to the tools they have for making decisions. It will lay out visually the steps and components in the process so the students can see the many alternatives more clearly.

3. Review the key vocabulary words and seek examples from students' prior experience with each word.

Clarify and Model the Task

1. Label each part of the organizer that you projected for the class to see: topic, need, alternatives, plus and minus consequences, choice.

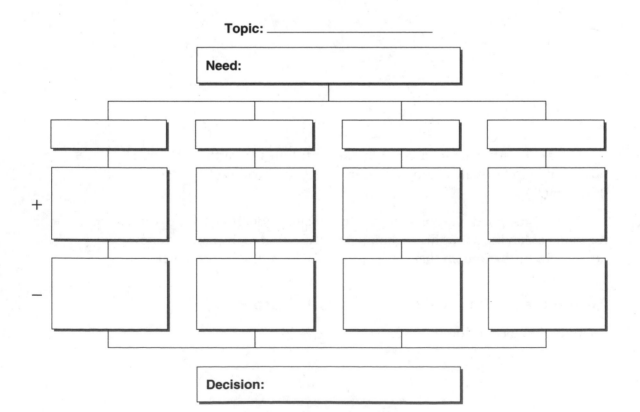

2. Select a story from the daily newspaper of a person faced with a decision. Use this story to fill in the sample chart. Trace the person's decision-making process.

3. Check for understanding of the key components of the organizer (e.g., topic, need).

4. Create student trios. Give each student two of the key vocabulary words and assign them to look up the meanings of each word, sketch it in a picture, and teach/quiz the others on the meaning.

5. After a round-robin teaching of the words, ask the tallest person in each group to check that all understand the words' meanings.

Complete the Task

1. Brainstorm a list of topics for the decision chart. You can facilitate this process by focusing the area of possibilities (e.g., limit it to the characters of a story you are reading, personal school decisions, decisions by a person in the news or a famous person being studied in history, science, or the arts).

2. Review the DOVE guidelines (p. 216) and roles of the recorder, checker, and encourager (pp. 216–217).

3. Distribute markers and newsprint to each learning group. Invite each group to select its own need statement from the brainstorm list.

4. Allow at least 15 minutes for the groups to finish the task. Monitor and coach those students who are having difficulty.

5. Post completed charts and allow several groups to explain them. Give praise and constructive feedback as needed.

Guide Reflection

1. **Focus on Process.** Ask each group to assess its teamwork in completing the chart. (How well did they work together? How can they work together better as a team?)

Assign each student the task of using the chart for making a decision related to the content of your course. Ask them to explain in writing why they choose the need and the final decision.

After writing their responses, students will engage in an all-class discussion of the value of the decision maker's chart. How is it helpful? Where else might they use it?

2. **Focus on Content.** Ask students, in groups of six, to agree on What was most difficult for the person making a decision to do? What was easiest?

Ask one or two groups to report on their understandings. Probe with "Why do you think that?"

DECISION MAKER'S FLOW CHART EXAMPLES

Elementary Grade Example

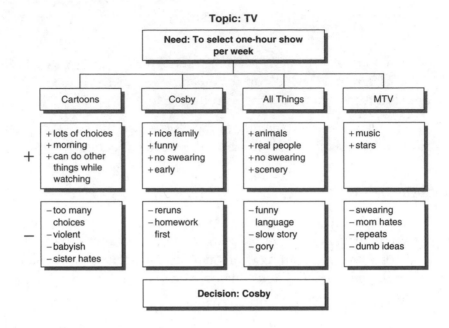

Topic: TV

Need: To select one-hour show per week

Cartoons	Cosby	All Things	MTV
+lots of choices +morning +can do other things while watching	+nice family +funny +no swearing +early	+animals +real people +no swearing +scenery	+music +stars
−too many choices −violent −babyish −sister hates	−reruns −homework first	−funny language −slow story −gory	−swearing −mom hates −repeats −dumb ideas

Decision: Cosby

Middle Grade Example

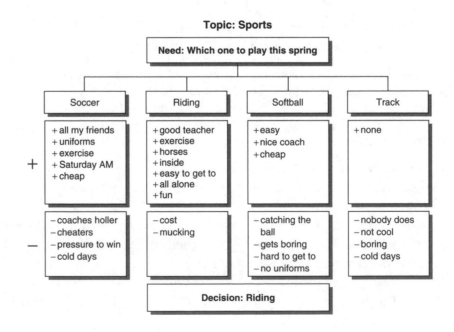

Topic: Sports

Need: Which one to play this spring

Soccer	Riding	Softball	Track
+all my friends +uniforms +exercise +Saturday AM +cheap	+good teacher +exercise +horses +inside +easy to get to +all alone +fun	+easy +nice coach +cheap	+none
−coaches holler −cheaters −pressure to win −cold days	−cost −mucking	−catching the ball −gets boring −hard to get to −no uniforms	−nobody does −not cool −boring −cold days

Decision: Riding

Secondary Grade Example

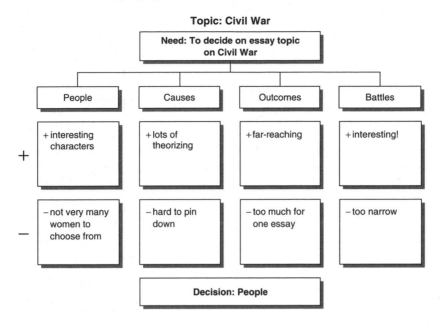

Topic: Civil War

| Need: To decide on essay topic on Civil War |

| People | Causes | Outcomes | Battles |

+
| + interesting characters | + lots of theorizing | + far-reaching | + interesting! |

−
| − not very many women to choose from | − hard to pin down | − too much for one essay | − too narrow |

| Decision: People |

MORE IDEAS

Elementary Grade Examples

Mathematics: Which problem-solving method to use?, Which visual project to use to show understanding of geometry shapes?

Language Arts: Which book to read during sustained silent reading?, What characters in a story show similarities?, What topic to choose for the next writing assignment?

Science: Which scientist's biography to read?, What way to present the results of an experiment?, What project topic to choose for the classroom science fair?

Social Studies: What decisions by a president to study?, Which action project on the environment to do?, Who to interview about school safety?

Other: Which medium to use for an art project?, When is the best time to practice an instrument for the school musical tryouts?, What foods to change for a more nutritional lunch?

Middle Grade Examples

Mathematics: Which consumer product to analyze and evaluate with data?, Which hypothesis to use to solve the "swimming pool tile" problem?, Which graph to use to illustrate a completed word problem?

Language Arts: What author to select for a book report?, What editorial position to take in the class newsletter on an emerging issue of bullying at the school?, What arguments to use in defense of a literary character put on mock trial?

Science: What science career to consider?, With whom to partner? For the end-of-year science project?, What science to study first in high school?

Social Studies: What topic to choose about global conflicts?, To whom to address a letter of opinion about a local conflict?

Other: When to do daily homework?, What school sports to try out for?, How to say no to peers about drinking at a party?

Secondary Grade Examples

Mathematics: How to model relationships involved in solving a "health" word problem about prescription drug dosages?, Which advanced courses in mathematics to take in grades 11 and 12?, What math-related careers to consider?

Language Arts: What topic to select for an essay comparing a literary character from a class-studied novel with a character from a current TV drama?, What research topic to consider for the required research paper in Junior-year English?, What theme to select for reporting about the major authors studied in the Senior curriculum?

Science: What position to take regarding a contemporary science issue such as use of laser research for military purposes?, Which data manipulation and analysis strategy to use with an assigned inquiry project?, Which modeling approach to use to distinguish between the value of science and the value of technology in pursuing new applications of theoretical insights?

Social Studies: Which mathematical tools and concepts to use to analyze the current flow of immigrants in the Western Hemisphere?, What principles of American democracy to apply to current electoral college issues?, Which biographies to use to contrast the beliefs and effects of social Darwinism and social gospel on nineteenth-century politics?

Other: What major to select for study in college?, What elements to include in a physical conditioning program?, What composer to select for a musical recital?

Make Your Own

Topic: _____

Need:

+

−

Decision:

Your Ideas

_____

_____

_____

_____

_____

_____

_____

_____

Decision Maker's Flow Chart

Topic: _____

Need:

Decision:

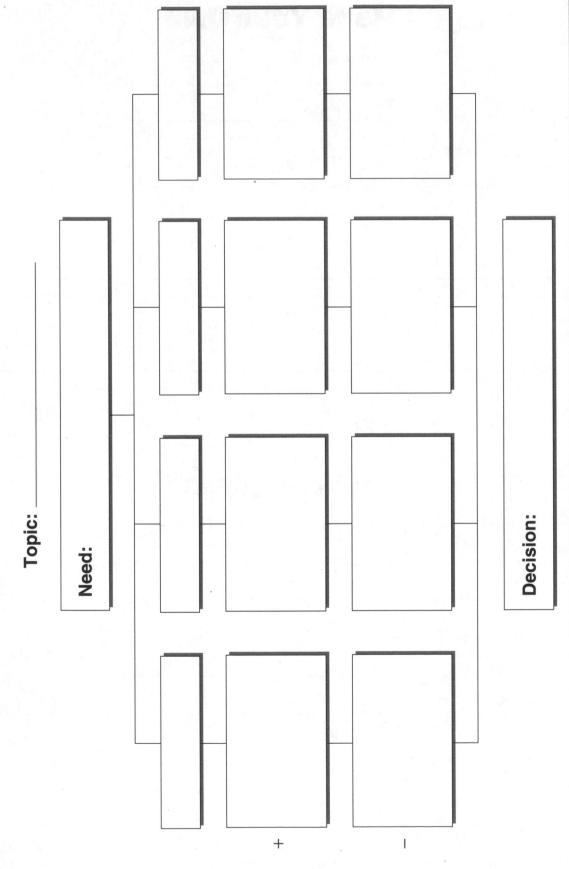

+

−

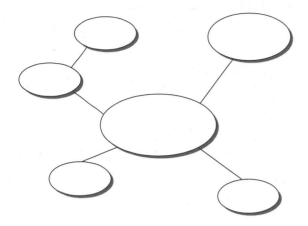

17

Concept Map

APPROPRIATE USES

1. Use as an advance organizer for a unit of study that builds on students' prior knowledge in an extensive way and will require frequent classroom discussions. Start with the map to collect students' prior knowledge on the topic. Encourage students to maintain the organizer through the unit, especially during all-class discussions.

2. Encourage students to use the map as they read textbook material or fiction books.

3. Use to map research studies.

4. Use to map thematic units.

5. Use to construct a concept map on a bulletin board. Expand it as the unit progresses.

Key Vocabulary

Connect, relationships, concept, fact

Attribution

The concept mapping strategy was developed by Joseph D. Novak (1998).

Learning Phases: Gathering information, making sense

Level of Difficulty: Challenging

Purpose: To enable students to find or make relationships among concepts and details collected from multiple and/or complex sources of information

Thinking Processes: Seeing relationships, similarities

LESSON DESIGN

Check Prior Knowledge of the Concept Map Organizer

1. On the overhead or board, show this statement: "A house is like a_____." Ask students to pick a second object to fill in the blank and complete the line with "because . . ." to show how their statement is true (e.g., "A house is like an airplane because both can have seats inside" or "both are people holders").

2. Explain to students that they are seeing relationships between the two objects. Some relationships or connections are factual, others more abstract.

3. Show a web on the board. Ask students to tell you what they know about the web as a graphic organizer. Put their responses on the sample web.

Web

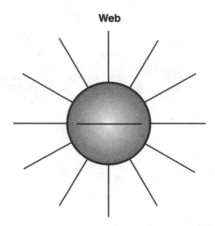

4. Tell the students that they are going to take the web a step further and use it as a tool to map relationships they see among similar ideas. The new organizer is called a concept map or a mind map.

Explain the Concept Map's Purpose

1. Using the emerging concept map, show the students how you have connected the items on the map. Select several and ask students to tell you why they think you made the connections. (If helpful, cue them with a reminder of the house-airplane analogy above.)

2. Explain that the purpose of the concept map is to improve the students' ability to make logical connections among ideas that may not seem connected at first glance. Check for understanding by asking for other examples of connected ideas that may not seem related at first.

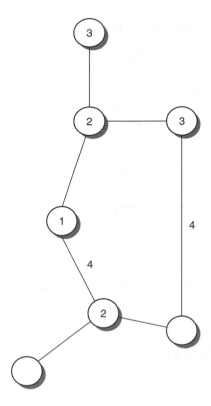

Key
1. Core concept or main topic
2. Sub-topics
3. Details or facts
4. Connection lines

Clarify and Model the Task

1. Display an age-appropriate sample map (see the following examples). Point out the examples of (a) the key idea, (b) sub-ideas, (c) connecting details, and (d) connecting lines. If possible, use different color markers to highlight the display.

2. Form mixed-ability groups of three. Assign three roles: the materials manager (gets and manages the newsprint and colored markers), the map-maker (draws the map elements and leads decision making), the word recorder (writes in the words agreed on by group). Review DOVE guidelines (p. 216).

3. Assign the reading task. Jigsaw the subtopics so that each student in a group is reading with a different focus, or have all three read the same material. Chunk longer reading tasks so that the groups alternate between working with the text and the map.

Complete the Task

1. Allow sufficient time for all groups to finish.

2. Monitor the map making and check that all are doing their jobs.

Guide Reflection

1. **Focus on Content.** When the map is completed, ask students to make journal entries completing this lead-in: "What were the most important contributing ideas that you learned about 'the big idea' in this task?" When finished, invite them to read round robin to other members in the group. Conclude with a class discussion of each subtopic: What does it mean? How does it support the big idea? Why is the sub-idea important?

2. **Focus on Process.** Select up to three groups to present their completed maps to the class. When finished explaining the map's content, each group will share its reasons for any three similarities among connected items.

Assess Student Learning

Ask students to complete a short essay that will assess understanding of both (a) the content and (b) how to form a concept map.

CONCEPT MAP ORGANIZER EXAMPLES

Elementary Grade Example

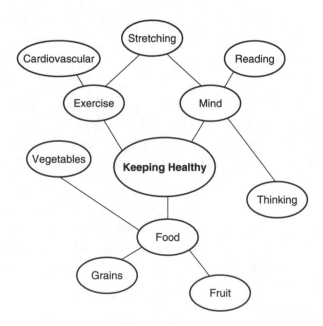

Middle Grade Example

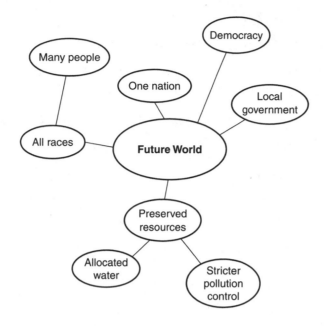

Secondary Grade Example

Concept Map Sample
English: Maya Angelou

MORE IDEAS

Elementary Grade Examples

Mathematics: Numbers, operations, basic geometric shapes

Language Arts: *Who Is in Rabbit's House?: A Masai Tale, Madeline's Adventures, The World of Peter Rabbit and Friends*

Science: Means of transportation, dinosaurs, food chain

Social Studies: Classmates, our town, the president

Others: Hobbies, our school, "Peter and the Wolf"

Middle Grade Examples

Mathematics: Problem-solving terms, factoring, stock market math project

Language Arts: Story writing, poems of Gwendolyn Brooks, *Of Mice and Men*

Science: Space travel, whales, scientific method

Social Studies: U.S. Constitution, Thurgood Marshall, Ryker's Island

Other: True friends, dream vacations, hobbies

Secondary Grade Examples

Mathematics: Linear equations, solving inequalities, algebraic symbols

Language Arts: T. S. Eliot, *Death of a Salesman*, Godfrey Mwakikagile

Science: Mole theory, endothermic reactions, photosynthesis

Social Sciences: Social class and poverty, biopolitics, destructive insects

Other: Date rape, impressionist painters, Leonard Bernstein's *West Side Story*

Make Your Own

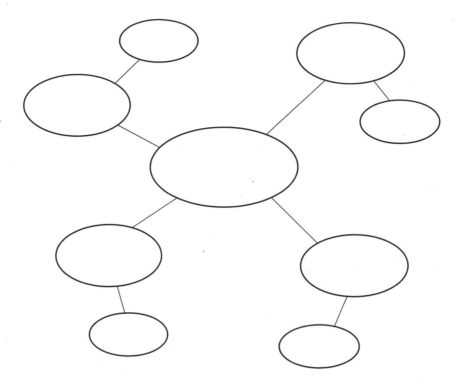

Your Ideas

_____

_____

_____

_____

_____

_____

_____

_____

_____

Concept Map Graphic Organizer

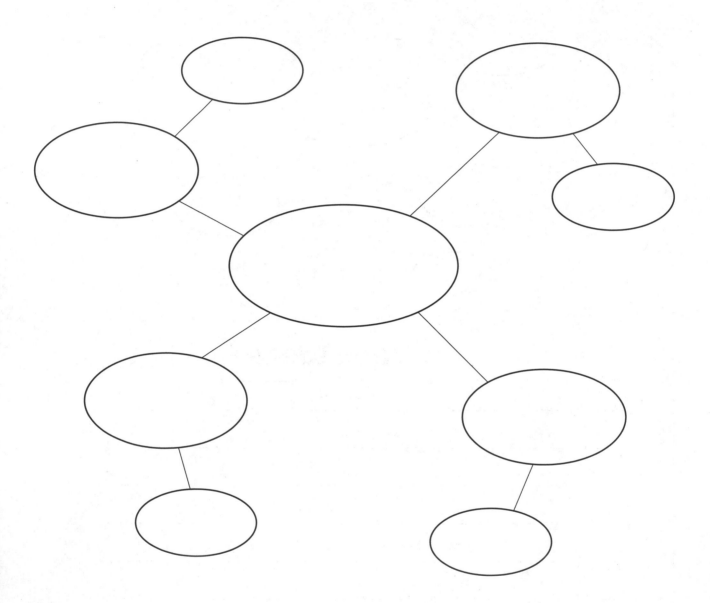

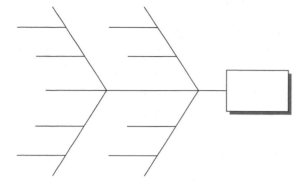

18

Fishbone Analyzer

APPROPRIATE USES

1. Use to introduce students to the concepts of cause and effect.

2. Use to introduce or overview lessons that connect events by cause and effect.

3. Use to summarize cause-effect patterns in scientific, historic, or literary events.

4. Use to facilitate students' analysis of cause and effect patterns of thinking.

Key Vocabulary

Cause, effect, analysis, impact, results

Attribution

This graphic organizer was developed by Kaoru Ishikawa in the 1940s for use in total quality management studies.

Learning Phase: Making sense

Level of Difficulty: Challenging

Purpose: To develop students' ability to establish causal connections

Thinking Process: Analyzing causes and effects

LESSON DESIGN

Check Prior Knowledge of the Fishbone Analyzer Organizer

1. Show a picture of the fishbone analyzer to the class.

2. Check to see how many *know* this as a graphic organizer by asking for thumbs up ("yes") or down ("no"). Repeat the check to see how many have *used* this organizer.

3. If any students can help, ask them to explain how the fishbone is used as an organizer, preferably with an example. If not, go to the next step.

Explain the Fishbone Analyzer's Purpose

1. See Purpose above. Review key vocabulary words with commonplace cause and effect relationships (e.g., hand in a fire, excess water in a closed container, hammer on a nail).

2. Ask students to identify cause-effect patterns from their experience.

Clarify and Model the Task

1. Post a blank fishbone for all to see.

2. In the head, write "car accident." At the end of each major bone, write the category labels: "people," "machines," "environment," "others." The categories will give clues to possible causes of the accident (the effect). Clues may include brake failure, misjudgment, wet road, darkness, and so forth.

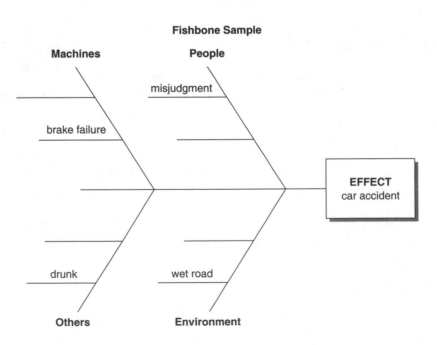

Fishbone Sample

3. Ask students to provide other possible causes. Enter these on the model.

4. Check that the students know how to set up the fishbone organizer.

Complete the Task

1. Set up learning groups of three. Review the DOVE guidelines (p. 216) and the roles of checker, recorder, materials manager (pp. 216–217). Distribute newsprint, markers, and tape to each group (p. 217).

2. Provide a cause-effect task selected from the content of an upcoming chapter. All groups should use the same task with print or video material providing the evidence that they will need. (For suggestions, see sample ideas below.)

3. Instruct students to read the material that contains the information needed to set up the fishbone organizer with the title you have provided in the "head." Use the same category labels as modeled with the "car accident."

4. When students in a learning group have completed their information gathering from the material provided, they will begin the task of placing possible causes in the appropriate category.

After a student provides an idea, the checker makes sure all agree on its placement in a category.

Continue with each student in a group taking a turn until all ideas are exhausted.

5. After all ideas are categorized, each person will select the three he or she believes to be the most likely cause. The recorder will list each person's ideas in a column before making an unduplicated master list.

Carl	Ray	Group List
1. wet road	1. drunk	• wet road
2. drunk	2. brake failure	• drunk
3. fell asleep	3. sun in eyes	• fell asleep
		• break failure
		• sun in eyes

6. Each learning group will vote on its master list. Each person has three votes. Each vote has a value point (1 = 3 points, 2 = 2 points, 1 = 1 point). Before casting votes, individuals may tell "why" for the votes they want. However, there is no disagreement about any reasons given.

7. The recorder will make a list of the final vote in the group.

8. Select one group to post its fishbone with only its final three ideas showing. In turn, ask others to add to the fishbone organizer without duplicating any ideas.

9. Hold a 10-minute "reasons why" discussion with the entire class.

10. At the end of the discussion, ask all to vote with the three-vote system for items listed on the organizer. What are the three most likely causes?

Guide Reflection

1. **Reflect on Content.** Ask each learning group to come up with reasons for the top three items on the class's fishbone as the most likely causes.

Ask each learning group to come up with reasons any of the top three should not be on this final list.

Require groups to go to their resource materials to back the arguments.

Allow one group to present one argument pro and the others to refute it with the arguments against its inclusion.

Repeat this step with each of the top three ideas, allowing no more than 7 minutes for each debate.

2. **Reflect on Process.** Ask each learning group to construct a fishbone on a cause-effect pattern with which its members are familiar.

Instruct individuals in each group to select the most likely cause of the effect selected and explain "why."

Provide a final stem for the fishbone: "The fishbone is . . ."

FISHBONE ORGANIZER EXAMPLES

Elementary Grade Example

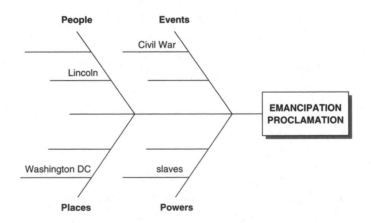

Middle Grade Example

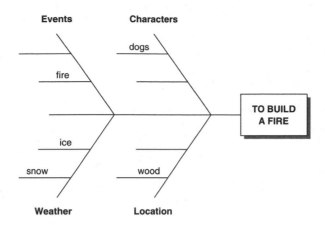

Secondary Grade Example

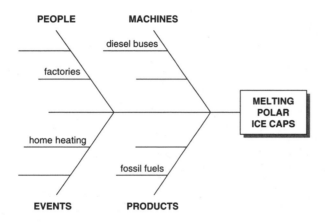

OTHER IDEAS

Elementary Grade Examples

Language Arts: *Louie's Search* (Ezra Jack Keats), *Paper Bag Princess* (Robert Munsch), *Amazing Grace* (Mary Hoffman)

Science: Fungi growth, plant growth, human health

Social Studies: Consequences of rule breaks, Declaration of Independence, Underground Railroad

Other: Damage to hearing, a trip to grandmother's house

Middle Grade Examples

Language Arts: Her stories: *African-American Folktales* (Virginia Hamilton), *The Lizard and the Sun* (Ada Alma), *Too Many Tamales* (Gary Soto)

Science: Man on the moon, avalanches, tsunamis

Social Studies: Slave trade, Westward movement, Trail of Tears

Other: Darfur crisis, melting ice caps, alcoholism

Secondary Grade Examples

Language Arts: Lost Generation poets, deaths of Romeo and Juliet, *Arrow of God* (Achebe)

Science: Doppler effect, conservation of energy, entropy

Social Studies: Magna Carta, Bill of Rights, terror, famine of the Ukraine

Other: Depression, STDs, college admittance

Make Your Own

Your Ideas

_____

_____

_____

_____

_____

_____

_____

_____

_____

Fishbone Analyzer Graphic Organizer

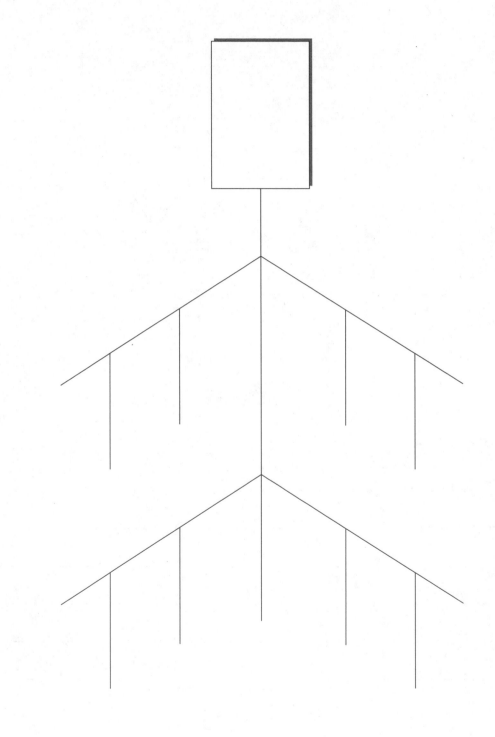

I	
D	
E	
A	
S	

19

Problem-Solving Chart

APPROPRIATE USES

1. Use to review the best ways to avoid "strangers" (K–8).

2. Use in social studies to create hypothetical peaceful solutions to wars.

3. Use in literature to help a main character solve a problem.

4. Use in writing to outline best ways to organize an expository essay.

5. Use in mathematics to develop concepts.

6. Use in mathematics to find ways to improve multiplication tables.

Key Vocabulary

Problem statement, analyze, sequence

Learning Phase: Making sense

Level of Difficulty: Challenging

Purpose: To provide students with a framework for solving problems

Thinking Processes: Problem posing, analyzing, evaluating by criteria and sequencing

Attribution

Adapted from James Bellanca and Robin Fogarty, *Patterns for Thinking* (1991). IRI/SkyLight.

LESSON DESIGN

Check Prior Knowledge of Problem-Solving Chart Organizer

1. Divide the class into groups of three. Review the DOVE guidelines (p. 216). Give each learning group one set of three index cards, all with the same job role written on the back.

2. Explain the IDEAS chart by uncovering one letter at a time. Select one of the examples at the end of this lesson to illustrate each point.

3. Invite each student to fill in a blank chart (p. 150). Use selecting "job roles" as the topic, and explain that all three persons in a group have cards with the same role. Ask the class members to figure out how to form groups that include each of the three job roles.

4. Instruct these groups with the same cards to use the IDEAS chart to come up with a solution.

5. Give each group a blank IDEAS chart on a transparency plus a marker. Allow 6–10 minutes.

6. Ask the materials managers from several groups to take turns and share their completed charts with the class. Instruct the listening students to search for similarities among the three to five reports you selected.

7. At the end of each learning group's report, ask its recorder to describe what he or she found hard in completing the project. Make a master list on the board.

Problem-Solving Chart Instructions

I	Index the facts as you see them.
D	Define the problem.
E	Expand on ideas or possible alternatives.
A	Adopt a criterion.
S	Select and sell your idea to others involved.

8. Complete the check of prior knowledge with an all-class discussion in which you ask students to tell how this approach was similar to or different from other ways they know to solve problems.

Explain the Problem-Solving Chart Organizer's Purpose

Select examples based on the prior knowledge check above.

Clarify and Model the Task

1. Walk back through the use of the IDEAS chart for coming up with solutions to the group roles problem.

2. Select a problem based on the material the students are studying in the current unit. (The sample ideas below may help you select a "problem" from your content area.)

Problem-Solving Chart Literacy Example

Topic: "The Lion and the Mouse"

I	Index the Facts As You See Them. (Students look for clues that describe the lion's predicament. "His foot is caught in a trap.")
D	Define the Problem. (Students infer the consequences for the lion who has his foot in the trap. What are the clues as to what will happen to him? Why do they think that?)
E	Expand on Other Possible Alternatives. (Ask students to hypothesize what else could happen. Could he escape? How? Why do they think so?)
A	Adapt a Criterion. ("Everyone should go free.")
S	Select Your Ideas and Sell Them to Others. ("Mouse will eat the ropes and the two will run from the hunters.")

3. The imbedded mnemonic (IDEAS) in this graphic gives students a way to recall the steps of the problem-solving process. It helps them break the story down as a problem to be solved. It is also a tool that enables teachers to examine underdeveloped cognitive functions. For instance, in this problem-solving sequence, students must draw inferences and develop hypotheses about the reading material. Inferring and hypothesizing are two important thinking operations that impact the quality of reading comprehension. Students may be strong, average, or weak in using these operations. To strengthen weak operations, teachers can select cognitive functions, such as blurred perception and accuracy. (For this problem-solving chart, refer to the chart of cognitive functions (p. 211) for a more complete discussion of the relevant cognitive functions.)

4. Using reading material selected for this unit (textbook, article, literature), instruct the groups of three to rotate their roles; review the DOVE

guidelines and the chart. Each group will construct an IDEAS chart for the material assigned.

5. When the groups have finished, ask each to share its chart with the class. Those listening will provide constructive feedback.

Guide Reflection

1. **Focus on Process.** Each group of three will reflect on these three questions. The recorder will write the composite response on a sheet of 8.5×11 paper.
   - What did we do well in following the IDEAS process?
   - If we used IDEAS again, how could we improve the process?
   - What help do we need to improve?

2. **Focus on Content.** On the reverse side, complete these three questions:
   - What did we learn about the material in this chapter?
   - How did IDEAS help us?

PROBLEM-SOLVING CHART ORGANIZER EXAMPLES

Elementary Grade Example

Topic: "The Little Engine That Could"

I	Train starts up the hill
D	Heavy load
E	More coal in the boiler, cut car off, less coal, extra effort
A	No help
S	Extra effort "I think I can."

Middle Grade Example

Topic: Noise in Cafeteria

I	– Students yell across table, clash trays, high pitch
D	– Students not controlling loudness
E	– Quiet signs and signals – Air raid siren – Ban the noisiest – Quiet checker at table
A	– Students can hear to the other end of table – Students use 6" voices
S	– Table checker and signal; have all students practice

Secondary Grade Example

Topic: Community Garbage

I	– Junk and food wrappers on lawns and streets
D	– Community looks dirty
E	– Ban junk food – Clean-up campaign – Containers on corners
A	– 100% no junk food wrappers
S	– Students have a clean-up day once a month

MORE IDEAS

Elementary Grade Examples

Mathematics: After completing a study of coin problems, asking groups of students to construct a sample problem; exchanging problems and use IDEAS as the way to solve

Language Arts: Brainstorming a list of problems for a character from a favorite story; in pairs, students use the IDEAS chart

Science: In class, construct an interview to give to parents, storeowners, or friends. What problems do they see in the community caused by pollution?

Social Studies: Field trip to a local park: ask the class to observe the park grounds and to find what they could fix

Other: Stranger danger, homework, fighting with a friend, TV time

Middle Grade Examples

Mathematics: Using proportions to solve problems, using number operations of positive fractions

Language Arts: Author's purpose, author's point of view, character's main challenge in story

Science: Junk food, tension, heart diseases, bullies

Social Studies: Indigenous cultures of North America

Other: Rules, cliques, gangs

Secondary Grade Examples

Mathematics: Quadratic formula, DeMoivre's theorem, Gauss-Jordan elimination

Language Arts: *Escape from Slavery* (Bok), *Maud Martha* (Brooks), *Romeo and Juliet* (Shakespeare)

Science: Alzheimer's disease, deforestation, nuclear proliferation

Social Studies: Genocide in Africa, illegal immigration, gender bias in science

Other: Dating, parties with alcohol, picking a college

Make Your Own

	THE PROBLEM-SOLVING CHART Topic:
I Index the facts as you see them.	
D Define the problem.	
E Expand on ideas or possible alternatives.	
A Adopt a criterion.	
S Select and sell your idea to others involved.	

Your Ideas

Problem-Solving Chart Graphic Organizer

	Topic:
I Index the facts as you see them.	
D Define the problem.	
E Expand on ideas or possible alternatives.	
A Adopt a criterion.	
S Select and sell your idea to others involved.	

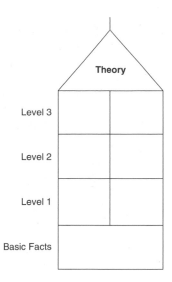

20

Two-Way Thinking Tower

APPROPRIATE USES

1. Use to provide a model that helps students understand the relationship between inductive and deductive thinking.

2. Use to help students connect specific facts to abstract theory.

3. Use to enable students to assess the validity of a theory.

4. Use to analyze data in support of a hypothesis.

Key Vocabulary

Induction, deduction, analysis, synthesis, theory, fact

Learning Phase: Making sense

Level of Difficulty: Challenging

Purpose: To enable students to use a visual model for understanding the complex processes of inductive and deductive thinking

Thinking Processes: Induction, deduction, analyzing, synthesizing

Adapted from Clarke, J. H., Raths, J., & Gilbert, G. L. (1989). Inductive towers: Letting students see how they think. *Journal of Reading, 33*(2), 86–95. Graphic Organizer created by Robin Fogarty.

Attribution

Adapted from Clarke, J. H., Raths, J., & Gilbert, G. L. (1989). Inductive towers: Letting students see how they think. *Journal of Reading, 33*(2), 86–95. Graphic Organizer created by Robin Fogarty.

LESSON DESIGN

Check Prior Knowledge of the Two-Way Thinking Tower Organizer

1. Post "comparison alley" organizer for all to see. Label the headers with "induction" and "deduction." Break down the vocabulary words with the prefixes and roots (to lead) for "to lead in" and "to lead out" (de). Identify the subject as "patterns for thinking."

2. Ask students to work to identify any familiarity they have with these words by identifying on the chart what they know are similarities between the words and what are the differences. Write these on the chart posted for all to see. After students have finished what they can offer (Don't forget lots of wait time!), fill in the missing elements. Note that many students who have experienced the words often "mix-up" the terms and their meanings.

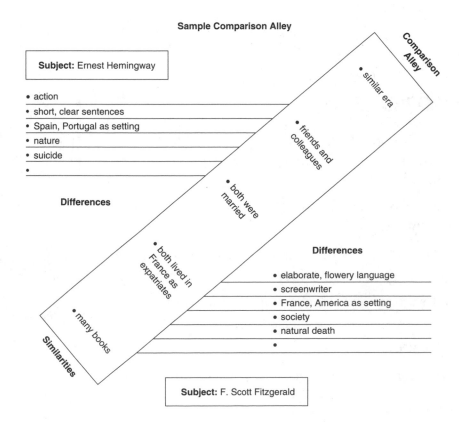

Sample Comparison Alley

Comparison Alley

Subject: Ernest Hemingway

- action
- short, clear sentences
- Spain, Portugal as setting
- nature
- suicide
-

Differences

- similar era
- friends and colleagues
- both were married
- both lived in France as expatriates
- many books

Similarities

Differences

- elaborate, flowery language
- screenwriter
- France, America as setting
- society
- natural death
-

Subject: F. Scott Fitzgerald

Explain the Two-Way Thinking Tower's Purpose

1. Show the blank tower organizer for all to see.

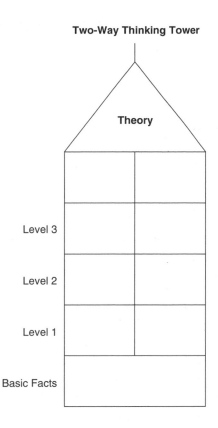

Two-Way Thinking Tower

Theory

Level 3

Level 2

Level 1

Basic Facts

2. Explain the tower as a model to show the inductive pattern of thinking, clarify the definition, and provide the purpose of this lesson (above). End with an indication of how they will next use the model in a follow-up task that you will assign.

Clarify and Model the Task

1. Enter a theory at the top of the map (e.g., *Tyrannosaurus rex* was a carnivore).

2. Go to the bottom of the map and enter factual data (e.g., claws, dung, socket teeth, long legs, short arms, jaws, olfactory space in brain, wounds, duck-billed remains, bone fragments of plant eaters).

3. Group like facts and label each group on the next level (e.g., smell, eaten food remains, appendages, mouth).

4. Continue up levels by forming new, more abstract groups with appropriate labels (e.g., chaser, top of food chain evidence, biter).

5. Determine if the facts actually lead to proving the theory. Adjust the theory as the gathered facts show new evidence.

Complete the Task

1. Form mixed-ability groups of three. Provide reading material to each group on a topic taken from their textbooks or other written materials you provide. (As an alternative, assign each group its own topic.)

2. Review the DOVE guidelines (p. 216). Assign and review the roles of recorder, reporter, and reader (pp. 216–217). Distribute large (3 × 4) newsprint and markers to each group. Instruct recorders to enter the top triangle (#1) for the organizer and the bottom box (#2). Allow large blank space between for the levels of labels. Younger students may want to draw pictures rather than write words. *It is important, however, that they do represent their own ideas rather than use preprinted cards.*

3. Present the topic(s) to the groups, which they will enter on their towers. Invite them to use the provided material to search out facts (#2).

4. Circulate among the learning groups as they gather factual information from the reading material. They can do this data collection in any random fashion as facts appear in the reading.

5. Allow sufficient time for the groups to gather enough information to group. Remind them to find how they can best agree (no one magic answer!) on words that have a similarity. They can then label those groups and write in both the grouped facts (#3) and the new label (#4). Challenge the learning trios to group the label categories in higher levels of abstraction. For each higher group, they must provide a label and place that on the next level (#5). This may result in some re-categorizing of lower-level groups.

6. When the learning trios have completed the last level of labeling, ask them to review the tower from bottom to top and determine if the top label categories make sense from bottom to top.

Guide Reflection

1. **Reflect on Process.** In journals, each group member can complete this stem starter: "In our project, the tower helped us to see the two-way connection between induction and deduction by. . . ." Each learning trio will share its completed stems.

2. **Reflect on Content.** In journals, each group member can write a summary paragraph that starts with the stem, "Three learnings I made about the topic _____ from completing this tower are. . . ."

3. Select one student from each trio to share the completed stem. On the board, use a web to record the statements for all to see.

Web

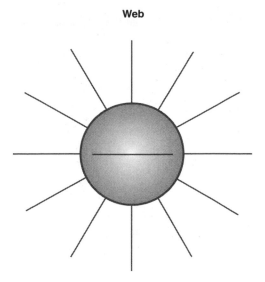

TWO-WAY THINKING TOWER ORGANIZER EXAMPLES

Elementary Grade Example

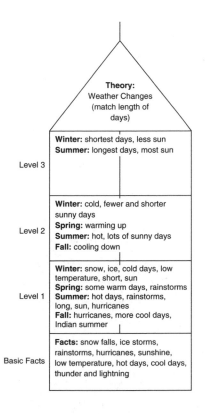

Middle Grade Example

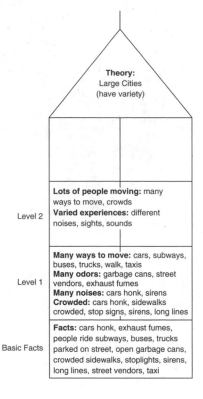

Secondary Grade Example

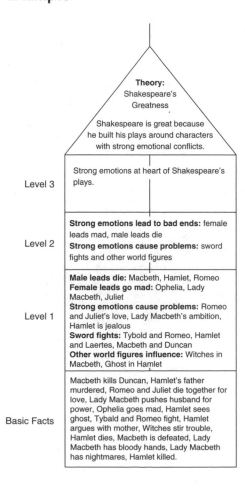

MORE IDEAS

Elementary Grade Examples

Mathematics: Volume relationships, landmark numbers, spatial relationships

Language Arts: *El Autobus Magico* (series), *Half-a-Ball-of-Kenki: An Ashanti Story*

Science: Food chain, sunlight, pulley power

Social Studies: Our town, traveling on an airplane

Other: Clean parks and playgrounds

Middle Grade Examples

Mathematics: Inverse relationships of numbers, nonstandard unit measurement

Language Arts: Archetypical patterns in myths, structural features of informative text, inferential thinking

Science: Life cycle of frogs, planets, simple machines

Social Studies: Incan architectural influences, Arabic language, imperial state of China

Other: Health effects of marijuana, hip-hop music, the Special Olympics

Secondary Grade Examples

Mathematics: Absolute value of real numbers, nonstandard units, inverse relationships

Language Arts: Figurative language, autobiographic narratives, *The Tree Where Man Was Born* (Mathiessen)

Science: Quantum theory of atomic structures, oil drop experiment, intermolecular force

Social Studies: Causes of war, the Industrial Revolution, colonial rule

Other: Andalusian architecture, compositions of Leonard Bernstein, city of San Francisco

Make Your Own

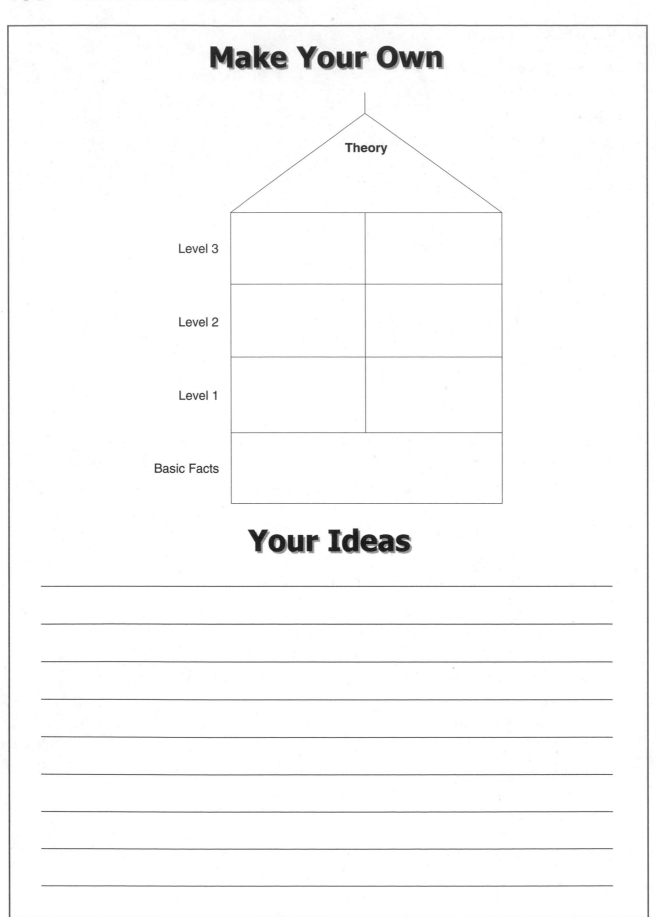

Theory

Level 3

Level 2

Level 1

Basic Facts

Your Ideas

_____

_____

_____

_____

_____

_____

_____

_____

Two-Way Thinking Tower
Graphic Organizer

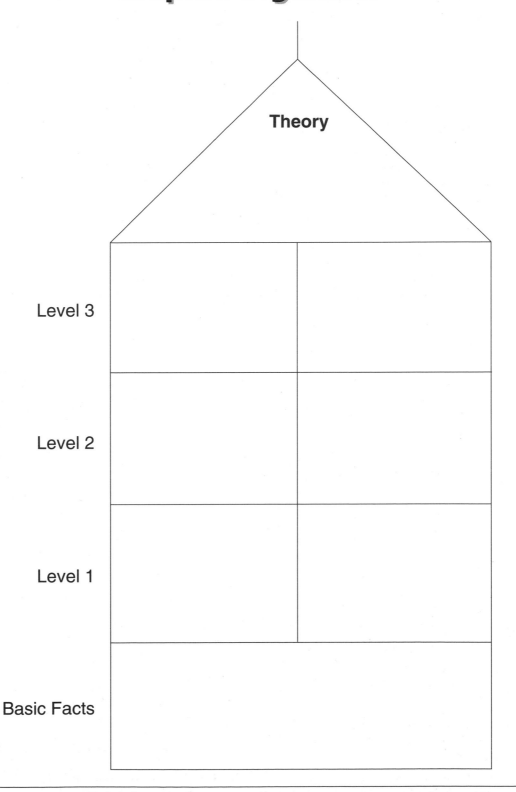

Theory

Level 3

Level 2

Level 1

Basic Facts

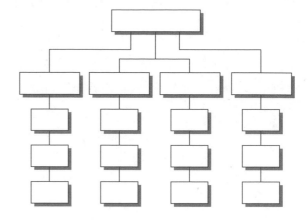

21

Classification Flow Chart

APPROPRIATE USES

1. Use to classify information in a textbook or its single chapters.

2. Use to classify information in a work of fiction such as a play or novel.

Key Vocabulary

Classify, compare, categorize, similarity

LESSON DESIGN

Check Prior Knowledge of the Classification Flow Chart Organizer

1. Show a simple version of the chart for all to see.

2. Ask students to tell you what they know about this organizer. Invite them to speculate on its value as a learning tool.

Learning Phase: Making sense

Level of Difficulty: Challenging

Purpose: To enable students to classify large amounts of related information in a unit or course

Thinking Process: Classification

3. Give a brief example of the chart's use asking the students to complete some of the details. Enter responses on the model for all to see (e.g., Red Riding Hood: characters, locations, events, symbols).

4. Invite students to ask questions about how to use this chart (e.g., "What headings?" "How much detail?").

Explain the Classification Flow Chart Organizer's Purpose

1. If using the flow chart with a fiction story (novel, short story, children's book), explain that this organizer will help them chart out and see the connections among the principle elements of fiction.

2. If using as an advance organizer for reading a textbook, explain how it will enable them to chart each chapter's important concepts and subconcepts in the appropriate categories. This will help them separate "the forest from the trees."

Clarify and Model the Task

1. Select the reading material that the students will chart. Provide the appropriate headers and place them on the flow chart for all to see.
   - Fiction Headers: characters, conflicts, locations, time, themes, symbols
   - Nonfiction Headers: individuals, conflicts, events, dates, places, topics of discourse

2. Invite students to read the first 3–5 pages of the selected passage.

3. After all have finished, begin the process of filling in the flow chart.

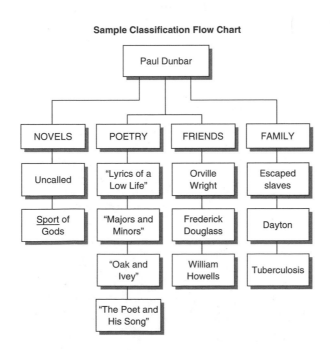

Sample Classification Flow Chart

Complete the Task

1. Form mixed reading ability learning groups of three. Review the DOVE guidelines, and assign the group roles (pp. 216–217).

2. Assign the next chapter for reading and charting. Provide the headers for the first row. If possible, have students read the material as a homework assignment and prepare ideas for the chart.

3. Distribute the chart materials (p. 217). Allow 20 minutes for the student learning groups to chart the assignment. Monitor and coach as needed with special attention to any learning groups that you predict might need assistance.

Guide Reflection

1. **Reflect on Process.**
   - Give each group additional newsprint. Ask them to respond to each of these questions: What did we do well in this task? How would we improve our charting? What help do we need?
   - Match groups of threes to form groups of six. Have these find the similarities and differences in the charts before each reviews its process evaluation.

2. **Reflect on Content.**
   - Ask each student to write a summary of the key points identified on his or her learning group's chart. Provide a rubric to guide the writing task (e.g., understands the key concept, supports the key concept with three or more sub-ideas, has sufficient factual detail).
   - Select two or three summaries to read to the class. Guide a discussion of the content by probing for sub-ideas, agreements, and disagreements.

CLASSIFICATION FLOW CHART ORGANIZER EXAMPLES

Elementary Grade Example

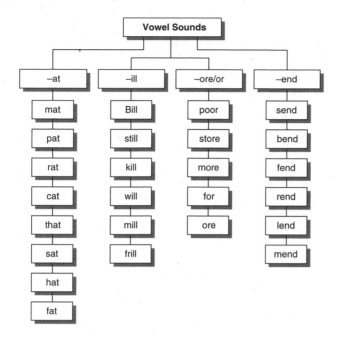

Middle Grade Example

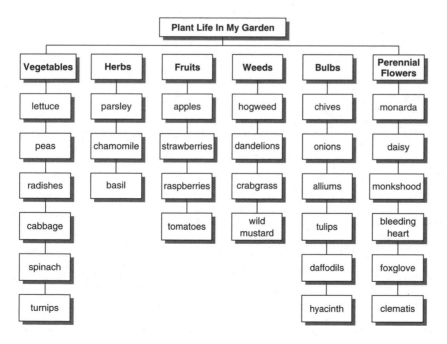

Secondary Grade Example

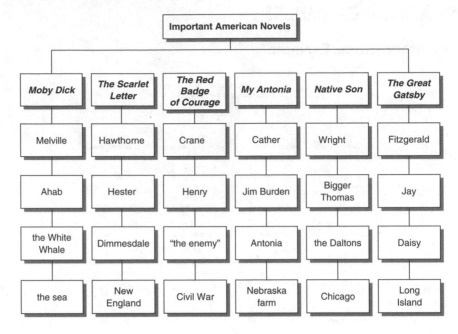

MORE IDEAS

Elementary Grade Examples

Mathematics: Number operations, geometric shapes, metric measurements

Language Arts: Parts of speech, oral report, homophones

Science: Forces, organisms, fossils

Social Studies: Representative democracy, the seven continents, symbols of the American democracy

Other: Buildings in our community, our parks, favorite TV shows

Middle Grade Examples

Mathematics: Algebraic functions, statistical measurement tools

Language Arts: *To Kill a Mockingbird,* Ruiz de Burton, Jack London

Science: DNA, Charles Darwin, life cycles

Social Studies: The Plains Indians, trade routes to North America, colonial settlements

Other: The Beatles, art elements and the principles of design, standards of dress

Secondary Grade Examples

Mathematics: Polynomials, quadratic equations, logarithmic laws

Language Arts: Figures of speech, the Russian novel, nonverbal communication

Science: Laser applications, nuclear proliferation, volcanic eruptions

Social Studies: Judeo-Christian view of law, effects of the Industrial Revolution, current religious-political conflicts

Other: American jazz, the French Impressionists, the prairie architects and the American skyscraper

Make Your Own

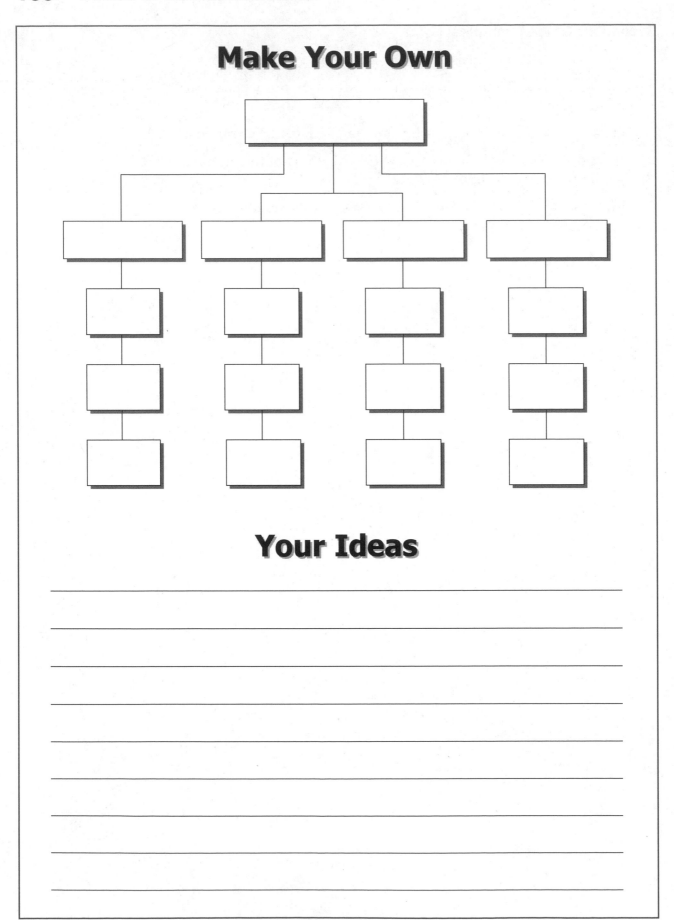

Your Ideas

Classification Flow Chart
Graphic Organizer

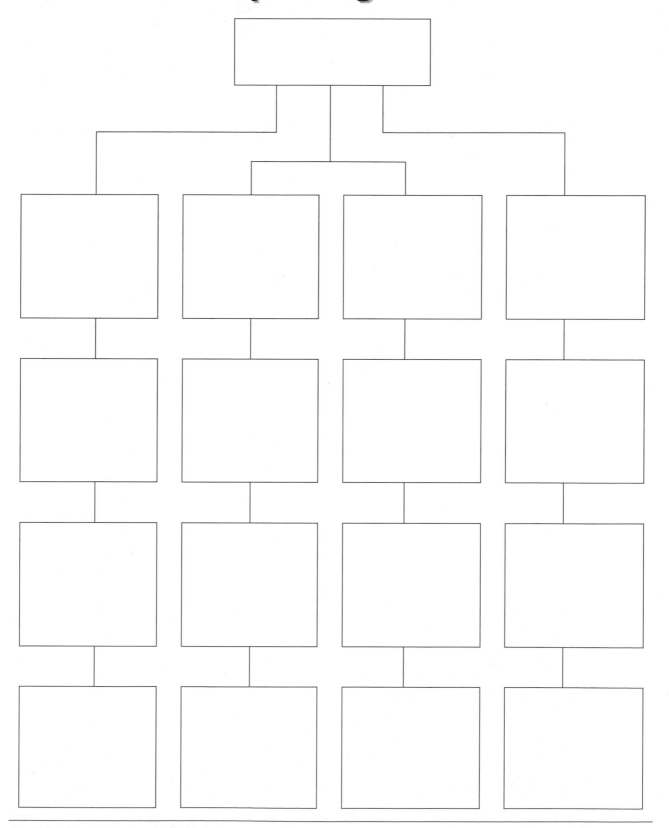

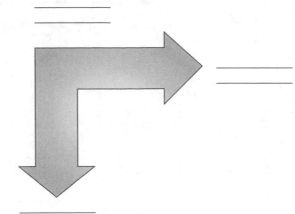

22

Right Angle

APPROPRIATE USES

1. Use to introduce/overview a chapter or topic of study.

2. Use to help students develop the implications of new ideas.

3. Use to help students deepen inferential thinking.

4. Use to help students make applications of ideas learned across the curriculum.

5. Use to summarize key concepts in a chapter or a topic.

Learning Phase: Making sense

Level of Difficulty: Challenging

Purpose: To help students develop implications of concepts learned or to make applications of ideas across the curriculum

Thinking Processes: Seeing implications, making applications

Key Vocabulary

Implications, inferences, applications

Attribution

Created by the author.

LESSON DESIGN

Check Prior Knowledge of the Right-Angle Organizer

1. Show the organizer for all to see. Ask for thumbs up by all students who have used this organizer before; thumbs down by all who have not seen or used it.

2. Enlist the assistance of any students who have used the organizer in the past. Ask them to tell you what the purpose is for each of the four areas marked A-E. Correct or add to their responses as needed.
   - Topic
   - Concept or subtopic
   - Research information
   - Implications of subject
   - Applications of subject #1 implications

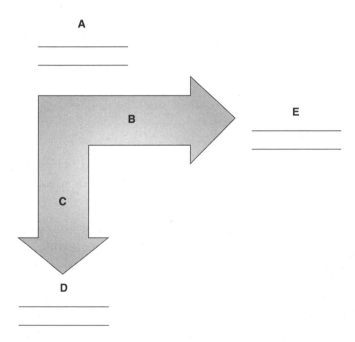

3. Select the topic that students will use. Enter it on the graphic model.

4. Ask students what is meant by an "implication." Build the definition from multiple student responses (to have an effect on, to result in, to suggest a possible outcome). Give examples (e.g., the president's speech implied that the law would pass easily).

Explain the Right-Angle Organizer's Purpose

1. Purpose: "to learn how the right-angle organizer helps them see the likely or suggested results of using a concept or making a statement."

2. Ask students what are some of the possible outcomes (implications) of driving under the influence of drugs, disobeying their parents, or helping a friend. What is likely to happen?

Clarify and Model the Task

1. Form cooperative learning groups of three. Review the DOVE guidelines (p. 216), the roles and responsibilities of the recorder, reporter, and materials manager (pp. 216–217), and provide each learning group with materials (newsprint, markers) for sketching a large right-angle organizer. Check for understanding of the elements of a right-angle organizer.

2. Use Leonardo Da Vinci as the model. On the organizer in space A (topic) write in "Da Vinci." In spaces B and C write in "scientist" and "painter." Read from an encyclopedia or Wikipedia excerpts about his inventions and his paintings.

3. Ask the class for ideas about how Da Vinci influenced the world through each of his talents. What were the implications of his talents? Write responses in D and E on the master right angle.

4. Review the procedures for completing the right angle and check for understanding.

Complete the Task

1. Provide each learning group with a name of a person that you have selected from the topics or concepts under study. (For ideas, see the examples below.)

2. Instruct each group to complete a right-angle organizer with that name. Color code the sections of the organizer so that they use a common schema for the sections similar to the schema of the other groups.

Sequence of Steps for the Right-Angle Organizer

1. Enter title of concept assigned to learning group.

2. Research accomplishments or facts.

3. Select accomplishments or facts and list on graphic (B and C).

4. Brainstorm implications of selected accomplishments (D and E).

5. Highlight most important implication.

---

3. Provide a list of the steps they will use to complete the organizer.

4. Wander among groups and coach. Spend time near any groups you predict may have more difficulty with this task. Ask questions. Do not give answers to their questions unless absolutely necessary. Respond with, "I don't know. What do you think?"

5. When 5 minutes remain in the period, end the task and put materials away for safekeeping.

6. Start the second day of focus on this organizer by having the learning groups complete the task.

Guide Reflection

1. **Reflect on Content.**
   - Match trios to form learning groups of six. Give each trio 5 minutes to share its completed right angle and to respond with explanations of "why?" posed by the partner group.
   - Allow each learning group 3 minutes to share its right-angle chart with the class. Remind all others to take notes about each topic that is core to their study of the chapter.

2. **Reflect on Process.**
   - Ask students to complete a stem about the key vocabulary words "About _____, I learned. . . ." and to share the completed sentence within the learning trio.
   - Ask students to summarize their rationales.

RIGHT-ANGLE ORGANIZER EXAMPLES

Elementary Grade Example

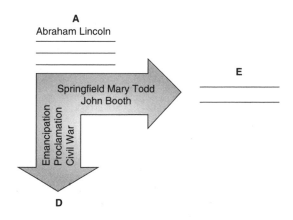

Middle Grade Example

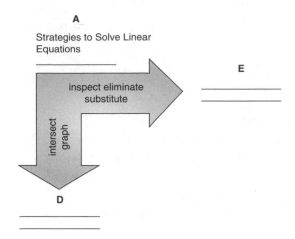

Secondary Grade Example

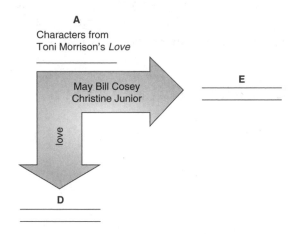

OTHER IDEAS

Elementary Grade Examples

Mathematics: Odd and even numbers, size-order patterns, geometric shapes

Language Arts: Letter names, blending sounds, story characters (e.g., "Koala Lou," "Who's Got Game?")

Science: Magnets, food chains, water cycle

Social Studies: Pyramids, the North Pole, the House of Representatives

Other: Seeds in the garden, hummingbirds, stranger danger

Middle Grade Examples

Mathematics: Polynomials, coefficients, equations

Language Arts: Comprehension strategies, Cuentos Chicanos, *The Ox-Bow Incident*

Science: Fungi, plant parts, volcanoes

Social Studies: Ancient civilizations of Africa, the mountains of the Western Hemisphere, the Bill of Rights

Other: Jazz composers, The Wyeths, Tiger Woods

Secondary Grade Examples

Mathematics: Location statistics, data representations, permutations

Language Arts: *Philadelphia Fire* (John Wideman), Fanny Hurst, *Portrait of the Artist as a Young Man* (Joyce)

Science: Cells, species variation, ecosystems

Social Studies: Sojourner Truth, Greco-Roman law, Tuskegee airmen

Other: Wynton Marsalis, the American Impressionists, vaudeville

Make Your Own

_____

_____

_____
_____

_____
_____

Your Ideas

_____

_____

_____

_____

_____

_____

_____

_____

_____

Right-Angle Graphic Organizer

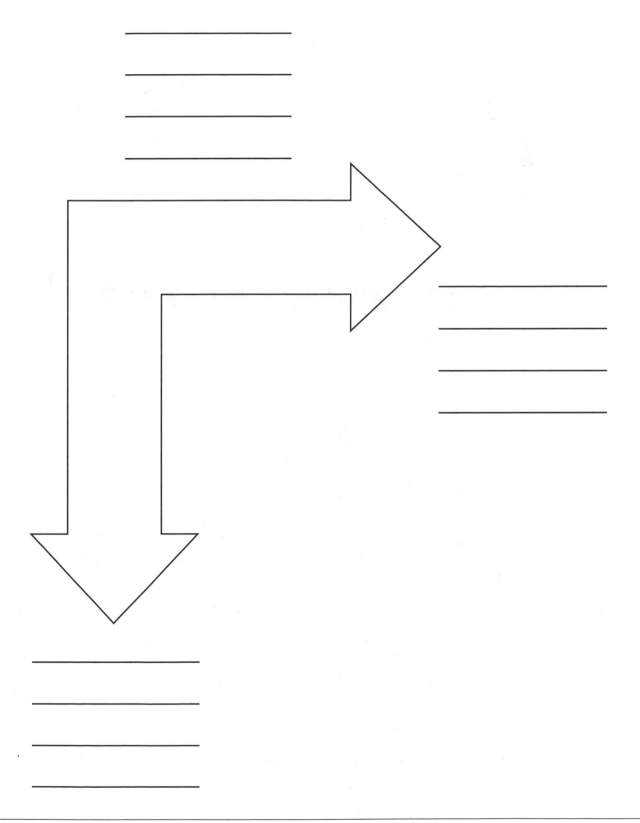

23

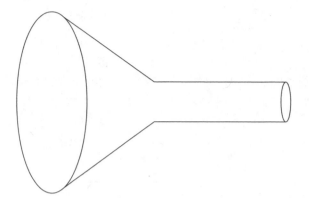

Inference Funnel

APPROPRIATE USES

1. Use for evidence in a reading passage (fiction or nonfiction) to draw a conclusion about a person, place, or thing.

2. Use with clues to form a hypothesis.

3. Use to gather data for reaching a conclusion in a scientific experiment.

4. Use to guess what is the best way home when lost.

Key Vocabulary

Inference, clue, conclusion, concept

Attribution

This organizer was developed by the author.

LESSON DESIGN

Check Prior Knowledge of the Inference Funnel Organizer

1. On the board, write the word *inference*. Ask for a show of hands from those who can explain the word. Use wait-time and ask for several different responses "in your words, with your examples." Distribute the opportunity to respond to students in various parts of the classroom.

2. If no one is able to respond, write a summary definition on the board. "Inference = evidence based guess" and provide an example (e.g., "Your brother comes into the house. He looks very sad. You know he was on a date. What inference could you make?"). Ask for other examples familiar to the students.

3. Post the organizer for all to see. Check to see how many have used it. Ask those that have to fill in the parts. If no one has had experience with it, explain its makeup.

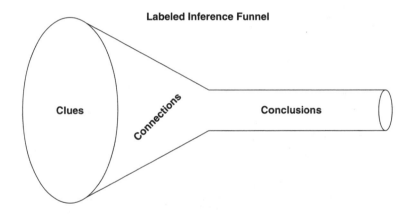

Labeled Inference Funnel

Clues | Connections | Conclusions

Explain the Inference Funnel Organizer's Purpose

1. Walk the students through the organizer to show them how it will help them track the connections between clues and their conclusions.

2. Explain how this is a sixth sense or intuitive sense used to solve a problem by forming a hypothesis. The organizer will give them a tool to help them be more skillful at drawing the nearest-to-correct conclusion.

Clarify and Model the Task

1. Start with an example. On the overhead, show this brief passage.

Passage

Who is this person? "He lived on a large plantation near the Potomac River. As a boy, he claimed to have cut down a cherry tree with his ax. He had crossed the frozen Delaware River during the war against Britain after spending many weeks at a campsite near Valley Forge."

---

2. Ask the students to tell you who they think this person might be. Ask them to use the clues provided in the story that enabled this decision. Do not let them use any information other than the facts they see in the story. After selecting these, ask them how they knew the facts added up to George Washington (prior knowledge, multiple clues). (For younger students, select an example that allows them to use their prior knowledge.)

3. Return to the previous funnel (p. 177). Ask the students to help fill in the chart: (1) What are clues? (2) What do they tell you? (3) What is the final conclusion?

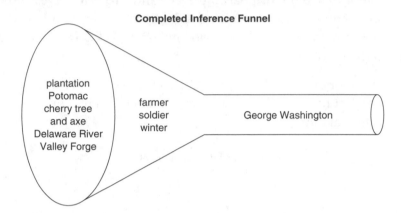

Completed Inference Funnel

plantation
Potomac
cherry tree
and axe
Delaware River
Valley Forge

farmer
soldier
winter

George Washington

4. Check for understanding for how to use the chart.

Complete the Task

1. Form cooperative work teams of three. Review the DOVE guidelines. Assign the roles of reader, recorder, and checker in each team. Invite the recorder to take two sheets of large newsprint and markers. The first part of the task is to sketch an outline of the chart that is displayed.

2. Assign a brief story or nonfiction piece to each team. The reader will read the passage assigned (all groups will have a different passage) while the others follow along. (Alternatively, all can read the passage silently or for homework.)

3. When the reading is complete, teams will complete the organizer with the information gathered from the assigned passage. All contribute.

4. Walk among the teams and monitor the discussions. Check that no one student dominates a team's responses.

Guide Reflection

1. Post the completed newsprint sheets around the room. Stand each team by its poster. At a signal, the reporter stays by the poster as the other two move to the next poster to the right. The reporters explain the poster to the visiting team, highlighting the clues and the conclusions.

2. After 2 minutes, signal a new move on the carousel. Only the reporters "stay home" so they can explain to the next visiting team. Continue for four or five rounds.

3. After all teams return to their seats, invite each student to make a journal entry: "I learned that drawing inferences helps with reading because. . . ." If time allows after they have written their entries, invite volunteers to share the statements.

INFERENCE FUNNEL ORGANIZER EXAMPLES

Elementary Grade Example

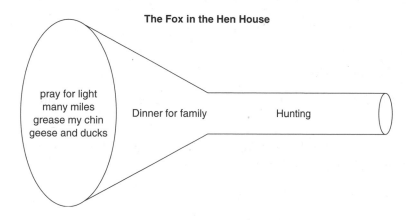

The Fox in the Hen House

pray for light
many miles
grease my chin
geese and ducks

Dinner for family

Hunting

Middle Grade Example

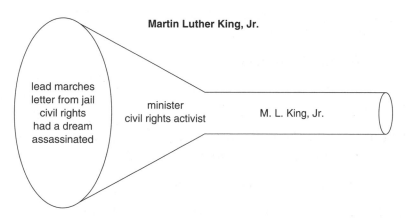

Martin Luther King, Jr.

lead marches
letter from jail
civil rights
had a dream
assassinated

minister
civil rights activist

M. L. King, Jr.

Secondary Grade Example

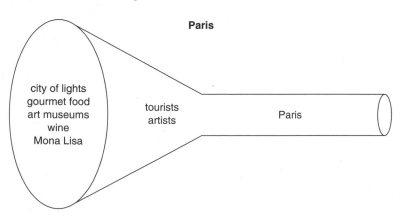

Paris

city of lights
gourmet food
art museums
wine
Mona Lisa

tourists
artists

Paris

MORE IDEAS

Elementary Grade Examples

Mathematics: Numbers, money, decimals

Language Arts: Irish folktales, "The Bremen Town Musicians," the Creation story

Science: Magnets, polar bears, clouds

Social Studies: Our state capitol, George Washington, Africa

Other: Safety signs, merry-go-round, the grocery store

Middle Grade Examples

Mathematics: Negative decimals, measures of central tendency, linear equations

Language Arts: "The Purloined Letter" (Poe), "The Lottery" (Jackson), "On the Gull's Road" (Cather)

Science: Solar system, molecules, CO_2

Social Studies: Woodlands peoples, Continental Congress, Louisiana Purchase

Other: Being popular, stem cell research, the Super Bowl

Secondary Grade Examples

Mathematics: Polar coordinates, fundamental theory of algebra, De Moivre's Theorem

Language Arts: *A Portrait of the Artist as a Young Man* (Joyce), *The House of Mirth* (Wharton), *Heart of Darkness* (Conrad)

Science: Newton's laws, electrons, mole theory

Social Studies: Russian Revolution, Holocaust, Warsaw Pact

Other: Stem cell research, the Million Man March, fossil fuels

Make Your Own

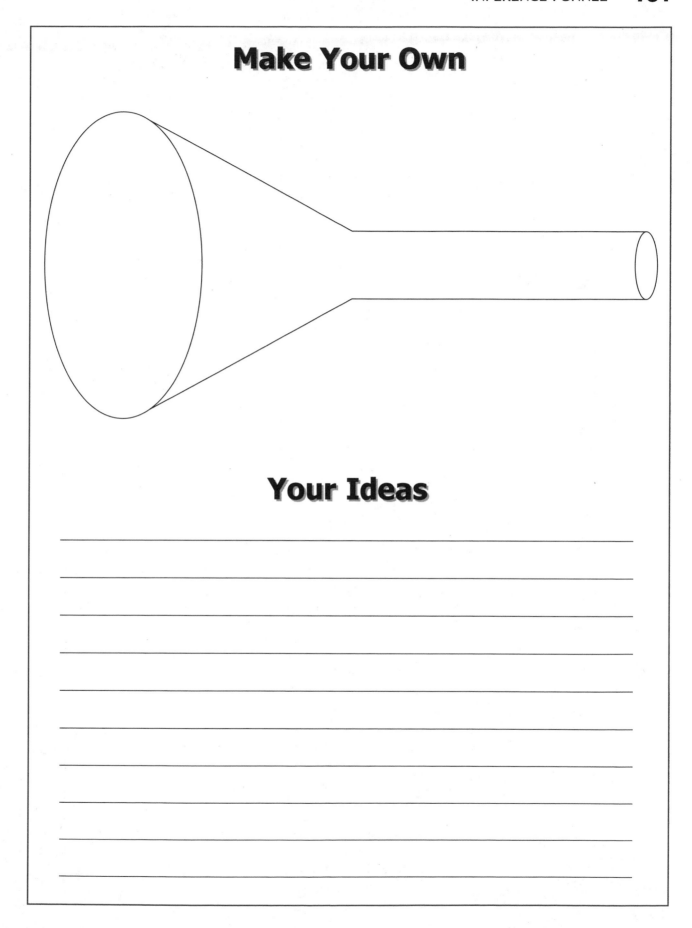

Your Ideas

_____

_____

_____

_____

_____

_____

_____

_____

_____

_____

Inference Funnel Graphic Organizer

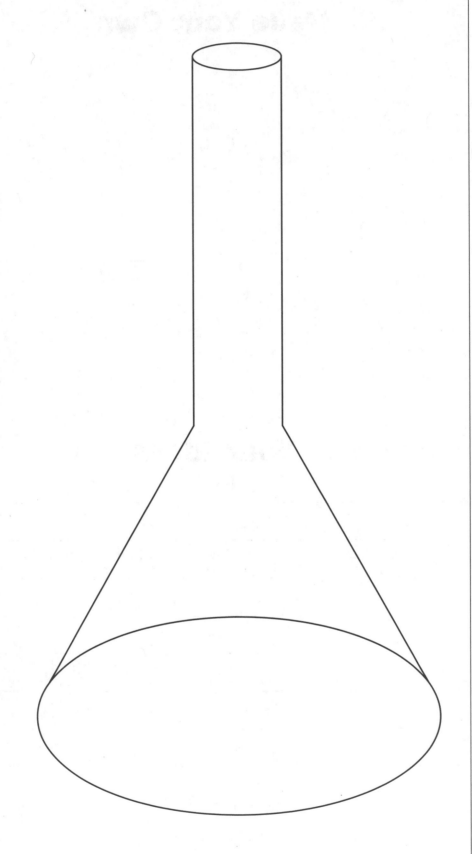

Topic: _____

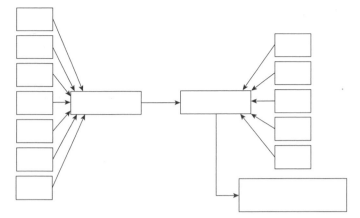

24
What's the Big Idea?

APPROPRIATE USES

1. Use to help students understand the thinking operations inherent in the scientific method.

2. Use to enable students to form generalizations gathered from evidence in the fields of science, mathematics, social sciences, and literature.

3. Use to foster cross-disciplinary study of critical issues related to the curriculum.

4. Use to enable students to experience the theory development process.

5. Use to facilitate students' understanding of possible reasons for inconsistent results from uncontrolled conditions.

6. Use to help students appreciate the usefulness and limitations of theories as scientific representations of reality.

Learning Phases: Gathering information, making sense, showing conclusions

Level of Difficulty: Challenging

Purpose: To facilitate hypothetical thinking

Thinking Processes: Generalizing, hypothesizing, proving, forming principles and rules

Key Vocabulary

Fact, opinion, theory, hypothesis, valid evidence, reliable evidence, principle, level of abstraction

Attribution

Adapted from Sinatra, R. C. (2000). Teaching learners to think, read, and write more effectively in content subjects. *The Clearing House, 73*(5), 266–273.

LESSON DESIGN

Check Prior Knowledge of the What's the Big Idea? Organizer

1. Use the KWL graphic organizer to determine what students know (K), want to know (W), and learned (L). See page 1 for explanation and guidelines for use of the KWL.

KWL

Topic: _____		
Know	Want to know	Learned

2. Post the organizer for all to see using newsprint that you can save. Use a student volunteer to record responses drawn from a wide number of students in the class, especially those sitting in the back of the classroom. Ask, "What do you know about the scientific method?"

3. After including all non-duplicated responses, ask "What else do you think may be important to know about the scientific process?" Have the responses listed in the "W" or "I want to know" column.

4. When these responses are completed, save the newsprint for use in the coming days of class.

Explain the Big Ideas Organizer's Purpose

1. Post the organizer for all to see.

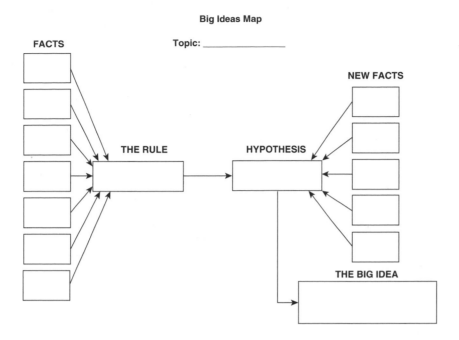

Big Ideas Map

2. Explain that the students will use this graphic to learn the process of the scientific method by doing. As they work with the organizer, they will have the opportunity to refer to the KWL each day to see which of their questions are being answered.

3. Mediate the value of using the graphic (segmenting the steps, analyzing the key elements and direct experience to help them move from concrete details to abstract concepts and deeper understanding). Also mediate the value of the scientific process as an important means for proving theory by means of the best available evidence or data.

4. Enter the key words from the vocabulary list and ask for definitions and examples from students. If no correct responses are provided, add the words to the second column of the KWL.

Clarify and Model the Task

1. Pick a topic from current events related to the content of your course (e.g., Social Studies/genocide; Science/drought; Literature/a missing person mystery).

2. Role-play with yourself as the investigator. Using a blank map, walk the class through the steps from selection of the topic. As the students follow your thinking, be sure they understand that this is a model that they can follow when they are assigned the next part of this project.

- Identify the topic (e.g., nature's impact on human migration).
- In row 2, enter some factual information (e.g., Oklahoma dust storms, droughts in Somalia and Kenya, tsunami in Indonesia, volcanic eruptions in Sicily, hurricanes in New Orleans). Ask students to provide additional events that they know impacted human lives.
- Encourage students to ask you questions about each incident so they can find a similarity that fits all. You are looking for a common feature(s) that ties all the disasters to human migration. "What is the relationship that connects these various disasters with human migration?"
- When the connecting factor is identified, enter it in the generalization box. Phrase it as a generalization (e.g., "Major natural disasters that kill large numbers of people cause many to flee to climate unaffected by the type of disaster they experienced.").

Big Ideas Map

Topic: Nature's Impact on Human Migration

FACTS

| dust storms |
| droughts |
| tsunami |
| volcano |
| hurricanes |

THE RULE

| kill people destroy environment |

HYPOTHESIS

| survivors look for safety |

NEW FACTS

| Houston |
| across U.S. |
| high ground |

THE BIG IDEA

| important to have safe havens |

- Show the students how to switch the generalization to a hypothesis. The wording is likely to be the same, but phrased as a question or with the word "all" added (e.g., "We believe that all major natural disasters that kill large numbers of a population cause most survivors to flee to other geographic areas they think are free of this danger.").
- Show students how they must now find additional evidence to prove their hypothesis. Select some examples that fit the criteria in the hypothesis statement (e.g., the destruction of Pompeii).
- Show some non-examples that fail to meet all the criteria such as "the Chicago fire" (not a natural disaster), "the Westward migration" (not a natural disaster), "the heat wave of 1995" (insufficient deaths, no property damage). Discuss four criteria "necessary" (an element that must be included) and sufficient (there are enough examples that fit exactly that make the hypothesis statistically likely to happen. Also discuss the terms *reliable* and *valid*.

- Modify the hypothesis based on the data found (e.g., "in the majority of cases," "at least half of the population"), write the principle or theory that applies.

Complete the Task

1. Divide the class into mixed-ability groups of three. Review DOVE (p. 216). Each learning group will draw straws for the roles of recorder, facilitator, and reporter (pp. 216–217). Provide each group with the materials it will need (p. 217) and review each other's responsibilities.

2. Select a topic for the class from your curriculum. Each group will use the map to guide its steps from facts to theory. When the learning groups are ready to gather evidence, encourage them to divide this responsibility so that each is looking for different pieces of information.

3. Monitor the groups' progress and check for their understanding of each statement entered on the chart.

4. After two to three class periods, students should have completed the Theory Maps. Match each learning group with a second to form groups of six. With the reporter for each group in the lead, the groups will review their charts and be asked by the other group to defend the reliability of the data presented, its validity, and its sufficiency.

5. If time allows, select one or two groups who received high marks for the three criteria (reliability, validity, and sufficiency) to present to the entire class.

Guide Reflection

1. **Reflect on Process.**
   - Provide students with the following stems. Select a volunteer from the back of the classroom and proceed in a sequence from one student to the next, completing the first stem. After hearing from six to eight students, switch to a new stem. Allow students to think for a moment before sharing with the class. "Today, what I learned about making a hypothesis was. . . ." "Today, what I discovered about forming a theory was. . . . " "Today, what I learned about evidence to support a hypothesis was. . . ."
   - As an alternative, allow students to select any one of the above stems for a journal entry. After 3 minutes of writing, invite volunteers to share entries with the class.

2. **Reflect on Content.**
   - Present students with two questions about the topic used with the Big Idea Map: (1) What do you think were the most important facts you gathered with this organizer? (2) What were the important connectors that helped you make sense of these facts? After students have time to write individual responses in a journal, invite as many as time allows to share one or the other with the class.

BIG IDEAS ORGANIZER EXAMPLES

Elementary Grade Example

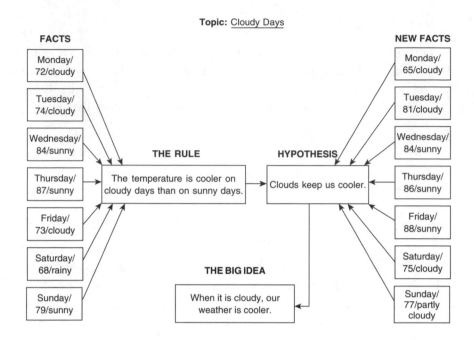

Topic: Cloudy Days

FACTS		NEW FACTS
Monday/72/cloudy		Monday/65/cloudy
Tuesday/74/cloudy		Tuesday/81/cloudy
Wednesday/84/sunny		Wednesday/84/sunny
Thursday/87/sunny		Thursday/86/sunny
Friday/73/cloudy		Friday/88/sunny
Saturday/68/rainy		Saturday/75/cloudy
Sunday/79/sunny		Sunday/77/partly cloudy

THE RULE — The temperature is cooler on cloudy days than on sunny days.

HYPOTHESIS — Clouds keep us cooler.

THE BIG IDEA — When it is cloudy, our weather is cooler.

Middle Grade Example

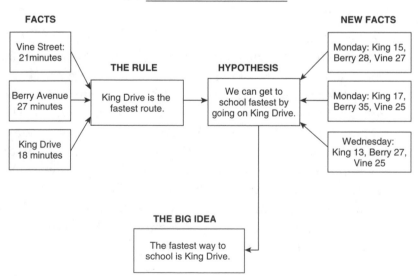

Topic: Routes to School From Our Home

FACTS		NEW FACTS
Vine Street: 21 minutes		Monday: King 15, Berry 28, Vine 27
Berry Avenue 27 minutes		Monday: King 17, Berry 35, Vine 25
King Drive 18 minutes		Wednesday: King 13, Berry 27, Vine 25

THE RULE — King Drive is the fastest route.

HYPOTHESIS — We can get to school fastest by going on King Drive.

THE BIG IDEA — The fastest way to school is King Drive.

Secondary Grade Example

Topic: The Odyssey

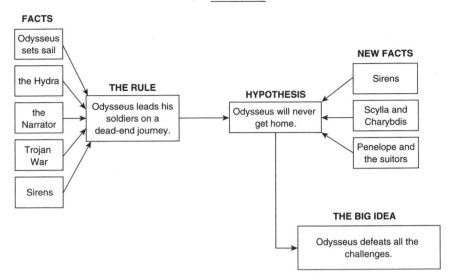

MORE IDEAS

Elementary Grade Examples

Mathematics: Theory of equivalence, place value of ten-sets, variables

Language Arts: Rhyme patterns, suffix rules, character traits

Science: Flow of current, magnetic forces, the effects of sound

Social Studies: School bus behavior rules, being fair, friends

Other: Pet care, answering the phone

Middle Grade Examples

Mathematics: Determining quality of peanut butter, best car for gas mileage, longest battery life

Language Arts: How to write an "A" paper, qualities of a good summary statement, how to tell a good book

Science: The best way to use a microscope, buoyancy of objects, impact of light on plant growth

Social Studies: Changes in population density, changes in performance of school sports teams, best vacation spots for a family

Other: A good TV comedy show, safe use of myspace.com

Secondary Grade Examples

Mathematics: Vectors as systems, number theory arguments with whole numbers, permutations

Language Arts: _____ as a classic "hero," what is a high-quality research paper?, reasons for a character's change in a novel

Science: Impact of accelerator speed on atomic particles, distance effects on star brightness, effects of water regulation laws on environment

Social Studies: Animal cloning by somatic cell nuclear transfer, selection of specific energy sources, immigration limits on various cultures

Other: Impact of copyright laws on music sales, changes in newspaper readership

Make Your Own

Topic: _____

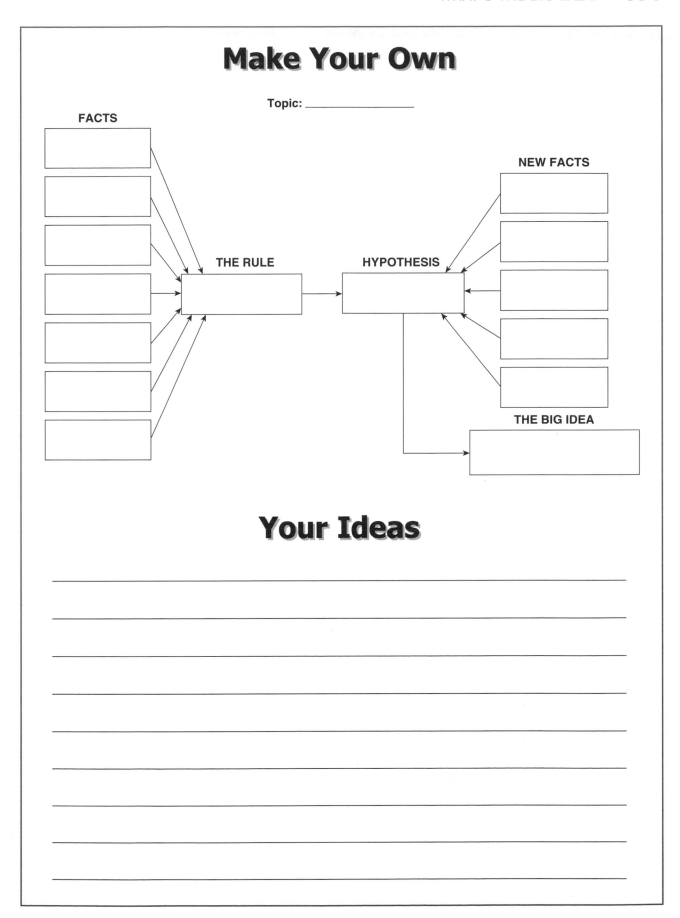

FACTS

THE RULE

HYPOTHESIS

NEW FACTS

THE BIG IDEA

Your Ideas

_____

_____

_____

_____

_____

_____

_____

_____

_____

Big Idea's Graphic Organizer

Topic: _____

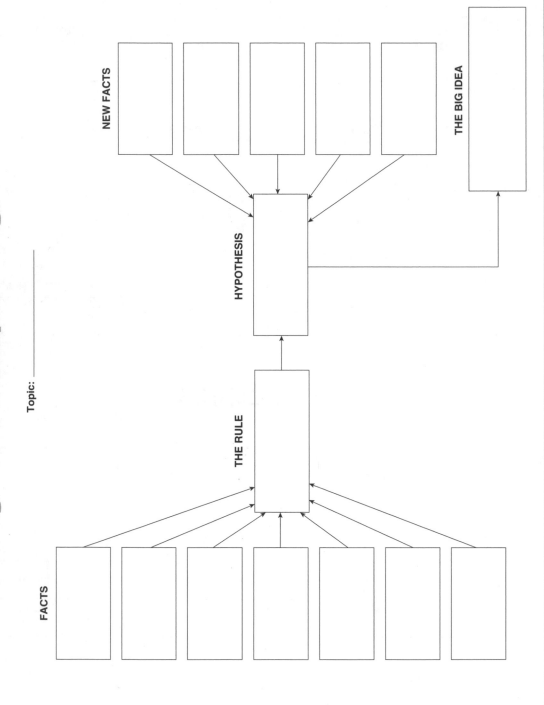

FACTS

THE RULE

HYPOTHESIS

NEW FACTS

THE BIG IDEA

192

25

Invent Your Own Graphic Organizer

Beyond the visual graphics for organizing thinking patterns are more thinking patterns and more graphics that are possible and, perhaps, yet to be invented. You may invent the next organizer, or you may help your students create the next ones. Here are the suggested procedures for "invent your own."

1. What thinking skills or thinking patterns need a graphic organizer? Brainstorm a list and select the skill or pattern that will help your students most.

2. What visual metaphors or graphic forms come to mind for the skill you have selected? For instance, how might a common organizer such as a desk or filing cabinet present the design you need?

3. What are the procedures that will enable students to think through a thoughtful task? For sample, review IDEAS. (Note that the framework for the problem solving is broken down into five procedures.)

4. What key verb or noun will help students recall the parts of the organizer? Play with synonyms of the thinking skill or patterns that you can create an acronym from, such as IDEAS. Note how the key instructional phrases begin with a work that creates the acronym. Instead of using a word like "gather" or "collect" to start the procedure instructing the thinker to "get the facts," use the term "index." It gives you an "I" and suggests both gathering of facts and ordering them.

5. Sequence your lesson design:
- Purpose of the organizer
- Vocabulary
- Thinking skills or patterns
- Introductory lesson

Determine:
- Group size
- Roles and instructions
- Guidelines
- Visual overheads
- Materials
- Task instructions (Keep the first task simple and fun.)
- Assessment of organizer task
- Assessment of cooperation
- Closure

6. Field test your lesson design. Teach the lesson to your class. After the lesson, ask students to evaluate the design. Use the PMI organizer (p. 71). Review the responses. Ask the students to clarify what difficulties they encountered and make adjustments in your design. If student groups are making designs, have them exchange their designs and use the PMI to evaluate each design. Use these criteria:
- To what degree does the organizer help visualize the thinking pattern?
- To what degree does the organizer make the pattern of thinking simple and structured?
- To what degree is the organizer usable with a variety of subjects?

7. Field test the schedule.

8. Make revisions.

Invent Your Own Graphic Organizer

26

Graphic Organizers: Tools for Lifelong Thinking and Learning

Teachers can strengthen students' immediate efficiencies as learners by helping them develop skilled use of graphic organizers. They can also facilitate students' capacities as lifelong learners. Like carpenters or surgeons who buy a new tool or instrument, the intention is not to use the tool once and then leave it in a toolbox or on an instrument tray. In like manner, it is shortsighted for teachers to use a graphic organizer as a tool in one lesson and then forget about it. It is more beneficial if students not only learn to use the tool, but also develop their capability to re-use it in other learning situations without teacher direction. To do this, teachers must teach for transfer so that students can develop high-level skill in using the tool across the curriculum and at the most appropriate times.

Teachers enrich students' transfer of graphic organizers by helping students reinforce, practice, and reflect on the use of these thinking tools and each tool's related cognitive processes. When teachers want students to develop expert use of a graphic organizer, they teach the organizer for transfer. Each time students repeat their use of the tool (practice), teachers can encourage them to assess that use. The assessment enables students to think about what they did well with the tool, what they could improve, and where they need help. With the insights from such an examination, students' take the responsibility to improve how they use the organizer. As they become more skilled and see more possible applications, students become empowered about when, where, and how they can take advantage of organizers.

Teachers do not have to teach every organizer for transfer. In many instances, teachers will use an organizer for a very specific, one-time purpose. Teachers will use other organizers that they want students to transfer and use in a variety of ways and instances throughout the school year. If each teacher in students' school lives were to select one organizer to add to the students' learning tool kits, students could end up with a well-stocked collection.

FIRST STEPS IN TEACHING FOR TRANSFER

When teaching for transfer, teachers intentionally facilitate improvement in how the student uses an organizer. With all intentional transfer instruction, teachers make clear to students that they are working on transfer, what is being transferred to where, and why this is important. There are no secrets. With this intentional approach, teachers have any number of different options to promote students' habitual transfer of organizers across the curriculum and beyond.

1. Check prior knowledge. Show the blank organizer and ask volunteers to walk you through the sequence for its use. Ask additional students to provide a why for each step.

2. Post the procedure for using an organizer in the classroom. Invite students to create a mnemonic to help them with procedural recall.

3. Use the same organizer to start off each chapter in the textbook or other reading tasks by assigning students to read each section and add to the organizer.

4. Make the organizer a part of the daily or weekly homework assignment. As students read the text, they will complete a chapter organizer with the intent to gather information or elaborate on ideas.

5. Start each class period by adding to the model organizer for the section assigned. Students may draw from the organizers completed for homework.

6. Brainstorm with students other reading materials in your course with which they could use this organizer. To encourage its use, assign the organizer's use to some of your other reading assignments. Brainstorm how students could use the organizer with reading or problem-solving assignments from other classes. Ask for specific examples.

7. Brainstorm what other types of data collection or elaboration with which they could use an organizer. Ask for specific examples.

8. Use organizers in a sequence. Start with a prior knowledge organizer before using another gathering organizer for collecting information.

9. Use a summarizing strategy that encourages students. Share in pairs or larger learning groups what they learned about the content that they organized and how well they used the organizer to guide their thinking.

10. Use an assessing organizer to encourage reflection on content learned and/or thinking process improved.

SUMMARY

Novice carpenters have a sound knowledge of the most important tools in their toolbox. Likewise, it is important for students to establish their knowledge of the most important cognitive tools they will use in their studies. Some tools the novice will use over and over. Others, the novice carpenter will use only occasionally. As the novices grow in experience, they also expand their tool kits to better meet a wider variety of work challenges. In a like manner, as students approach more and more difficult studies, they must expand their tool kits to meet a wider array of challenges. Graphic organizers are important tools for lifelong learners.

27

Skillful Thinking Is Not an Accident

When experienced Formula 1 race car drivers get behind the wheel on the race track, they enter a special high-speed world of super-fast driving. What ordinary people do as they drive to and from work or the store on city streets is far removed from how these drivers function.

Like most athletes, race car drivers, male and female, take many years of hard, intense study and work to master the driving requirements of these high-speed cars. While much of what they do can be attributed to natural skill, their mentors coach them in the fine points of driving at breakneck speeds. In a like manner, students must take time and study to develop the learning skills that produce classroom success. High-gear driving is difficult. It requires concentration, practice, persistence, and intrinsic motivation with sound advice from a coach. So, too, does high-gear thinking.

Thinking like *driving* is a generic word. It can only suggest what the specific skills and operations are that lead to success. Under the umbrella of thinking are those operations, functions, and tools that the student must develop in order to drive the track.

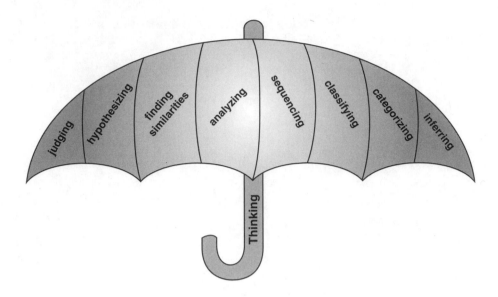

When teachers present the curriculum in any classroom, more often than not, students see what they must learn in the printed textbooks or hear it from the words of the teacher. The students' challenge is to decipher that information and make sense of vast amounts of data. As they advance through school, students discover that there is no such thing as raw content. In each discipline, they discover there are specific operations of the mind that are best suited to the challenge of making meaning from the data they gather.

THE THREE PHASES OF LEARNING

It seldom happens that teachers build their lesson plans on the framework of improving cognitive ability. Most lesson designs come from looking at segmented and separate strategies that often ignore the basis of learning in cognition. For instance, in direct instruction, teachers learn to start with an anticipatory set to ready students for the topic. They then proceed through the lesson's objective, information, checks of procedures and information, and guided practice. This model does not consider the thinking operations or the cognitive functions that students must use to understand and apply the content. At best, teachers are encouraged to ask "higher-order" questions as a tool for promoting student thinking.

By using Feuerstein's three phases of learning as the framework for instruction, teachers create lessons that make thinking central to the task of learning content. In each phase, these teachers have a dual agenda.

For each phase, students must use thinking operations to obtain maximum understanding of the content they are asked to learn. In the behaviorist model, these phases are not recognized. Instead, learning is a function of receiving information, memorizing key elements, and taking a test to show recall. Students with the best memories receive the best grades, even on essay questions that may ask them to analyze or evaluate what they recall. In the behavioral framework, transfer and application do not exist (Feuerstein et al., 2006).

Feuerstein's Three Phases of Learning

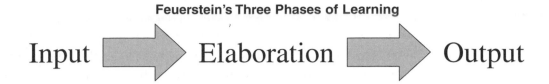

Input → Elaboration → Output

First Phase: Students Construct; Teachers Mediate

In Feuerstein's three-phase, cognitive model, the student is a constructor or maker of meaning. This is an active role. Students, however, develop more rapidly and skillfully when the teacher assists as a mediator of the students' thinking processes and does not leave them to sink or swim alone.

In the first phase, called "input," students faced with a question, problem, or challenge search out information. Some of this search may require students to call on the memory banks that store prior knowledge and experience. Other parts come as the students gather new information from appropriate sources. Such sources can include textbooks, other print materials, video, music, conversations with peers or experts, lectures from teachers, and so forth. The more skilled students are in accessing these data, the closer they come to constructing meaning through the learning process. When students run into difficulty with the construction task, the effective teacher intervenes with help that makes them more efficient "information gatherers."

Mrs. Ramirez faced her math class. For the first time, she was going to teach her students about the operations with exponential expression by focusing on their mathematical reasoning. In prior years, she had followed a simple formula. First, she would ask the students how many knew such rules as $a^0 = 1$ and $a^1 = a$. Then she would write the full set of five rules on the board. Next, she gave them a problem and showed them how to use the rule to solve the problem. She repeated this for each rule after first checking how many had followed what she did. After explaining that this lesson would give them practice in using these rules, she handed out worksheets and asked them to complete the first two problems. When all looked ready, she asked a student in the front row to do the first sample on the board. When that was done, she asked another student to do the second sample. She corrected any mistakes and asked all the students to use a thumbs up to show they understood. Finally, she instructed the students to complete the practice sheet as she moved among them to help as needed. When the bell rang, she gave two assignments. She wanted them to memorize the formula and to complete the second page of the worksheet.

Mrs. Ramirez started her lesson by asking the students to tell her what they knew about exponential expressions such as the five she wrote on the board. After giving them a minute to think, she posted a web on the board. She told the students that all their names were in a hat. When a name was called, that student was to give an idea or say "I pass." She continued calling names and writing ideas on the web until there were no more ideas.

(Continued)

(Continued)

"That is quite a list," Mrs. Ramirez said. "You know a lot. Now, I see all of the rules on the board. That is great. And you have also shown that you are familiar with all the important notations such as = and power. But I want you to understand more. We are going to do some work to show you how important it is to have a standard order of operations. Since algebra deals with the unknown quantities, some of which may be grouped together and are subject to the same transformation, it is important that we understand what happens and how we set off the differences."

With these last words, Mrs. Ramirez showed an overhead with the last sentence. She labeled it "What we are going to learn."

"This is the purpose of this lesson that we will work on for the next few days. Now I want you to get into your learning groups and take out your notebooks. Go to the back and review the DOVE guidelines and make sure that in each group a new person is doing each of the three roles."

While the students moved their desks into triads, she distributed a sheet of newsprint and markers to each set. Then she flashed a large Venn diagram on the screen. "You have seen this before. Please copy it onto your worksheets."

The students helped each other prepare the sketch. "Mark the right circle 'Operations with Exponential Expressions.' Mark the second 'Absolute Value.'"

Mrs. Ramirez replaced the Venn with two lists headed by the same marks.

Algebra

Concept	Purpose	Rules
Operations with exponential expressions	Scientific notations Simplified operations	$a^0 = 1$ $a^1 = a$ $1/a = a^{-1}$ $\sqrt{a} = a^{1/2}$ $n^{-1} a = a^{1/n}$
Absolute value	Measure of the distance of a number to the origin {The expression: $\lvert x - 2 \rvert \leq 1$ refers to all the real numbers that are not more than 1 unit apart from 2}	$\lvert x \rvert = \lvert -x \rvert$ $\lvert x \rvert = a$, then $x = -a$ or $x = a$ $\lvert xy \rvert = \lvert x \rvert \bullet \lvert y \rvert$ $\lvert x/y \rvert = \lvert x \rvert / \lvert y \rvert$ $\lvert x \rvert^2 = x^2$ $\sqrt{x^2} = \lvert x \rvert$ $\lvert x \rvert > a$, then $x < -a$ or $x > a$

"Look at these two lists. I want you to tell me what is the same and what is different about each of the lists. You will use the Venn to make a picture of what is similar and different. Let's start with one example. Tell me where to place it on the graphic organizer, Donna?"

Mrs. Ramirez instructed the learning groups to begin. Although they debated within some of the groups, Mrs. Ramirez concentrated on taking notes of what she was hearing students give as reasons for their placements. Occasionally, when a group asked her to give her opinion, she responded with "I don't know. What do you think?"

Noting that more than 90 percent of the groups had completed the task, she gave her "one minute more" sign before saying "Time's up. Let's talk."

"Manny," she addressed a student in the back of the classroom. "Bring your group and your chart to the front. I want you to tell us what you found was special about the first group of expressions."

After the first group finished and others had added a few points, Mrs. Ramirez called on two additional groups to explain the remaining two columns. When there was disagreement from other learning groups, she asked for reasons. "Why do you say that? What is your thinking behind that statement?" When a student gave a general answer, she probed for precision and accuracy.

When Mrs. Ramirez noted that only 3 minutes remained in the class period, she stopped the group discussion. "This is as far as we can go today. Tomorrow, we will review the similarities and differences that you found. In addition, I want us to do some thinking about the thinking you did with the Venn. Let's be ready to talk about finding similarities and why that was important here. More important, I want to talk about some of the impulsive decision making I noticed and marked in my notes. We will also talk about how some of the imprecise and inaccurate statements some of you made got in the way and what you can do about that the next time. So, until tomorrow, great job thinking!"

Students do not all come to the first phase of learning with equal efficiencies of gathering data from real, virtual, or read information. Some do come with the very well-developed cognitive functions that make data gathering easy and proficient. They are precise and accurate as they take in information from multiple sources of information and they focus accurately on the most important data. Others, however, look at the same information and see a jumble of details. They are unable to separate important facts from the unimportant.

Feuerstein firmly disagrees with the psychometric approach that postulates learning as a fixed process, in which the IQ is set at birth mostly by genetic inheritance (Feuerstein et al., 2006, p. 12). Instead, he notes that most children, given the proper mediation by parents, teachers, and other caregivers, will develop their cognitive functions. "Except in the most severe instances of genetic and organic impairment, the human organism is open to modifiability at all ages and stages of development" (Feuerstein et al., 2006, p. 13).

Second Phase: Making Sense of New Information

The input phase of learning leads into the second phase in which students make sense of or elaborate the information they have gathered. In this phase, they again will use a variety of mental operations. Even when some students have performed well in the prior information-gathering stage, they may underperform in the elaboration stage. Once again, undeveloped cognitive functions get in the way. By strengthening these, Feuerstein asserts, students helped by parents and teachers can more deeply understand or make sense of the information they have gathered.

"What are the connections between part A and part B of a concept?" "How is idea A like idea B?" "What is the relationship between Hamlet and Ophelia?" "In what phylum would you place this animal?" "What reasons support this conclusion?" are examples of the kind of questions students are trying to answer in the second phase. Yes, in the short run, they can memorize the responses for quick recall. In the long run, however, as they are bombarded with more and more information, students who have not developed the mental operations to do the analysis, find similarities, or classify will find it more and more difficult to perform well with advanced schoolwork. Beyond the school years, these students will lack the effective thinking operations to problem solve their way through the increasing complexities of life in the twenty-first century.

The Third Phase: Communicating New Understandings

In the third phase, output, students express in many different ways the ideas they have formed. Students may elect a variety of media as the means for expression. Some will speak or write in words; others will paint abstract expressions, impressions, or realistic representation of their new understandings; others may elect to speak through music, dance, or some other of the multiple intelligences. However, what is most important is that they use sound logic, precise expression, and accurate information. As in the prior stages, some students will communicate their newly formed concepts efficiently; others, many of whom were efficient thinkers in the first two phases, will have trouble with the output.

THE ROLE OF GRAPHIC ORGANIZERS IN THE THREE PHASES

In all three phases, graphic organizers provide visual tools that help students make their thinking more efficient as they

1. Gather information from one or more sources including their prior knowledge

2. Construct visual, concrete frameworks for thinking about abstract information and concepts

3. Search for relationships or connections among different facts, opinions, and concepts

4. Sharpen their cognitive abilities to use a wider range of thinking operations

5. Improve the quality of their thinking by developing their cognitive functions

6. Improve academic achievement by applying higher-quality thinking to ever more difficult content across the standards-based curriculum

Graphic organizers enable students to more easily see the thinking that they are doing. Organizers group the words in patterns that show or illustrate the relationship between and among words and phrases. It is important for teachers to enable students to use these organizers to illustrate the specific operations of thinking, such as comparing, hypothesizing, or summarizing, that students are asked to use in each learning phase. When using the learning tools, it is important that teachers guide the students in using the specific organizers that match up to the specific cognitive operations within a phase. When students are not precise or accurate in this use, teachers must "step in" and mediate the correct use. Leaving students to guess at how to construct an organizer is inappropriate.

SUMMARY

Feuerstein's three phases of learning are like road signs that tell teachers how to help students gather information, make sense, or understand that information and communicate new insights. As mediators, teachers do not allow struggling thinkers to construct new ideas on their own; rather they guide the thinking operations and strengthen the students' cognitive functions. One set of very effective tools at the mediator's disposal is the graphic organizer.

28

Promoting Students' Thinking About Their Thinking

Teachers have many opportunities to develop their students' habits of effective "thinking about thinking." After teachers have stimulated students' thinking by using graphic organizers in daily lessons, they begin to do what the neurological and educational researchers have noted is most important for the substantive improvement of learning. Teachers mediate these changes by promoting their students' metacognition or "thinking about thinking."

TIME TO THINK

The time allotted for metacognition is an important instructional decision. Time taken for metacognition by teachers cannot be incidental. Nor can it be a haphazard or occasional "add-on" stuck at the end of a lesson. There are three critical moments in this decision-making process.

Selecting the Targeted Thinking Spectrum

By starting with an understanding of what thinking operations are central to students grasping the deep meaning of core curricular concepts, teachers select the most appropriate graphic organizer with the same care that they select the material that will uncover the concepts.

As they allot time for the graphic organizer in the lessons they are designing, teachers must ensure that students have at least equal time among the three phases as they gather, make sense, and communicate what they are learning. Throughout the students' engagement time with the content and the organizer, teachers must schedule ample time for reflection on both the content and the thinking processes used. This means time devoted at the start of the lessons, in the middle, and at the end.

Time allotted for thinking also requires teachers to allow sufficient "think-time" when students are asked to respond to questions that start their minds working. When teachers are asking only factual questions, they get accustomed to calling on the students who raise their hands fastest. They also tend to call on the same students who sit in the front rows ready and eager to respond (Rowe, 1987). When thinking is the goal, it is important for teachers to allow sufficient wait-time. They must allow all students the chance to reflect on what they will say and then give all students an equal chance to respond to the start-up questions and to the follow-up questions that probe for deeper thinking and the development of students' cognitive functions.

Reflections on Thinking: The Benefits

What are the benefits that students derive from greater reflection on what and how they are learning, the guided "thinking about thinking" that alert teachers capture at every teachable moment?

1. Metacognition improves the quality of specific thinking capabilities. These include such curriculum-imbedded, cognitive operations as sequencing, comparing, classifying, predicting, hypothesizing, making judgments, and inferring.

2. Metacognition improves student achievement dramatically. Among the most powerful ways of knowing in the standards-based curricula are those cognitive operations identified by Robert Marzano and his associates at the Mid-Central Regional Education Laboratory (*Classroom Instruction That Works*, ASCD, 2001): finding similarities, hypothesizing, and summarizing. According to this meta-analysis of instructional strategies, the more proficiently teachers attend to development of these cognitive processes, the better students will perform across the curriculum. The research on metacognition emphasizes that thinking about thinking adds to the effects.

3. Metacognition enriches students' motivation to learn. As students build habits of reflection, they change from being passive receivers of information who perceive that others control what and how they learn. They move to becoming "active generators" of knowledge who are themselves responsible for how and what they learn (Feuerstein et al., 2006, p. 4).

4. Metacognition enables students to engage in specific thinking operations (e.g., analyzing, estimating) that are most appropriate to specific curricular areas (e.g., math, science, language arts). Rather than "thinking about thinking" (the generalized term), these students "think about estimating" or "think about analyzing."

5. Metacognition encourages students to refine the quality of their thinking. As the teachers help students focus on cognitive functions, they facilitate development of students' efficiency as learners.

Teachers as Mediators of Thinking

Teachers mediate metacognition in all three phases of learning: gathering information, making sense of information, and communicating ideas. Feuerstein's term *mediator* defines the teacher's role as questioner and cue-maker in each of these phases. Questioning, cueing, and use of advance organizers are additional high-effects strategies described in Robert Marzano's meta-study on achievement (Marzano et al., 2001).

Effective mediation with its intense questioning and in-depth student responses does present a dilemma for those teachers who are compelled to lecture as the primary means for "covering" the prescribed curriculum. It also presents a dilemma for those teachers who are being mandated by their district leadership to use scripted lessons in reading and mathematics with little or no time for use of those thought-producing instructional strategies that research shows are the true achievement score raisers.

There is no question that script-restricted teachers have too little time allowed for student reflection. This follows the lack of time for learning groups, graphic organizers, or extended discussions to promote deeper understanding of curricular topics created by the scripted approach to instruction. Unless these teachers are able to "selectively abandon" low-effect, scripted instructional strategies, they will have little time for the all-important reflective practice.

The Pathway to Reflection

When promoting "thinking about thinking," teachers can start students on the pathway to reflection by coupling metacognitive prompts with students' use of the graphic organizers.

The following guidelines facilitate best use of these tools in various content areas:

1. Focus students on thinking about the central thinking operation highlighted by the graphic organizer. For instance, with the Venn, teachers focus on mediating the process of finding similarities. With the starburst, they focus on the process of classifying.

2. Lead questions that focus on a specific thinking operation sound like "What did you do well when you were *predicting?*" A strong response would sound like "I asked myself the question, *what will happen next in the story?* After I read the next page, I looked back to see how accurate my prediction was."

3. When students give a partial answer, teachers ask the next student to add to the first's response.

4. Encourage full participation by respecting students' right to say "I pass."

5. Ensure that the classroom is a safe place for students to think out loud when they respond to your questions. Dissuade side comments, judgmental statements, or put-downs from other students.

6. Use sufficient wait-time to distribute the opportunity to respond around the class. As you wrap around the classroom, ask each student to respond in turn. For ensuring equal distribution, use tactics such as drawing names from a hat, drawing name cards from a deck, or picking numbers from a tumbler.

7. Respect all answers, especially when you disagree. Put more emphasis on seeking clarity and depth in student answers.

8. Play devil's advocate. Say "I don't know. What do you think?" when students try to get you to do their thinking.

9. Manage the discussion and the time. Develop skills for keeping everyone "on point." Don't allow any one student to dominate.

Tactics to Stir Thinking

Multiple questioning and cueing tactics also promote enrichment of multiple intelligences. If students are using a graphic organizer with a textbook, they can enrich both their visual and their verbal intelligences as they organize their thoughts through the graphics. Other organizers, helped by astute questioning tactics, develop the interpersonal and intrapersonal intelligences.

1. **Draw-pair-share:** Students sketch their ideas before talking with a partner.

2. **Write-pair-share:** Students write a response to the questions.

3. **Journal stems:** Students respond to "About (specific thinking process), I learned. . . ." "I improved . . ." "I need help to . . ." "I am pleased that . . ." Allow sufficient time for the written response in the journal before ending the class or calling on students to complete a round-robin read within a small group or for the entire class.

4. **Assessment patterns:** Students respond to a sequence of questions such as Mrs. Potter's:

- What did you do well?
- If you could do it over again, what would you do differently?
- What help do you need to make better use of this process?

Assessment organizers such as DeBono's PMI (p. 71), the ranking ladder (p. 55), and Fogarty's Jigsaw (p. 47) facilitate the visual and intrapersonal intelligences when coupled with a structured sequence of self-analysis questions:

- What were you trying to do with this thinking process?
- So, how did you do?
- Now what else can you do to improve its use?

SUMMARY

Habits of metacognition develop best when teachers teach students the tactics and strategies that make the control of reflective practice more efficient. Rather than simply use these tactics to facilitate a one-time discussion, teachers foster the development of the metacognitive habit by scaffolding instruction of the tactics. After initial use and discussion of the tactics, teachers provide ample opportunity for students to practice, receive feedback, and improve the quality of their thinking about thinking.

29

Developing the Quality of Student Thinking

In addition to mediating the thinking operations inherent in most graphic organizers, teachers can focus students' metacognition on cognitive functions related to each of these processes. As identified by Reuven Feuerstein, the cognitive functions are the quality indicators of deeper levels of thinking (Feuerstein et al., 2006).

When students' cognitive functions are weak or underdeveloped, teachers can change the quality of students' thinking for the better. As Feuerstein teaches in his Theory of Structural Cognitive Modifiability (Feuerstein et al., 2006, 2ff), intelligence is neither fixed nor immutable. With appropriate mediation, teachers can change intelligence. With increased intelligence comes increased achievement. Smarter students make better learners because they are more efficient thinkers.

When a function is weak or deficient, it prevents a student from learning well. When a function is strong, it contributes to the students' more powerful learning performance. The following chart is a diagnostic tool that teachers can use to assess the quality of a thinking operation (e.g., comparing, differentiating, inferring). With this practical assessment tool, teachers can go a step beyond the minimal practices of metacognition by placing the language of the cognitive functions into students' metacognitive vocabulary and helping them refine the quality of their thinking.

When teachers are helping students to develop any of these functions within specific thinking operations such as predicting or finding similarities, they take note of what students are saying or doing as the best clues to the quality of how well students are using the operation. After determining which of the cognitive functions need the most immediate attention, teachers can target the entire class, small groups of students, or individuals who need differentiated mediation.

TACTICS FOR DEVELOPING COGNITIVE FUNCTIONS

How can a teacher mediate development of a cognitive function? Teachers who pay attention to the quality of thinking called for in the standards can mediate cognitive development with a well-designed instructional flow that includes the following:

1. Graphic organizers are used to structure how students think about the content they are studying.

2. With each graphic organizer, teachers focus students on specific thinking operations. When possible, teachers focus that attention on those operations that research says most facilitate higher student achievement.

3. When students struggle to perform a cognitive operation well, teachers work to strengthen students' underdeveloped cognitive functions.

4. Teachers plan how they will facilitate improved student thinking with ample time provided for students to think about their thinking throughout every lesson.

5. Teachers help students build a repertoire of graphic organizers that strengthen thinking habits.

6. Teachers help students refine their use of these tools for thinking.

Within the flow of each lesson, teachers have multiple tactics that they can select to help their mediation of student thinking focused on developing cognitive functions.

1. **A mini-lesson:** 10–20 minutes of instruction that focuses on developing the targeted cognitive function. For instance, if geometry teachers diagnose multiple students in the classroom as *imprecise* with measurement, they can select word problems related to a required concept such as diameter of a circle. The problems will require students to use *precise*

Fishbone Chart: The Cognitive Functions

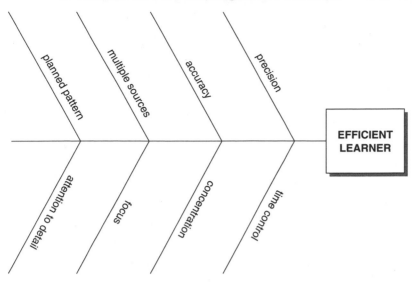

Cognitive Functions: A Sample List

Impulsive Thinking	Reflecting Deeply
Episodic thinking	Seeing relationships and connections
Imprecise data collection	Attending to precise details
Low-risk taking	Hypothetical reasoning
Inaccurate reporting	Providing accurate facts and figures
Wild guessing	Predicting with reasons
Literal interpretations	Making inferences
Unconnected facts	Summarizing with support
Unconnected concepts	Seeing similarities
Illogical arguments	Logical understanding
Poor common sense	Judging with evidence

numbers as they measure and calculate circumference. Before starting the measurement task, the teacher uses an advance organizer that requires students to think about the importance of precision. The class constructs a web of the tactics they will use to ensure precise measurement. Students select three tactics (e.g., double checking each problem) that they think will help improve their *precision* and pay attention to these throughout the task. After the task is completed, the teacher helps the students assess their attention to *precision*.

2. **PMI assessment:** At the end of a task, the students attach a PMI (p. 71) that assesses how they checked for *precision*. Students in a language arts or English class check for *precision* in grammar, usage, punctuation, spelling, and so on.

A Sequence Chart to Guide Lessons That Develop Thinking

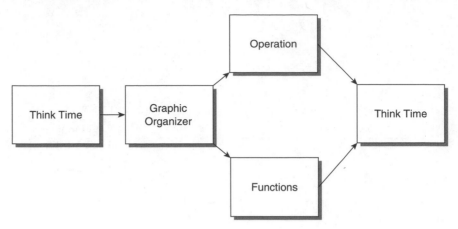

3. **Class motto:** The class brainstorms a saying that promotes development of the targeted cognitive function. For instance students make posters for the room with the saying (e.g., *Precision* Counts).

4. **Written feedback:** Teachers provide written feedback on the students' "corrected" work. "Your *precision* is improving. I only found this one *imprecise* measurement in your lab report. Note these other precise measurements you made."

5. **Paired check-ups:** Students work in *"precision"* check-up pairs. Before they turn in any work, they proofread each other's work for precise facts, grammar, computations, and so on.

6. **Function focused tactics:** Teachers ask students to reflect on assessing their individual functions. Teachers use the same tactics as those used to promote reflection on use of the graphic organizers. Instead of focusing the reflection on the organizer, teachers focus the tactics on the cognitive function. "Let's focus for a moment on the word *'precision.'* Remember that it was a goal to be more *precise* with our choice of words. In this task, how *precise* were you?"

SUMMARY

Instructional tactics that focus on improvement of a cognitive function are not add-ons. The best instruction intentionally integrates these tactics into each lesson. Teachers build the gathering of information around an organizer, use additional organizers to help students understand the information, and guide reflection that provides the students with the practice and feedback for overcoming any cognitive shortcomings and for making the organizer a lifelong learning tool. As a goal for this lesson, teachers stress the improvement of select cognitive functions such as increased *precision,* using many sources of information, or greater control of impulsive thinking.

30

Using Graphic Organizers With Learning Groups

Teachers can structure membership in learning groups in two ways: by mixed ability and by same ability. From the research view, the most effective groups for increasing student achievement are the mixed-ability groups in which the students have a common academic goal. By definition, mixed-ability groups with a common academic goal are "cooperative groups." When teachers imbed graphic organizers as the primary tool to help learning groups achieve their shared group goal, they are likely to see even better results (Marzano, 2001).

Marzano and his associates reinforced what other researchers have shown for several decades. Roger and David Johnson, Robert Slavin, Robin Fogarty, James Bellanca, and others who developed various cooperative learning models have pointed out the superiority of cooperative groups over other forms of instruction such as individualized learning and large-group lecture. It was the Johnsons' pioneering research that compared cooperative group learning with individualized learning and showed the overriding power of the former to increase student achievement.

Cooperative learning groups enable students to help other students, build their interactive social skills, and gather more effort by working together as opposed to learning alone. The farm-raised Johnson brothers developed a humorous acronym PIGS-FACE that describes the characteristics of and the benefits to students who work in cooperative learning groups.

1. **Positive Interdependence.** Students who work in groups learn how to work in a constructive way with students from different racial, economic, and ethnic groups.

2. **Individual Accountability.** Students learn together to help each other understand the material. However, they also learn that all individuals in the learning group will be responsible or accountable for showing what they each know.

3. **Group Process.** Students learn that each group task has a structure. They learn what it takes to function as a team with give and take.

4. **Social Skill Development.** Students develop the social skills needed for collaborative work.

5. **Face-to-Face Interaction.** Students learn conflict resolution skills as they work with each other on difficult tasks and resolve differences of opinion.

D. W. Johnson and R. T. Johnson, *Nuts and
Bolts of Cooperative Learning*, Edina, MN:
Interaction Book Company, 1994

INSTRUCTIONAL TACTICS IN COOPERATIVE LEARNING GROUPS

To help them structure learning group work that results in the best achievement, teachers have a selection of tactics available:

1. **The DOVE Guidelines.** These guidelines remind students of those behaviors that are most likely to promote the engagement of all members of the group in the task.
   - Do respect different ideas.
   - Opt for the Offbeat. As a thinker, think outside the box.
   - Vast Numbers Are Needed. Go for a big quantity of ideas from which you can select the best.
   - Expand. Piggyback or hitchhike with others' ideas.

2. **Trios.** With graphic organizers, groups of three make the best number. This ensures that there is someone to arbitrate conflicts constructively.

3. **Roles and Responsibilities.** Post a standard set of roles that students can use in learning group tasks:
   - Recorder: has the responsibility to fill in the graphic that is the official document of the group.

- Reader: has the task of reading the material and the instructions to the class.
- Leader: has the task of making sure all understand their roles, the instructions, and the ideas from the group. Specific organizers may have other roles that fit the task.
- Materials manager: obtains markers, newsprint, and tape as instructed. Sets out lab equipment in science tasks. Collects completed assignments and turns in to teacher.
- Checker: checks for understanding and agreements.
- Other: roles and responsibilities that fit specific tasks in a lesson.

4. **Assessing Cooperation.** From time to time, use a rubric to assess the group interactions. Talk about how individuals can improve the quality of the group work by improving role performances, social skills, following guidelines, matching the elements of PIGS-FACE, and other factors that help the students achieve the group's stated, shared goal.

5. **Shared Materials.** Positive interdependence is enriched when the group shares a single graphic on a large sheet of newsprint (or butcher paper). The members agree on their ideas for the organizer, their reasons for each idea, and what they will present to the class. The large sheet enables group members to see what they are recording. It also enables other students to see what a learning group is presenting to the class. If teachers wish to grade the results, group members sign the newsprint. In most instances, it is better for group cohesion that students make their own sketches of the organizers. When a graphic figure is too complicated to replicate in a large sketch, the instructions direct teachers to duplicate the master. Otherwise, the master provided at the end of each lesson is reserved for use with the overhead projector.

6. **The T-Chart.** Teachers use this graphic organizer to build students' understanding of social skills. After naming a social skill such as good listening, the teacher asks "What does listening look like?" and records the answers in column 1. Next, the teacher asks, "What does listening sound like?" and records the responses in column 2. Teachers post this T-chart for reference throughout the learning group tasks. In a no-frills classroom, it is important that students generate these ideas. Purchased charts, no matter how attractive, do not allow for student "ownership" of the ideas generated.

The T-Chart: Listening

Looks Like	Sounds Like
eye contact	silence
head nod	run home
leave in	
sit still	

7. **The Monitor Role.** When students are working in the learning groups, teachers walk among the students to note that every student gets to contribute, that students are using their interactive social skills, that all are doing their assigned roles, and that all understand the material.

8. **Reinforcing "Good Thinking."** By taking note of what students are saying as they work on the organizers, teachers can hear the quality of thinking. When teachers "catch students thinking," they tell students what they like. "I'm glad to hear you thinking carefully before you speak" (controlled impulsivity). "I like the way this group started with a plan" (planning behavior). "Glad to see how you have rechecked your numbers" (precision and accuracy).

9. **Journals.** Journals are an important tool for use with cooperative groups. Teachers ask students to divide the journals into three parts: Part I for reflections on content, Part II for reflections on cognition, and Part III for reflections on collaboration. Additional assignments of prior knowledge assessments go on the right side pages and post-task reflections on the left. These distinctions make it easier for teachers to review student reflections. Students may discuss responses to teacher prompts and cues in their groups, but make their individual journal entries.

DIFFERENTIATING INSTRUCTION WITH SAME-ABILITY GROUPS

Teachers should not forget that homogeneous groups sometimes have a place in the classroom. However, they should use these like-ability groups with care. The largest danger is that homogeneous groups become a ready excuse to retrack untracked classes. This occurs when teachers set students into same-ability groups and leave the groups together for long periods of time.

Like-ability groups work best under specific conditions:

1. They are short term with a very specific purpose. Teachers form the groups as a way of providing direct instruction and guided practice for students who need special attention in learning the content of a lesson, receiving instructions, or reviewing for a test. Same-ability groups are also helpful for extension projects by students who are able to go beyond the core material in a unit.

2. They do not allow anyone to "label" any group of students as "the dummies" or "the brains." Classroom labels, especially with older students, usually do not need an official sanction, but they do stick.

3. There is high intrinsic task motivation for any group not under direct contact with the teacher. This motivation is based on students' high interest in the task assigned or the group's high level of concern about completing the task in a scheduled time. Using ability groups to complete worksheets is a direct road to discipline disaster.

4. When devoting time to one group, teachers must remember the rule of proximity. This rule predicts what happens in many classrooms when the teacher's attention is consumed by one group. Other students can feel unconstrained. Their on-task behavior declines. Such conditions may explain why the research on achievement gives low marks to this grouping mechanism.

SUMMARY

Learning groups are a *high-effect* learning strategy. Graphic organizers imbedded in a cooperative learning task become all the more effective as tools to promote higher achievement and richer thinking.

Marzano's High-Effect Instructional Strategies

Identifying Similarities
Summarizing
Reinforcing Effort
Homework and Practice
Nonlinguistic Representation
Cooperative Learning
Setting Objective/Feedback
Testing Hypothesis
Cues, Questions, and Organizers

31

The Multiple Uses of Graphic Organizers in Assessment

Teachers use graphic organizers mainly as instructional tools. However, they also find them useful as assessment tools that adapt to a variety of classroom learning objectives. In addition, when teachers intend that their students build a box of "learning to learn" tools for use in and outside of the classroom, they include assessment of students' improvement in how they apply these tools in different learning situations.

USING GRAPHIC ORGANIZERS AS EVALUATION TOOLS

The PMI (p. 71), the KWL (p. 1), the web (p. 8), and the scale (p. 63) are organizers that teachers can use to assess students in three dimensions: content, cooperation, and cognition.

ASSESSING CONTENT

To assess content in a lesson, teachers can use the organizer in the middle of a lesson or at the end. For use in the middle, they focus on what the students have learned so far in relation to the objectives. Consider this KWL example in a lesson on Harriet Tubman. Having checked out what the students knew (K) and wanted to know (W) at the start of the lesson, midway in the lesson teachers return the class to the KWL chart. They ask the question, "So far in relation to what you wanted to know, what have you learned?" After students list their ideas, teachers can ask "And what else have you learned about Harriet Tubman?"

Topic: The Underground Railroad		
K	*W*	*L*
Harriet Tubman, safe houses, abolitionists, Canada	dangers, accomplishments, states, other people involved, effect on Lincoln	Frederick Douglass, Susan B. Anthony, Emancipation Proclamation, routes, places

The web also works well as a mid-lesson assessment tool. Teachers start with a write-pair-share tactic after the students have completed the information-gathering phase in the lesson. They ask students to write a short paragraph summarizing the information gathered. After reviewing their summaries with a partner, students volunteer a brief statement to the teacher. On the web, posted for all to see, the teacher lists each new idea. The teacher concludes by checking for understanding of the five most important ideas.

At the end of a lesson, teachers may use the scale to assess understanding of a unit's content. Teachers provide a blank scale to each student. For instance, in a World History class in a unit on the Middle East, the teacher can assess students' understanding of the rationale for the U.S. interventions. Using the scale graphic organizer, students who are working in trios list what they have learned about the reasons for the military interventions. They then apply points (+ or −) to each intervention on a 1–5 scale. They conclude with a summary statement that explains the final balance.

Teachers review the group's assessment and grade it according to a rubric that may include a number of ideas presented, accuracy of information, depth of detail, completeness of summary, and so forth.

ASSESSING COGNITION

Teachers also may use a graphic organizer to assess targeted cognitive operations. For instance, they can ask students to construct a PMI chart in their journals. At the end of each day, teachers ask the students to reflect on the targeted operation by adding to the PMI. At the end of the lesson, they ask the students to write a summary paragraph about the entries from one or more of the columns.

The assessment of cognition can focus on three areas for these reflections: (1) cognitive operations such as identifying similarities or classifying that the teachers targeted in the lesson; (2) cognitive functions such as precision in labeling data or the conservation of constants; or (3) the use of the graphic organizers in the lesson.

A Sample PMI on Cognitive Functions

Function: **Improving My Planning Behavior**

P (+)	Think before asking
M (−)	No homework plan
I (?)	Why didn't I do this before?

P (+)	Using web to get ideas
M (−)	Reviewing steps in plan (daily schedule)
I (?)	When will I start plans in other courses?

ASSESSING COOPERATION

Teachers can also use graphic organizers to help students assess their cooperation during group tasks. They can also use organizers to assess cooperative social skills individual students were developing during group work.

The PMI, the web, and the scale work well when used with a summary statement. Consider this example of the web used by a teacher that gathered feedback from group members on its cooperative work. The group used the group processes learned to complete this web. Each student then wrote a summary.

As the examples show, teachers can select which organizers to use and whether to focus the assessment on cooperation, cognition, or content. At some time in a unit, teachers will reinforce their expectations in each of these areas by doing at least one formative assessment. They have the option of gathering these assessments from individuals or teams or they can use the organizer to communicate their own feedback to the students.

ASSESSING GRAPHIC ORGANIZER USE

When teachers' goal is to enable each student to master a "mind tool," they can choose to assess students' use of the selected organizer in three dimensions. First, teachers can assess the progress students are making with a graphic organizer as a key tool in their "learning tool box." Second, they

A Group Assessment of Cooperation

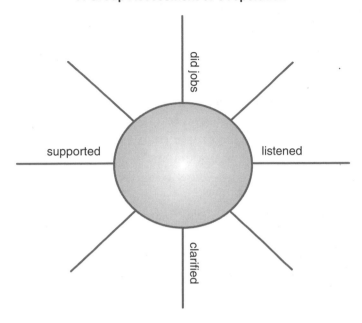

A Group Assessment of Cooperation

More Examples: group spirit, left out, off task, had materials

Student 1 Summary: Our group generally did a good job with cooperation. That was clear from the way we listened to each other, supported each others (sic) ideas, and did our jobs. Sometimes we got off task with disagreements and we needed more examples.

Student 2 Summary: I liked our group. We all pitched in. The materials manager had our paper and markers. The rest did their jobs. Sometimes I felt left out.

can focus on improvements students show in the processes and procedures for correct use of the organizer. Third, they can assess how the students use the organizer as a product that helps communicate their ideas.

One of the easiest ways to assess how much improvement students are showing in their use of graphic organizers is to look at "homework" or unguided practice. After teaching the use of the organizer and guiding its application in a classroom task, teachers can assign students to use the organizer for out-of-class reading assignments. For instance, a language arts teacher can ask students to use a spider map when reading a short story or a concept map when gathering ideas for a research paper. With this assignment, teachers will hand out a rubric that focuses on those cognitive functions most important to use of the organizer and the content. How *accurate* was the information included? How *precise was the language?* How well did the student *coordinate multiple sources of information?* How *spontaneous were the comparisons* made?

In addition to improving the organizer's use, teachers should reinforce the idea that the organizer is a purposeful tool. One purpose is to gather information. A second is to make sense of that information. The third is to communicate new understandings.

When it comes to making sense of information with an organizer, rubrics should highlight the quality of thinking that occurs. For instance, when students use an inference funnel in social studies, do they pick up all the salient clues that lead to a major event? Do they make the correct inferences and show subtle connections between the clues and the outcomes of the event? When using a sequence chart in science, do they place the procedures for a complex experiment in the proper order? Can they branch the order?

Graphic organizers used to understand a complex concept make helpful tools in communicating these new insights. When students make presentations of their findings from a survey, the conclusions they drew from a lab experiment or the thematic relationships they see between characters in a story, they can use graphic organizers as the visual tool to explain their discoveries to others. Teachers can use rubrics that include benchmarks ranging from artfulness and visual clarity of the organizer to how well it communicates the relative importance of main and sub-ideas connected to content standards.

SUMMARY

Teachers can look at graphic organizers and assessment from two points of view. Graphic organizers make effective assessment tools for examining content, cognition, and cooperation in a lesson. Teachers who are expecting students to use selected organizers as independent learning tools can assess students' improvement as they use the tools for out-of-class assignments.

Experienced teachers assess best by planning lesson sequences that require the least amount of record keeping. In a lesson sequence with graphic organizers as the integrating tool, six grade entries are more than enough in a unit. This means that they will limit "graded" documents to two or three products that show their understanding of key concepts. In addition, they may collect a summative self-assessment from each student focused on cognitive improvements and a peer review of cooperation.

Designing From the Rear

When teachers start their planning for lessons, it is helpful if they start at the rear by asking what it is they want their students to know and do. Once they have these questions answered, they proceed to design lessons that outline the content, the cognitive processes, and the cooperation that will enable students to know and do what is expected.

After selecting the outcomes, keeping in mind the importance of high challenge (content), high support (cooperation), and high thought (cognition), it is time to segment the lesson and pick indicators of success for

Sample Content Outcomes

Primary	Journal entries with daily "I learned . . ."
Middle	Student-made math problems in portfolio.
Secondary	Essays that summarize key concepts of each unit.

Sample Complex Cooperation Outcomes

Primary	Student-observer checklist on group's behavior.
Middle	Base groups solve disagreements with five-step model.
Secondary	Student teams use group investigation method.

Sample Complex Thinking Outcomes

Primary	Student portfolio contains student evaluation of best work.
Middle	Students create prediction questions to literature.
Secondary	Students use graphic organizers in weekly journal entry.

each element. Here is an appropriate use for the sequence chart (see p. 15). To see the sequence, lay out eight to ten frames. The first frames will picture (1) the end product and outcomes, (2) what students are learning about cooperative structures' skills and strategies, and (3) the graphic organizer for the unit. In frame 4, the picture will show the intermediate assessment. Frames 5 through 8 will illustrate the transfer tasks in which students are applying the cooperative/cognitive tools. This segment ends with a second intermediate assessment. The final segments will show students imbedding the cooperative/cognitive tools into the completion of the final product. The very last frame will show the final assessment.

After focusing this sequence, the teacher can pinpoint at each intermediate assessment and at the final assessment what he or she will see as the success indicators.

Once the teacher has identified the indicators, he or she will design the daily-weekly lesson with structures and strategies as described in the book. When ready to indicate the unit, the teacher will provide students with an outline including (a) the final product description, (b) the final cooperative and cognitive outcomes, and, if a grade is required, (c) a description of the final grade. In general terms, this grade, where necessary, will reflect both the noted ongoing progress and the final product's value. Once the teacher has reviewed these with the class (a copy for parents is also helpful), he or she can set up the first task in the sequence and the student portfolio.

If a teacher wants to avoid being buried in paper, portfolio development must follow the KISS principle. The more students begin to understand the implications of being classroom doers, the more work they

Assessment

	Assessment (1)	*Assessment (2)*	*Assessment (3)*
Content	three-sentence paragraph	three-paragraph essay	clear beginning, middle, and end
Cooperation	student knows words to encourage	student starts to use encouraging words	student uses only encouraging words
Cognition	student can label steps with Venn	student follows directions to make Venn	student makes own Venn

produce. Quantity precedes quality. With student work, a plan that saves you work and shifts responsibility for assessment to students is important.

If students can produce the quality work you desire, they can assess its quality. Students have the primary responsibility for assessment. The teacher's responsibility is to structure quality self-assessment by students, observe and give professional feedback, coach, make professional judgments that are reported to parents, and in too many cases—even in schools making significant reforms—reduce all products and assessments to a single grade.

To encourage student self-assessment, there are a variety of tools available. The easiest tool to use is the Likert scale. When students complete a task or at the end of today's work, groups first will use an indicator to review what they have done. Because the lessons have a triple agenda, it is not sensible to use the three scales at once. In the long run, you want information for all three agendas; in the short run, one thing at a time.

Begin by demonstrating one scale, against one group criterion. Point out that there are three scale marks: NOT YET, OK, and WOW!

Next, the indicators:

Instruct the teams to list what they did in the task or unit to meet the indicator. For novices, it helps to post or brainstorm a list of possibilities before they begin the task. When they do the assessment, they can select and use the pre-made chart as a starting point. After listing what they did well, the group will agree on its scale score. All sign the assessment form and put it with the product into the portfolio.

NOT YET   OK   WOW!

Cooperation	does roles, follows team rules, focuses social skill, uses conflict resolution skills
Thinking	uses organizers, shows persistence, flexibility, high fluency
Content	understands concept

Set up the threefold expectations for each group task. As the students develop facility in self-assessment, you may consider using two or three scales for major tasks. Provide each group with a portfolio large enough to hold the paperwork from each task. Allow time for each group to use the portfolio cover for team-building activities such as a team name, a team logo, a team motto, or team flag. They will include task work and their dated written assessments in the portfolio. In addition, have each individual keep a smaller portfolio. Individual assignments and self-assessments are saved here.

Once a week, or at the end of a unit, ask each group to select its best work for that time period and write the reasons "why" for you. Collect these and add your feedback before returning to the group. If you have assigned individual tasks or assessments, make a similar "my best" assignment each week. Instead of reviewing all students' work each week, develop a random selection pattern that allows you to focus on one quarter of the class each week. This will give you time to write more detailed and precise comments.

At the end of 8 weeks, instruct each individual to pick the three best work samples for the time. Instruct the students to use at least one criterion from each element—cooperation, thoughtfulness, and product—to measure their achievement. Ask students to write their reasons. If you can plan the time, confer with each student on these products and assessments.

If you don't have to provide a grade, you can add your comment to the students' summary work and send those home to parents. If grades are required, use the scale to identify the quarter mark.

When using this approach to develop complex products or exhibitions, be clear with students that the final semester grade will be based on what they do to improve along the way and the quality of the final product. When using the triple-agenda outcomes, clarify also the relationships among cooperation, thoughtfulness, and content mastery in the grade. In addition to the criteria and indicators of success you discuss in the classroom, it will help if you provide parents with a written explanation of your grading system and the rationale.

Evaluating student performance is a necessary task. However, more important is the opportunity for students to learn self-assessment.

The ancient Chinese proverb says, "Give me a fish and I'll eat for a day. Teach me to fish and I'll eat for a lifetime." So it is that when they teach students to self-assess, teachers give the students tools they will use throughout their lives to become better and more self-directed learners.

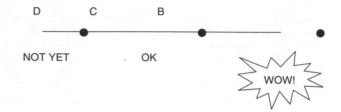

SUMMARY

Teachers have multiple opportunities to use graphic organizers to enrich their instruction and increase student achievement. The best uses of these visual tools are found in combination with other high-effects instructional strategies. Integrating these organizers with cooperative learning and the content to promote critical thinking and problem solving is most likely to produce the strongest results and highest motivation for students. The possible combinations are only limited by teachers' imagination in wrapping content, cognition, and cooperative learning into unified lesson designs geared to obtaining the most powerful outcomes.

32

No Child Left Behind and Research

How does use of graphic organizers fit with No Child Left Behind (NCLB) legislation? The answer is not difficult. The intent of NCLB is to hold teachers and schools more accountable for increasing achievement of all students, especially English-language learners, students of color, students of poverty, and students with special needs. The question classroom teachers and school administrators must ask is "by what means?"

In specifying an answer to this question, NCLB dictates that the means selected must meet the criterion "proven by scientific research." For reading, it mandates that schools develop students' reading comprehension by using research-based strategies. Graphic organizers in conjunction with other well-researched instructional strategies meet this guideline. Teachers who integrate graphic organizers into daily lessons can exceed this mandate in ways that raise expectations for student comprehension to the highest degree.

NCLB requires schools to make increased student achievement the number one instructional priority, especially in reading, science, and mathematics. The question is "by what means?" In the primary grades, NCLB does

229

emphasize providing students with the reading "basics" via phonics and phonemics. This emphasis with its attention to memory seems to put graphic organizers and thinking outside the reach of elementary students. However, unless a school district is so foolish as to limit all early grade instruction to the memorization of sounds and the exclusion of sense, elementary teachers have ample opportunity to use graphic organizers as a highly effective tool for attaining standards in other areas of the curriculum.

Graphic organizers are part of the top nine "high-effects" instructional strategy called "nonlinguistic representations." Others in this list of nine are hypothesizing, summarizing, identifying similarities, and use of questions, cues, and advance organizers. Although these strategies were isolated for research purposes, it makes sense that combination strategies such as question asking and graphic organizer use would increase the effect size and be stronger enablers of student understanding, especially in reading. In fact, Marzano's meta-analysis supports those combinations that give teachers a "two for one" increase in test scores.

What does this all mean? Simply this: If teachers want to comply with NCLB, they can do nothing better than make regular use of graphic organizers coupled with questions and cues as the primary strategies for raising student achievement scores and deepening their understanding. Better yet, they should increase the likelihood of stronger academic performance by imbedding instruction in cooperative learning tasks with an emphasis on helping students use those organizers that identify similarities, test hypotheses, and summarize.

Even if a school district interprets NCLB in the most literal sense, teachers can incorporate organizers, thinking processes, and questions into daily lessons, especially if students obtain most of their information via the reading pathway. Marzano's research makes it clear that graphic organizers are among the most practical strategies for facilitating the jumps in achievement students need to make.

NCLB's goal is to enable all students to meet more rigorous academic standards at higher levels of mastery. NCLB mandates that each state publish rigorous standards in reading, math, science, and social studies. Although standards for what students should know and do are a state responsibility, there is much agreement among the states that the most rigorous standards require students to perform complex thinking and problem-solving tasks. Note this example from mathematics:

Not every graphic organizer will facilitate higher mathematics achievement. However, as the research indicates (Ben Hur & Bellanca, 2006), the best math instruction relies on the use of multiple representations of abstract concepts. These include a selection of graphic organizers such as the Venn diagram (invented in the last century by Thomas Venn as a tool for displaying sets) and the classification matrix.

In addition, the metacognitive questioning described earlier (in Chapter 27) holds special significance for mathematics teachers as they develop students' mathematical thinking through visual, concrete representation of abstract concepts via appropriate graphic organizers.

Major Mathematical Concepts

Major Mathematical Concepts for Grades 6–8			
I = Introduce Concept M = Maintain Concept			
	Grade 6	**Grade 7**	**Grade 8**
Algebra and Algebraic Thinking	Properties		Properties of Rational Numbers (I)
	Expressions		
	Equations		
	Functions (I)	Absolute Value (I)	Step (I)
	Graphing: Integers and Functions (I)	Inequalities and Slope (I)	Inequalities (I)
	Integers	Absolute Value, Multiply and Divide, Equations (I)	
			Polynomials
			Rational, Irrational, and Real Numbers (I)
	Decimals (M)		
	Scientific Notation (I)		
	Fractions (M)		
Geometry and Spatial Reasoning	Angles (M)		
	Constructions: Congruent Segment, Parallel and Perpendicular Lines (I)	Perpendicular and Angle Bisectors, Congruent Angles (I)	
	Polygons: Different View (I)	Pythagorean Theorem (I)	
	Transformations: Translations, Rotations, Reflection (I)		Dilations (I)
	Coordinate Geometry (I)		

(Continued)

Major Mathematical Concepts for Grades 6–8 (Continued)

I = Introduce Concept   M = Maintain Concept

	Grade 6	Grade 7	Grade 8
Measurement	Area: Composite Figures (I)	Composite Figures and Trapezoids (I)	
	Surface Area: Prisms (I)	Cylinders (I)	
	Volume	Volume: Cylinders (I)	Volume: Cones, Pyramids, Spheres (I)
	Indirect Measurement: Scale Drawing, Using Similar Triangles, Ratio in Right Triangles (I)	Pythagorean Theorem (I)	Trigonometric Ratios (I)
Number Sense and Quantitative Reasoning	Compare and Order: Integers (I)		Rationals and Irrationals (I)
	Exponents	Negative Numbers (I)	
	Scientific Notation		
		Square Number and Square Roots (I)	
Probability	Independent and Dependent Events	Odds (I)	
	Theoretical Probability (I)		
	Probability of Complements		
	Permutation and Combinations		Factorial Notation and Pascal's Triangle (I)
Proportional Reasoning	Ratios	Equal Ratios (I)	
	Rate: Unit Price (I)		Dimensional Analysis (I)
	Proportions		
	Proportions in Similar Figures		
	Percentages		

SOURCE: From Meir Ben Hur and James Bellanca, *Making Mathematics Matter,* International Renewal Institute, Inc. 2005. Reprinted by permission.

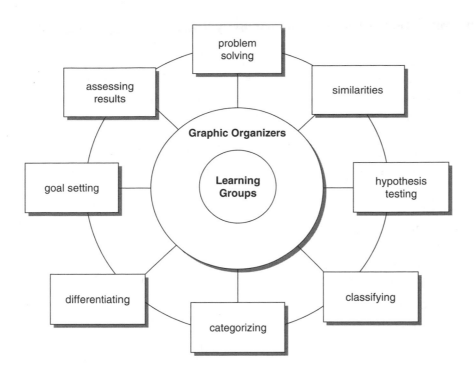

A SHORT LOOK AT THE RESEARCH

Research on the effectiveness of graphic organizers comes from a variety of sources. These include the studies of individual graphic organizers, brain research, reading research, research on learning disabilities, and research on instructional strategies. When used as a part of a formal lesson with other high-effect strategies, the impact of organizers on learning increases dramatically. Yet, in spite of this evidence, Marzano reports that the graphic organizer is the most underused of the high-effects strategies (Marzano, 2001).

The best-known meta-analysis of achievement results appears in *Classroom Instruction That Works* (Marzano, Pickering, & Pollack: ASCD, 2001). Chapter 6 focuses on the use of graphic organizers as a high-effects instructional tactic within the framework of "nonlinguistic" strategies. The researchers included seven major studies conducted from 1980 to 1999. They found that graphic organizers were reported with an average effect size of .75, with an average percentile gain of 27. The effect sizes reported ranged from .50 to 1.16.

One element that Marzano and his colleagues could not include because of the current emphasis on "scientific" research was the *combination factor*. Among the other high-effects strategies in the meta-analysis that produced the nine most effective strategies were "finding similarities," cooperative learning, questioning, and hypothesis testing. These had average effect sizes ranging from 1.61 (similarities) to .73 (cooperative learning) and .59 for questioning, cueing, and advance organizers. What the study could not show was research on combined strategies such as use of graphic organizers in a cooperative learning setting with a focus on finding similarities as students would do if they used the Venn diagram or comparison alley to find similarities as they worked in cooperative teams.

Since the publication of *Classroom Instruction That Works,* the Institute for Advancement of Research in Education (IARE) examined the instructional effectiveness of graphic organizers (2003). IARE conducted its study using criteria for scientifically based research studies set down by NCLB. It selected 29 studies that met the criteria for rigorous, systematic, and objective studies that had obtained reliable and valid information.

IARE's basic conclusion was that graphic organizers improved student performance in:

- Reading comprehension
- Student achievement across grade levels and content areas
- Thinking and learning skills for organizing information, seeing relationships, and categorizing of concepts
- Retention of information
- Achievement among learning disabled students

This study corroborated a 1984 meta-analysis (Moore & Readance) that graphic organizers did impact vocabulary scores. In addition, the study showed the positive impact on students' thinking and learning processes *when teachers were careful to preteach the strategies to the students* before asking them to use the organizers as learning tools. Among the thinking operations recognized were students' ability to see relationships, patterns, and connections; highlight important ideas; classify concepts and information; and comprehend the events in a story or book. Interestingly, the study also showed that using the graphic organizer improved social interaction among groups, facilitated group work, and peer collaboration.

Additional support for graphic organizers comes from the report of the National Reading Panel (2000). This report cites graphic organizers as one of the seven categories of instruction that are most effective in improving reading comprehension.

IMPLICATIONS FROM BRAIN RESEARCH

In the past decade, many educators have looked to brain research for guidance in how to best enrich student learning. While a great deal of brain research remains highly speculative in its impact on learning, some studies are suggesting the importance of visual-verbal connections.

One promising line of investigation by neurologists focuses on the plasticity of the brain. Plasticity is the lifelong capacity of the brain circuitry to change with experience. Plasticity enables the brain to modify its organization, neurochemical systems, cell assemblies, and behavior. Imaging techniques are being used to study neural plasticity in learning and development. Neurologists are hypothesizing about the nature of the connections between neural structures and cognitive processing.

Graphic organizers structure new ways for students to understand and process information. Although it will be many years before neural science catches up to classroom practice, it makes sense to hold that graphic tools do facilitate expansion of the neural systems.

SUMMARY

The strongest support for the use of graphic organizers as an instructional tool comes from recent meta-analyses of their effects on student academic performance. The effect sizes of those studies determined to be scientifically based in NCLB standards show that graphic organizers used appropriately (after instruction in how to use the tool) do result in significant gains. Although brain research implies that graphic organizers should help student learning, none yet exists to make this direct connection 100 percent certain.

Appendix

ELECTRONIC RESOURCES

Reuven Feuerstein

Background, Research, and Professional Development
www.iriinc.us

Research and Information Articles
www.icelp.us

High-Effects Instructional Strategies

Research and Information
www.ascd.org

Information
www.ed.gov/pubs

Research and Professional Development
www.marzanoandassociates.com

Cognitive Instruction

Research
www.questia.com

Research and Information
www.ncrel.org
www.mcrel.org

Professional Development
www.robinfogarty.com
www.iriinc.us

Cooperative Learning

Research and Professional Development
www.co-operation.org

Basic Strategies
www.edtech.kennesaw.edu

Information
www.ed.gov/pubs

Graphic Organizers

Mind Mapping Software
www.smartdraw.net

Sample Organizers
www.ncrel.org

Organizers in Bilingual Classrooms
www.everythingesl.net

Rubrics for Organizers
www.uwstout.edu/soe/profdev/rubrics.shtml

Research
www.cast.org

Special Needs Research
www.ncset.org/default.asp
www.nichcy.org

Electronic Graphics
www.inspiration.com
www.ael.org
www.mindservegroup.com

For additional electronic resources, Google "graphic organizers" or "nonlinguistic representations" or any of the subtopics listed in this appendix.

Bibliography

Alvermann, D. E., & Boothby, P. R. (1986). Children's transfer of graphic organizer instruction. *Reading Psychology, 7*(2), 87–100.

Anderson-Inman, L., Knox-Quinn, C., & Horney, M. A. (1996). Computer-based study strategies for students with learning disabilities: Individual differences associated with adoption level. *Journal of Learning Disabilities, 29*(5), 461–484.

Armstrong, J. O. (1993). Learning to make idea maps with elementary science text. *Technical Report No. 572.* Center for the Study of Reading, Urbana, IL.

Bellanca, J. (1990). *The cooperative think tank: Graphic organizers to teach thinking in the cooperative classroom.* Thousand Oaks, CA: Corwin Press.

Bellanca, J. (1992). *The cooperative think tank II: Graphic organizers to teach thinking in the cooperative classroom.* Thousand Oaks, CA: Corwin Press.

Ben Hur, M., & Bellanca, J. (2005). *Making mathematics matter.* Glencoe, IL: International Renewal Institute, Inc.

Berliner, D. (1986). Use what kids know to teach the new. *Instructor, 95,* 12–13.

Black, H., & Black, S. (1990). *Organizing thinking: Graphic organizers (Book II).* Pacific Grove, CA: Critical Thinking Press & Software.

Bos, C. S., & Anders, P. L. (1992). Using interactive teaching and learning strategies to promote text comprehension and content learning for students with learning disabilities. *International Journal of Disabilities and Development and Educations, 39*(3), 225–238.

Boyle, J. R., & Weishaar, M. (1997). The effects of expert-generated versus student generated cognitive organizers on the reading comprehension of students with learning disabilities. *Learning Disabilities Research & Practice, 12*(4), 228–235.

Bromley, K., & Irwin-DeVitis, L. (1995). *Graphic organizers: Visual strategies for active learners.* New York: Scholastic Books.

Brown, A. (1980). Metacognitive development and reading. In P. Spiro, B. Bruce, & W. Brewer (Eds.), *Theoretical issues in reading comprehension.* Hillsdale, NJ: Erlbaum.

Brown, A., Campione, J., & Day, J. (1981). Learning to learn: On training students to learn from texts. *Educational Researcher, 10.*

Brown, A., & Palincsar, A. (1982). Inducing strategic learning from texts by means of informed, self-control training. *Topics in Learning and Learning Disabilities, 2.*

Buzan, T. (1984). *Make the most of your mind.* New York: Simon & Schuster.

Cassidy, J. (1988). Using graphic organizer to develop critical thinking. *Gifted Child Today, 12*(6), 34–36.

Cassidy, J. & Hossier, A. (1992). A critique of graphic organizer research. *Reading Research and Instruction, 31*(2), 57–65.

Clarke, J. H., Raths, J., & Gilbert, G. L. (1989). Inductive towers: Letting students see how they think. *Journal of Reading, 33*(2), 86–95.

Clements-Davis, G. L., & Ley, T. C. (1991). Thematic pre-organizers and the reading comprehension of tenth-grade world literature students. *Reading Research & Instruction, 31*(1), 43–53.

Darch, C. B., Carnine, D. W., & Kammeenui, E. J. (1986). The role of graphic organizers and social structure in content area instruction. *Journal of Reading Behavior, 18*(4), 275–295.

Davidson, N., & Worsham, T. (1992). *Enhancing thinking through cooperative learning.* New York: Teachers College Press.

De Bono, E. (1983). The direct teaching of thinking as a skill. *Phi Delta Kappan, 64*(1), 703–708.

Deming, E. (1986). *Out of the crisis.* Cambridge: MIT Center for Advanced Engineering Study.

Dunston, P. J. (1992). A critique of graphic organizer research. *Reading Research and Instruction, 31*(2), 57–65.

Feuerstein, R., Feuerstein, R. S., Falik, L., & Rand, Y. (2006). *Creating and enhancing cognitive modifiability: The Feuerstein Instrumental Enrichment Program.* Jerusalem, Israel: ICELP Publication & the Company of the Enhancement of Mediated Learning Ltd.

Fogarty, R. (1997). *Brain: Compatible classroom.* Thousand Oaks, CA: Corwin Press.

Fogarty, R., & Bellanca, J. (1991). *Patterns for thinking: Patterns for transfer.* Palatine, IL: IRI/SkyLight Publishing.

Gardill, M. C. & Jitendra, A. K. (1999). Advanced story map instruction: Effects on the reading comprehension of students with learning disabilities. *The Journal of Special Education, 33*(1), 2–17.

Griffin, C. C., & Tulbert, B. L. (1995). The effect of graphic organizers on student comprehension and recall of expository text: A review of the research and implication for practice. *Reading and Writing Quarterly: Overcoming Learning Difficulties, 11*(1), 73–89.

Hawley, R. (1976). *Evaluating teaching: A handbook of positive approaches.* Amherst, MA: Education Research Associates.

Herl, H. E., O'Neil, H. F., Jr., Chung, G. K. W. K., & Schacter, J. (1999). Reliability and validity of a computer-based knowledge mapping system to measure content understanding. *Computers in Human Behavior, 15*(3–4), 315–333.

Hyerlye, D. (1998). Thinking maps: Seeing is understanding. *Educational Leadership, 53*(4), 85–89.

Hyerlye, D. (2000). *A field guide to using visual tools.* Alexandria, VA: Association for Supervision of Curriculum Development (ASCD).

Ishikawa, K. (1986). *Guide to quality control.* Tokyo: Asian Productivity Organization.

Johnson, R., & Johnson, D. (1998). *Cooperative learning in the classroom.* Minneapolis, MN: Interaction Book Co.

Jones, B. F., Palincsar, A. A., Ogle, D. S., & Carr, E. G. (Eds.). (1987). *Strategic teaching and learning: Cognitive instruction in the content areas.* Alexandria, VA: Association for Supervision and Curriculum Development.

Jones, B. F., Pierce, J., & Hunter, B. (1988a). Teaching students to construct graphic representations. *Educational Leadership, 46.*

Jones, B. F., Pierce, J., & Hunter, B. (1988b). Using graphic representation as a strategy for analysis and problem solving. Paper submitted to the Association for Supervision and Curriculum Development, Alexandria, VA.

Lavert, G. (2000). *The shaking bag.* Morton Grove, IL: A. Whitman.

Lavert, G. (2005). *Reading comprehension: What has thinking got to do with it? A manual for balanced reading instruction.* Glencoe, IL: International Renewal Institute (IRI), Inc.

Marzano, R. J., Pickering, D. J., & Pollock, J. E. (2001). *Classroom instruction that works: Research-based strategies for increasing student achievement.* Alexandria, VA: Association for Supervision and Curriculum Development (ASCD).

McTighe, J., & Lyman, F. (1992). Mind tools for matters of the mind. In A. Costa, J. Bellanca, & R. Fogarty (Eds.). *If minds matter: A foreword to the future (Vol. II).* Palatine, IL: International Renewal Institute (IRI)/SkyLight Publishing.

Merkley, D. M., & Jefferies, D. (2001). Guidelines for implementing a graphic organizer. *The Reading Teacher, 54*(4), 350–357.

Moore, D. W., & Readance, J. E. (1984). A quantitative and qualitative review of graphic organizer research. *Journal of Educational Research, 78*, 11–17.

National Reading Panel (NRP). (2000). *Teaching children to read.* Bethesda, MD: National Reading Panel.

Novak, J. D. (1998). *Learning, creating, and using knowledge: concept maps as facilitative tools in schools and corporations.* Mahwah, NJ: L. Erlbaum Associates.

Ogle, D. (1986). K-W-L group instruction strategy. In A. Palincsar, D. Ogle, B. Jones, & E. Carr (Eds.), *Teaching techniques as thinking (Teleconference resource guide).* Alexandria, VA: Association for Supervision and Curriculum Development.

Palincsar, A. S., & Brown, A. L. (1985). Reciprocal teaching: Activities to promote reading with your mind. In T. L. Harris & E. J. Cogen (Eds.), *Reading, thinking, and concept development: Strategies for the classroom.* New York: College Board.

Pearson, P. D., Hansen, J., & Gordon, C. (1979). The effect of background knowledge on young children's comprehension of explicit and implicit information. *Journal of Reading Behavior, 11*, 201–209.

Rico, G. (1983). *Writing the natural way: Using right-brain techniques to release your expressive powers.* Los Angeles: Tarcher.

Rose, D. H., & Meyer, A. (2002). *Teaching every student in the digital age: Universal design for learning:* Alexandria, VA: Association for Supervision and Curriculum Development (ASCD). Available at http://www.ascd.org

Rowe, M. B. (1987). Wait time: slowing down may be speeding up. *American Educator, 11.*

Salyer, B. K., Curran, C. & Thyfault, A. (2002). What can I use tomorrow? Strategies for accessibility math and science curriculum for diverse learners in rural schools. In *No Child Left Behind: The Vital Role of Rural Schools. Annual Conference Proceeding of the American Council on Rural Special Education (ACRES):* 22nd, Reno, NV, March 7–9, 2002.

Scanlon, D., Deshler, D. D., & Schumaker, J. B. (1996). Can a strategy be taught and in secondary inclusive classrooms? *Learning Disabilities Research & Practice, 11*(1), 41–57.

Senge, P. (1990). *The fifth discipline: The arts and practice of the learning organization.* New York: Doubleday.

Sinatra, R. C. (2000). Teaching learners to think, read, and write more effectively in content subjects. *The Clearing House, 73*(5), 266–273.

Sinatra, R., et al. (1994). Using computer-based semantic mapping, reading and writing approach with at risk fourth graders. *Journal of Computing in Childhood Education, 5*(1), 93–112.

Vacca, J. L. (1986). Working with content area teachers. In R. T. Vacca & J. L. Vacca (Eds.), *Content area reading.* Boston: Little, Brown.

Vacca, R. T., & Vacca, J. L. (1986). *Content area reading.* Boston: Little, Brown.

Vygotsky, L. S. (1978). *Mind in society: The development of higher psychological processes.* Cambridge, MA: Harvard University Press.

Index

CORWIN PRESS

The Corwin Press logo—a raven striding across an open book—represents the union of courage and learning. Corwin Press is committed to improving education for all learners by publishing books and other professional development resources for those serving the field of PreK–12 education. By providing practical, hands-on materials, Corwin Press continues to carry out the promise of its motto: **"Helping Educators Do Their Work Better."**

Science

Through

CHILDREN'S LITERATURE

An Integrated Approach

Second Edition

Carol M. Butzow

Educational Consultant

and

John W. Butzow

Dean, College of Education
Indiana University of Pennsylvania

Illustrated by
Hannah L. Ben-Zvi

2000
TEACHER IDEAS PRESS
A Division of
Libraries Unlimited, Inc.
Englewood, Colorado

To our daughters, Karen and Kristen

TEACHER IDEAS PRESS
A Division of
Libraries Unlimited, Inc.
P.O. Box 6633
Englewood, CO 80155-6633
1-800-237-6124
www.lu.com/tip

Library of Congress Cataloging-in-Publication Data

Butzow, Carol M., 1942-
    Science through children's literature : an integrated approach / Carol M. Butzow and John W. Butzow ; illustrated by Hannah L. Ben-Zvi.--2nd ed.
        p. cm.
    Includes bibliographical references and index.
    ISBN 1-56308-651-4
    1. Science--Study and teaching (Elementary) 2. Activity programs in education. 3. Children--Books and reading. I. Butzow, John W., 1939- II. Title.

LB1585 .B85 2000
    372.3'5044--dc21

                                                            99-088098

Contents

List of Figures

Preface

In 1989, we published the first edition of *Science Through Children's Literature*. It was intended to assist teachers in instructing young children about science, using materials that were familiar to them. We have been gratified with the overwhelming response teachers have made to the book. In the decade since it was published, we have seen many more teachers implement activity-based, literature-oriented teaching units in the primary grades. Teachers have told us that science is more approachable with our methods. Children use the knowledge they gain through reading as a foundation for studying academic content in the curriculum.

During the last 10 years, we have talked to countless teachers at workshops and conferences. The response was overwhelmingly positive as were comments from critics and reviewers. We have heard which activities worked best and which activities needed some retooling, along with suggestions for future volumes.

In reworking *Science Through Children's Literature*, we paid particular attention to the concept of the integrated unit, being careful that each unit contains activities in science, language arts/writing, math, social studies, and art or music. The biggest change was to accommodate the technological revolution that has occurred during this time by suggesting computer programs, word processing projects, or Internet-based investigations.

During this period, some of the books included in the original *Science Through Children's Literature* went out of print, and therefore other works with similar themes have been substituted. *Arthur's Eyes* replaced *Spectacles,* a story of a young boy getting his first pair of glasses. *Simon Underground* centers on the topic of soil as the home of an underground mole, while *The Gift of the Tree* portrays the process of producing new soil. *Mousekin's Birth,* which tells of animal reproduction, has been replaced by two books: *Before You Were Born* and *Everett Anderson's Nine Month Long. Sadie and the Snowman* chronicles events of the long winter, as does *The Big Snow,* and the poems of *Space Songs* have given way to the adventures of *The Magic School Bus Lost in Space.* Finally, the force and motion of *Mr. Gumpy's Motorcar* was replaced by efforts needed to dislodge *The Enormous Carrot.* And another new book, *Verdi,* has been added to round out the coverage of animals by including reptiles.

One of the criticisms of the first book was that it did not address the upper elementary student. This was done in 1994, with the publication of a more challenging work called *Intermediate Science Through Children's Literature.* By focusing on students in grades 5–8, we were able to target chapter books, many of which were often used in the reading curriculum: *Julie of the Wolves* by Jean Craighead George, *The Cay* by Theodore Taylor, *The Island* by Gary Paulsen, *The Black Pearl* by Scott O'Dell, and many others.

Over the years, teachers have suggested additional books that they considered suitable for integrated units. Visits to bookstores also kept us up to date and led to the publication of *More Science Through Children's Literature* in 1998. Books in that volume include *One Morning in Maine, Stellaluna, The Ice Horse,* and *Katy and the Big Snow.*

Additional books that never quite fit into the classifications of earth, life, and physical sciences found their own niche in *Exploring the Environment Through Children's Literature* in 1999. This work includes *The Little House, A River Ran Wild, Letting Swift River Go,* and *Island Boy,* along with many other environmental pieces. In this work, we also added a game or puzzle with each unit, along with computer activities.

We have recently signed a contract for a fifth book to be called *The World of Work Through Children's Literature*. It will feature the methods of work in both preindustrial and industrial societies, the assembly line method, industrial pollution, and specific occupations. A publication date of 2001 is planned.

Acknowledgments

To our parents, for their encouragement and support, especially Eunice Hollander, who read many manuscripts and took over many of our responsibilities so we could work on this project.

To our friends, especially Mary Schmidt, for sharing their ideas on books and activities and how they can be integrated into the classroom experience.

To Charles Mack, Elaine Davis, and the third-grade students of United Elementary School, Armagh, Pennsylvania, for allowing Carol the pleasure of teaching *Mike Mulligan and His Steam Shovel* as an integrated unit.

To the many teachers who have attended our workshops, conference presentations, and classes, for accepting and implementing our ideas and encouraging us to compile them into a book.

To Susan Sewell and Scott Palermo of the Delaware Valley Middle School, Milford, Pennsylvania, for sharing bibliographies and ideas about our mutual interests of science and children's literature.

To Nancy Nicholls of the Bangor Public Library, Bangor, Maine, and Jean Blake of the University of Maine Library, Orono, Maine, for their assistance in locating books and bibliographies during the initial phase of this work.

To the workers of the Pinocchio Bookstore, Pittsburgh, Pennsylvania, for recommending and obtaining many of the books we used in our work.

To the Northern New England Marine Education Project, University of Maine, for permission to adapt the illustrations related to ocean life.

To the graphics staff of the Media Resources Department, Indiana University of Pennsylvania (IUP) Library, for designing the concept maps included in this book.

To Paul Kornfeld, for analyzing and evaluating our proposed illustration list.

To Rich Nowell, for advice and information pertaining to Chapter 15, "The Ear and Hearing."

To Michael T. Pierce, for help in locating musical references.

Especially, to Kathleen Gaylor and the student workers of the IUP College of Education Dean's office, for their assistance in the preparation of this manuscript.

Introduction

Reading is the interaction among the reader's experiential background and knowledge, the author's background and purpose for writing, and the text itself. The reader actively constructs comprehension as these three elements interact. Reading skills, such as making inferences, comparing and contrasting, and drawing conclusions, are interdependent within this process and cannot exist alone as a child reasons and forms relationships.

Science also builds upon the reader's background knowledge as the student interacts with the author's knowledge, his or her purpose, and the text itself. To limit science instruction to memorization of facts would be akin to working with reading skills in isolation. Such an experience would not necessarily provide an increase in knowledge or facilitate the ability to reason and see relationships. While it is necessary to acquire factual knowledge, it is more important that children understand the conceptual framework that relates these facts one to the other and to the world in which they live. As the extent of human knowledge expands, reliance on factual memorization will become insufficient to produce citizens who can understand the role and use of science in a technological world.

Scientific study involves the acquisition of facts, principles, theories, and laws through a process or method that investigates problems, makes hypotheses, and evaluates data. The scientific method is similar to what individuals do when they seek to understand a new phenomenon. Children must experience learning and be allowed to build meanings and relationships for themselves. Only then will they have learned to read, not decode, and to understand concepts, not memorize facts.

The purpose of this book is to suggest an alternative approach to the teaching of elementary science in light of more contemporary definitions of both reading and science. This method utilizes well-selected and conceptually and factually correct works of narrative children's literature. Although the method is most easily applied with picture books aimed at grades K-4, it is also possible to employ it in higher grades using chapter books or by excerpting longer narrative works such as biographies, journals, or narrative accounts of real-life events.

Part I of this book describes an integrated approach to scientific instruction using children's fictional literature as its foundation. The discussion considers the developmental needs of young students and how well-chosen fiction can enable children to understand and remember scientific concepts. It presents criteria for judging such books and suggests appropriate activities for their use. It also suggests ways to work with the school library media specialist. A sample unit utilizes a classic children's book as the basis for an integrated science unit in the classroom.

Parts II, III, and IV contain activity units that cover life science, earth and space science, and physical science, respectively. Thirty-one children's books that can easily be adapted to the elementary curriculum are suggested and specific activities are provided for teachers to use in the classroom.

At the end of the book is an appendix containing answer keys to the puzzles included in some of the activity units.

Part I

Using Children's Literature As a
Springboard to Science

Chapter 1

INTEGRATING SCIENCE AND READING

The purpose of providing science instruction in the elementary school is to enable the learner to develop an understanding of the everyday events that constitute our world and to solve problems relating to these events. During this process, teachers must concentrate on providing opportunities for children to make firsthand observations, formulate inferences, and draw conclusions.

Children learn science best when they make observations about everyday events that they experience. After they have developed a conceptual foundation based on their own experiences, they will be able to learn technical scientific vocabulary.

Traditional and Contemporary Science Teaching

Typically, science is taught using traditional textbooks and worksheets. Subject matter is often broken into isolated "bits" to be memorized. Conceptual and practical application of ideas may be omitted or touched on only briefly. Vocabulary, a major element of comprehension, is typically taught for its own sake. In the following list, traditionally used methodology that emphasizes recall of specific information is described as "traditional science," in contrast to a conceptually based approach, which represents a more contemporary philosophy of science instruction.

Traditional Science

Emphasizes recall of specific vocabulary

Does not emphasize applications

Prepares students for later learning

Provides explanations

Requires understanding to precede activities

Does not consider student motivation essential

Contemporary Science

Is conceptually oriented

Emphasizes applications

Emphasizes problem solving

Has learner develop explanations

Allows activities to precede understanding

Considers motivation paramount

Fiction can be used as a foundation for contemporary science instruction. Children may find it easier to follow ideas that are part of a story line than to comprehend facts as presented in a textbook. A story puts facts and concepts into a form that encourages children to build a hypothesis, predict events, gather data, and test the validity of the events. Using fiction, the lesson becomes relevant and conceptually in tune with the child's abilities.

Literature can provide an efficient means of teaching because students' interest is sustained and the story structure helps them to comprehend and draw relationships between the material world and their own personal world. For example, trees are a common sight for most children. A nonfiction book dealing with trees may be totally objective, abstract, and stripped of relevance to the child's world. In this case it might be appropriate to use a fictional work such as Janice Urdy's *A Tree Is Nice* or Shel Silverstein's *The Giving Tree* to help children assimilate the concept of "treeness."

Well-chosen fiction reinforces the idea that science is a part of the lives of ordinary people. The scientific concepts come from a story about characters and places, which enables children to understand and remember them more easily than when a textbook approach is used.

Science/literature instruction can be taught using an integrated lesson that involves science and reading, as well as language arts, writing, math, social sciences, computer activities, music, and art. This integration breaks down the artificial barriers of subjects as individual units locked into specific time frames. Learning strategies to be targeted during the unit include observing, inferring, comparing, measuring, using time/space relationships, interpreting, communicating, predicting outcomes, making judgments, and evaluating.

It is also possible to use a children's literature selection in conjunction with a school curriculum or required science book, as long as the concepts involved are compatible and the fiction story book is not treated as a supplementary text. That is, when specific concepts (such as buoyancy) are being taught using the textbook, various story books can be used to illustrate those concepts and make them more real to the students. For example, *The Very Busy Spider* by Eric Carle can form the basis of a life science activity on spiders; *Who Sank the Boat?* by Pamela Allen focuses on buoyancy; and *Choo Choo: The Story of a Little Engine Who Ran Away* by Virginia Lee Burton adventure teaches about energy and motion.

Developmental Stages of Children

By selecting a narrative book with a scientific theme, a teacher can develop a science lesson that presents scientific information in a manner that is understandable, motivating, and conceptually compatible with the child's developmental stage. Educators must be aware of the developmental stages of children in the early elementary grades (K–4) when formulating instructional curricula.

Piaget (1970) tells us that before the age of eight, children are in a pre-operational stage. This means that:

1. Children are egocentric and view the world from their own perspective.

2. Children view phenomena concretely, and are not able to abstract information and ideas or use formal logic to understand scientific concepts until they reach the concrete operational stage when they can think of a world beyond their own.

3. Children have not developed the ability to think logically or abstractly; reasoning is unsystematic and does not lead to generalizations.

4. Children can focus only on the beginning or end state of a transformation, not the transformation itself.

5. Children are not able to recognize the invariance of objects when the spatial relationship of those objects changes.

Student participation in scientific activities is particularly useful to enhance logical thinking and facilitate cognitive development (Piaget, 1970). This active method of teaching utilizes direct instruction in reasoning, which cannot occur if we require objective thinking or abstract understanding that is beyond the child's conceptual level. We cannot expect a child to learn passively by observing experiments performed by the teacher, any more than we can expect that child to learn to play a musical instrument by watching someone play it.

Science is not the stockpiling of isolated experimental results and vocabulary words, but a means of producing intellectual explorers who are able to reason competently at their operational level in problem solving. If we try to teach children using only the realistic explanation of an adult, they are often left confused because they cannot understand the adult's abstract reasoning process. Therefore, we need to teach in terms of children's existing knowledge and abilities, not only to foster their conceptual understanding but also to provide them with security in the immediate human environment. Children will be ready to engage in rational investigations as more complicated reasoning processes develop and they pass into the concrete operational stage.

References

Piaget, Jean. *Science of Education and the Psychology of Children.* New York: Orion Press, 1970.

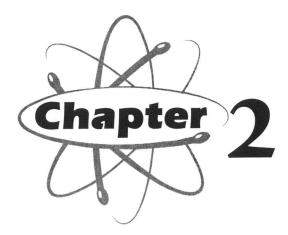

Chapter 2

TEACHING THE INTEGRATED UNIT

Judging Books

When choosing selections for an integrated thematic unit, it is necessary to develop criteria by which to judge children's literature. The following questions provide an outline for this process:

Content

Is the coverage of the book appropriate for the purpose: teaching science as an integrated unit?

Is the material within the comprehension and interest ranges of the age of the children for whom it is intended?

Is there a balance of factual and conceptual material?

Does the book encourage curiosity and further inquiry?

Does the work fit into one of the divisions of science; life science, earth and space science, physical science?

Is there enough scientific content in the book to develop an integrated unit based on it?

Is the use of fantasy confined to the development of the story, or does it spill into the content area?

Accuracy and Authenticity

Is the science content of the book up to date?

Are the facts and concepts presented accurately and realistically?

Theme

Does the story have a theme?

Is that theme worth imparting?

Is the theme too obvious or overpowering?

Setting

Is the setting clearly indicated?

How is the setting relevant to the plot?

Is a time frame delineated?

Does the time frame follow a clear temporal sequence?

Can students identify with the time and setting?

Characterization

How does the author reveal the characters?

Are they convincing? Do we see their strengths and weaknesses?

Do they act consistently with their ages?

Is there development within these characters?

Is anthropomorphism used? Is it appropriate?

Are the characters portrayed without racial, cultural, age, or gender stereotypes or bias?

Plot

Does the book tell a good story? Will children enjoy it and become involved?

Is the plot well constructed, fresh, and plausible?

Is there a logical series of happenings?

Are cause and effect demonstrated?

Are there identifiable conflict, problem, or other reasons to justify the actions of the characters?

Do events build to an identifiable climax?

Is there a satisfying resolution of events?

Style

Is there a consistent, discernible writing style appropriate to the subject?

Is the dialogue natural and balanced with narration?

Does the author create a mood? How?

Is the point of view appropriate for the book's purpose?

Illustrations

Are the pictures an integral part of the book? (Do the illustrations reinforce the facts and concepts expressed in the writing?)

Is the action of the book reflected in the pictures?

Are the illustrations authentic, accurate, and consistent with the text?

Do the illustrations create or contribute to the mood of the book?

Activities for an Integrated Unit

Reading Activities

Read to children every day, selecting both narrative and expository works.

Schedule sustained silent reading for children on a regular basis.

Use partner reading: children reading aloud together or to each other.

Use assisted reading: a student and the teacher reading together or taking turns.

Have the students read additional works by the author who wrote the book for the unit.

Have the students read other narrative or expository books on the same topic.

Use "big books" and predictable books to encourage student participation in reading.

Have the students read a biography of the author of the book.

Arrange for older children to read to younger children.

Have a "real world" reading corner: magazines (adults' and children's), telephone books, catalogs, signs, television guides, reference books, newspapers, and so forth).

Set up a classroom library of recreational reading books that represent all literary genres; include books written by the children.

Have the students listen to a story on tape and then read along with it.

Have the students practice reading a story, then tape it.

Writing Activities

Have the children read each other's writings.

Ask the students to edit each other's writing, using a word processor if possible.

Provide for sustained silent writing time, using self-selected topics or ones you specify, such as "If I had my choice, I would like to be . . ." or "My favorite character in the book was . . ."

Have the children write stories, including language experience stories.

Ask the students to keep journals (for example, to describe stages of plant growth).

Have the students keep reading logs (for example, titles and summaries of books they have read).

Assign the children to write poems, short stories, and descriptions.

Ask the students to draw and label maps, charts, and diagrams.

Have the children write letters to each other, authors, characters in books, and so forth.

Have the students sequence the events of a story using words or pictures.

Ask the children to predict the ending of the story and write it out.

Assign the students to rewrite the story's ending or create a sequel to the existing text.

Have the students create multiple endings for the same story and see which one is most popular.

Have the children "publish" a class newspaper.

Ask the students to adapt stories into radio dramas, plays, and television programs.

Assign book reviews.

Have the students summarize the story for a book jacket or bulletin board display.

Assign the children to think of interview questions to ask a guest who will visit the class.

Have the children rewrite the major action of the story from the viewpoint of a different character in the book.

Ask the students to keep personal dictionaries of key words from stories or words of special interest.

Have the children make up or complete word searches, crossword puzzles, word games, and acrostics that are related to the lesson.

Instruct the students to write out directions, for carrying out a specific task, for someone to follow.

Keep a card file of books read by you and the children on each major topic; classify them as fiction and nonfiction.

Make a question box to hold inquiries on the topic being studied; once a week, open the box and answer the questions.

Ask the students to help create a bulletin board using new words from the unit.

Have the students make time lines using long sheets of shelfpaper or heavy twine, knotted every few inches to represent a certain number of years. On these time lines, students should indicate events that take place in books that are studied.

Set up a letter-writing corner and a post office; have each child make a milk carton mailbox to receive mail.

Have the children write out and attach directions for plant care, animal feeding, turning on the computer, and so forth.

Post explanations or rules for fire drills, going to the library, special class changes, and so forth.

Provide a message board for communication between you and the students and among students.

Set up a school store, including sales slips, shopping lists, and an inventory of available items.

Ask the students to help make a gallery of children's and teachers' biographies. Attach recent or baby photos.

Have the children help set up a weather station, including devices to measure temperature, wind speed, and wind direction; ask them to study daily weather maps from the newspaper or on television.

Ask the students to help keep track of classroom events, news happenings, birthdays, honorary weeks, and so forth on calendars.

Discussion Activities

Have the children retell a story as a comprehension check.

Ask the children to identify text components (plot, setting, character, and theme).

Utilize learning strategies such as inference, cause and effect, observation, prediction, sequencing, comparison, and drawing conclusions.

Hold panel discussions and debates.

Have the students conduct interviews and discussions with outside speakers, other students, or "characters from the book."

Play "Who Said That?" to identify important lines from the book or "This Is Your Life" to review the accomplishments of the characters.

Have the students surf the Internet for additional information on the topic being studied.

Discuss the historical and geographical setting of the story if it is integral to the concepts covered in the story.

Ask the students what the author's purpose for writing this book was.

Ask the children how the author integrates scientific concepts into the book.

Art Activities

Have the students make cartoons of the action in the story and sequence them.

Ask the students to draw pictures depicting characters or events in the story.

Have the children design book jackets.

Ask the children to create an informational bulletin board about the concepts learned from the book.

Assign the students to write a commercial to encourage people to buy or read "their" books.

Have the students build dioramas or paint murals suggested by the setting or plot of the book.

Ask the children to design a coat of arms for a major character using symbols to show the accomplishments of his or her life.

Have the children label exhibits and collections of objects pertaining to the book.

Ask the students to sketch or make costumes similar to those worn by the characters (use dolls or people as models).

Show photos or slides to provide background knowledge for the book.

Have the children make "movie rolls" from shelfpaper and paper toweling tubes to illustrate scenes from the story.

Ask the children to construct puppets from paper bags, felt, or paper plates.

Have the students assemble a collage of pictures showing concepts and/or events in the story.

Invent a competitive board game about the story; include questions on vocabulary, events, characters, plot, time sequences, and so forth.

Bring in current magazine and newspaper articles that have relevance to the story.

Encourage students to initiate a fan club for their favorite authors or book characters; they should include membership cards, buttons, newsletters, and so forth. (Marc Brown's "Arthur" has his own fan club.)

Drama and Media Activities

Have the students present choral readings; they should include parts for large groups, small groups, and soloists.

Help the children tape dramatizations of the story in the style of the old radio shows.

Help the students produce videotapes in which the story is acted out.

Ask the students to pantomime events or concepts found in the story.

Teach the children how to improvise or role-play a section of the story, an alternate ending, a scientific happening, and so forth.

Have the students compare the book to a recording, filmstrip, or video of the same story.

If the book is long enough, have the children serialize it and present it over several days.

Pretend to be a movie director and cast the characters in the book for TV or a film.

Ask the students to select appropriate music to go with the reading or dramatization

The Activities Planner

The following planning list was developed to aid the teacher in structuring the integrated unit.

Activities Planner

Title of book: _____

Author: _____

Science concepts found in the book: _____

_____

_____

Vocabulary relevant to the unit: _____

_____

_____

Possible activities/science: _____

_____

_____

Possible activities/reading, language arts,
    writing, social studies, math, art, and music: _____

_____

_____

Computer connection: _____

_____

_____

Library media center work: _____

_____

_____

Puzzles or games: _____

_____

_____

Concept Mapping

When using literature in the classroom, it is necessary to understand that the concepts contained in the written materials, not just the facts and details, must be the focus of instruction. Children must be helped to recognize the concepts or ideas that the author is developing and relate them to each other and to their own backgrounds.

This strategy can be enhanced by a procedure known as "concept mapping," which helps learners to recognize and link concepts or ideas. Concept maps are simple visual diagrams or road maps that allow the student to relate the major ideas in a text, a fiction book, the mind, or any other source (Novak and Gowan, 1984). Concept maps clarify the major ideas students must focus on to accomplish a specific learning task. There are several advantages to using concept mapping in the classroom:

1. It shows that ideas are interconnected or radiate from a key concept, rather than being ordered linearly, such as in an outline.

2. It can be used to introduce a story or build background.

3. It increases comprehension.

4. It expands vocabulary.

5. It serves as a basis for writing activities.

6. It promotes cooperative or group learning.

7. It explores relationships within what was learned.

8. It provides a schematic summary of what has been learned.

The first time children are involved in concept mapping, they can be guided through the process by the teacher, who records their responses on the chalkboard. The teacher should stress the hierarchy of concepts, linking concepts and using verbs. If the children do not readily see relationships, they should be pointed out.

To create a concept map:

1. Use word association or brainstorming to select a key concept or idea to be studied, write this word on the board, and draw an oval around it. This is the subject of the concept map.

2. Work downwards from the key idea to major concepts, minor concepts, then specific facts or examples. Draw an oval around each concept or example.

3. Join all closely related concepts with lines, adding connecting verbs on the lines to explain the relationships (see figure 2.1).

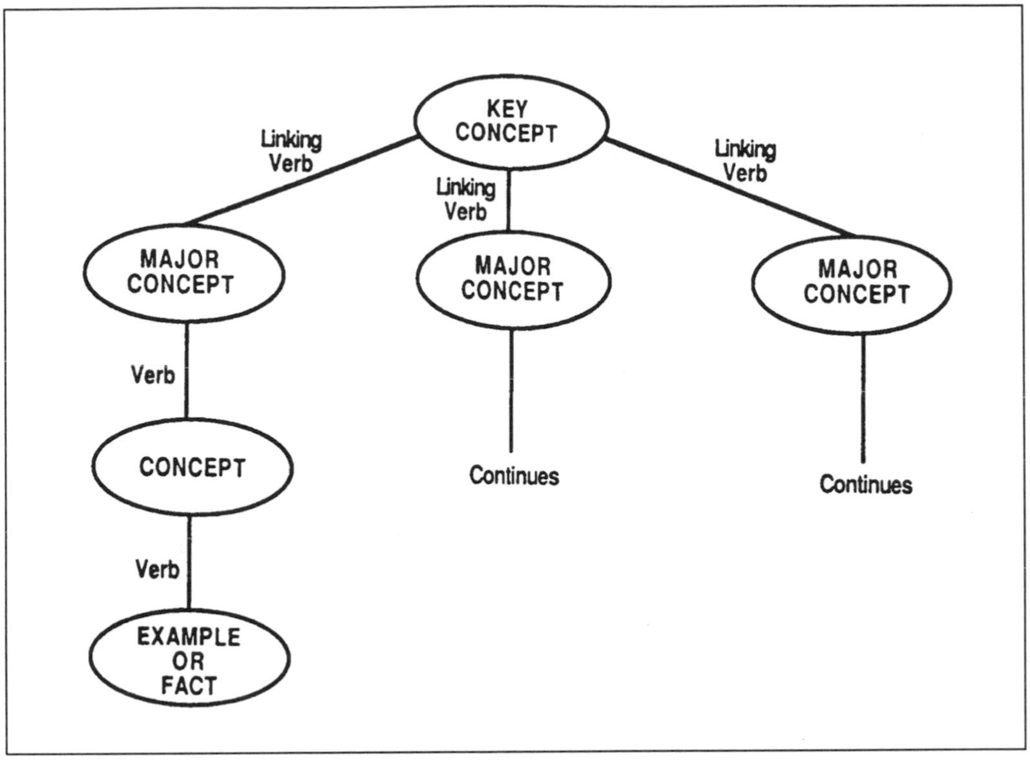

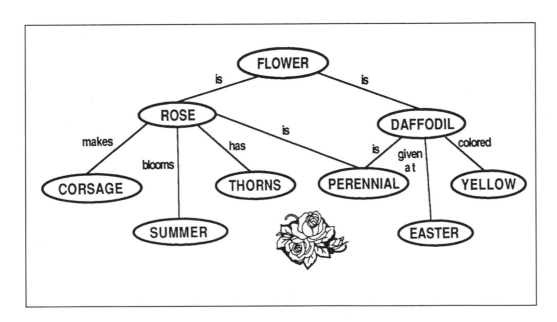

Fig. 2.1. Generic Concept Map

4. Identify any cross-links or relationships between the concepts and examples (see figure 2.2).

Fig. 2.2. Sample Concept Map

Concept maps may also be drawn after the teacher reads a short selection from a work of narrative literature or a non-narrative subject is to be explored. The teacher can initiate a discussion about the main ideas of the selection and the author's purpose for writing the piece. If the children can remember only factual information, the teacher should stimulate the conversation with questions such as Who? When? Where? Why? How? What were the results? Were there any connections between events? The next step is to work together and brainstorm one or more concept maps based on the selection. Children should see the connections and relationships and understand that these represent not just facts but also ideas. This process can be done with students from the earliest primary grades right through college.

For evaluation purposes, teachers can use a score sheet to see if students have included in the map the key concept, general and secondary concepts, linking words, cross-links or relations, a hierarchy or pattern, and examples. Evaluating concept mapping in this way is somewhat subjective, however, because no two concept maps will be the same.

Research and experience both indicate that children comprehend better when there are cross-links or relationships in the material presented to them. The ability to recall isolated facts and details does not indicate whether children have truly comprehended the meaning or concepts contained in the text. Higher-level thinking skills are not tapped or developed when only factual recall is elicited. Learning should include the linking of concepts.

Mike Mulligan and His Steam Shovel: A Sample Unit

Mike Mulligan and his steam shovel, Mary Ann, exemplify outstanding personal attributes and virtues, but there is much more for us to learn from these characters. First, the book is an outstanding source of scientific concepts and facts and can be used as the basis of an instructional unit on machines and energy. Second, it is an excellent model for language arts activities and process-writing classes, which can be integrated with the science instruction. Third, the underlying theme of the book, obsolescence, can be examined in terms children can easily understand. What is the effect of change on our society? How does technology affect the way we live? What happens when a machine becomes outdated or is replaced by a technologically advanced piece of equipment?

Mike Mulligan and Science

To use *Mike Mulligan and His Steam Shovel* by Virginia Lee Burton as the basis of a science unit, it is first necessary to identify the major scientific concepts contained in the book:

1. Machines make work easier for people.

2. Machines need energy to produce movement.

3. Various fuel sources produce energy.

4. It is possible for one machine to perform a variety of tasks.

5. People power simple machines.

6. Simple machines combine to become complex machines.

7. Machines can become obsolete.

A map of these concepts and their relationship to each other is shown in figure 2.3.

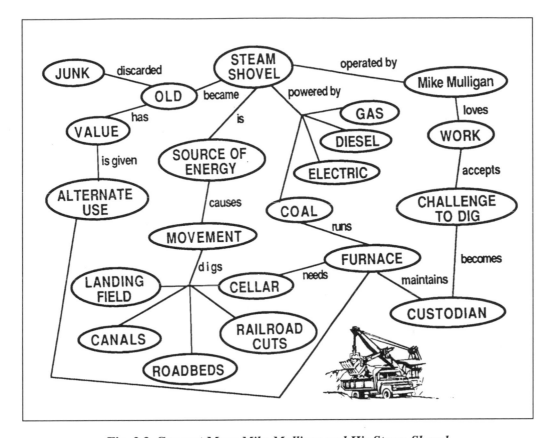

Fig. 2.3. Concept Map: *Mike Mulligan and His Steam Shovel*

The story line of a book such as *Mike Mulligan and His Steam Shovel* is in tune with the thought processes of the elementary student. Children can understand the concept of work and the use of machines as they follow the adventures in this book. Simple machines, force, motion, and energy can also become part of the lesson.

The story can be read to the group or shown on slides or video. The teacher may wish to do this two or three times before drawing a concept map of the story and engaging students in a general discussion of what the story is about and what can be learned about machines.

The first activity of the Mike Mulligan unit might be an investigation of the use of simple machines. This would stimulate interest in the topic and illustrate the role of machines in everyday life. Each child is given an object along with an index card bearing an instruction. For example:

    a.   a nail in a piece of wood at an angle/remove the nail and pound it in straight

    b.   a piece of wood with a screw in it/remove the screw

    c.   a rough stick of wood/make it smooth

    d.   an egg white/whip it until foamy

    e.   a carrot/peel it

    f.   a ball of yarn/crochet a chain

    g.   a dressmaker's pattern pinned onto cloth/cut it out

    h.   two flat sticks/glue into the shape of a sword

    i.   a ball of yarn/make a scarf

    j.   a cork in a bottle/remove the cork

    k.   a piece of wire/cut a specified amount

    l.   a plastic or metal can/pry open the top

    m.   a piece of cheese/slice it very thinly

    n.   a small board/saw it in half

To perform these tasks, students must use an implement. Display various household tools, including extras that will not be needed. Include pliers, hammers, screwdrivers, wrenches, wire cutters, small crowbars, scissors, saws, garden tools, wire whips, carrot peelers, C clamps, crochet hooks, knitting needles, bottle openers, corkscrews, wood planes, wire cheese slicers, and pizza cutters. Perhaps a mystery tool could be added if one is available, such as an old-fashioned curling iron or a shoe button hook.

Let the children select a tool to perform the task. Discuss why each child chose a particular tool and how it helped do the job. Would another tool have worked as well or better? From this demonstration of how tools work, it is possible to introduce the six simple machines: wedge, lever, pulley, inclined plane, wheel and axle, and screw. Some tools are a combination of one or more simple machines; for example, a hand can opener uses a wedge, a lever, and a wheel and axle. Students should be instructed in the use of sharp and heavy objects before being allowed to proceed on their own.

Following are additional science activities related to this sample unit:

1.   Ask students to identify and label, on a bulletin board display, simple machines that are part of a steam shovel.

2.   Have students discuss machines with family members and share the information with the class. Ask them: How do machines help us to do work? How have machines changed in your parents' or grandparents' lifetime? Are there old machines around the house or garage? Do machines ever cause problems?

3.   Have the children design and make a machine using plastic or wooden construction toys. They should be able to explain the purpose of the machine.

4.   Have the students use pulleys or boards (inclined planes) to move heavy objects.

5.   Fuel is consumed to produce the school's energy supply, for example, electricity for lights and natural gas for heat. Ask the children: Why are these fuel sources used? What are the school energy expenditures for a year? Have them graph these figures monthly. (See figure 2.4 for an example.)

6.   Have the students read other books about machines. **Note:** These can be nonfiction reference books.

7.   Provide catalogs about tools and machines for reading during free time.

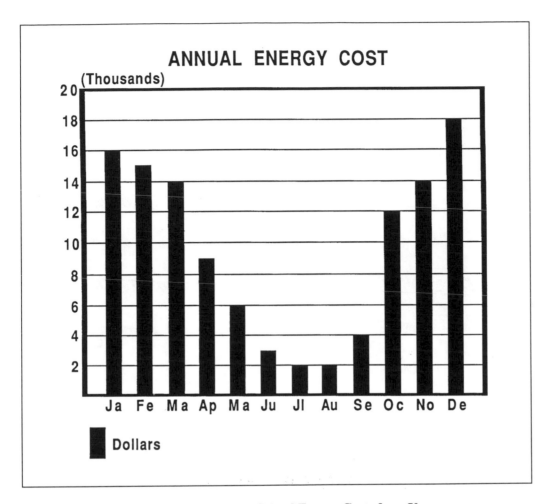

Fig. 2.4. Sample Graph: School Energy Costs for a Year

Mike Mulligan and Writing

Reading and writing strategies are used in both science and language arts. They can be taught as integrated units, which enables students to become critical thinkers and problem solvers. All reading and writing lessons should be done as a means to achieving these goals, not as isolated exercises that are an end in themselves.

Writing is a major element in learning science because it provides a continuous opportunity to learn more about the topic during the actual act of composing. In this way, students are "writing to learn" instead of the traditional "learning to write." Students can use strategies such as observation, description, comparison, evaluation, and forming relationships between concepts and ideas. As students continue writing, they review and edit each piece. Ideas are formulated, tested, and reflected upon to bring full meaning to the text, developing the student's comprehension.

Writing can be a superior means of examining what students have learned from a unit. A daily journal can aid students in reviewing and summarizing the activities of each day's lesson or discussing conceptual development (see figure 2.5).

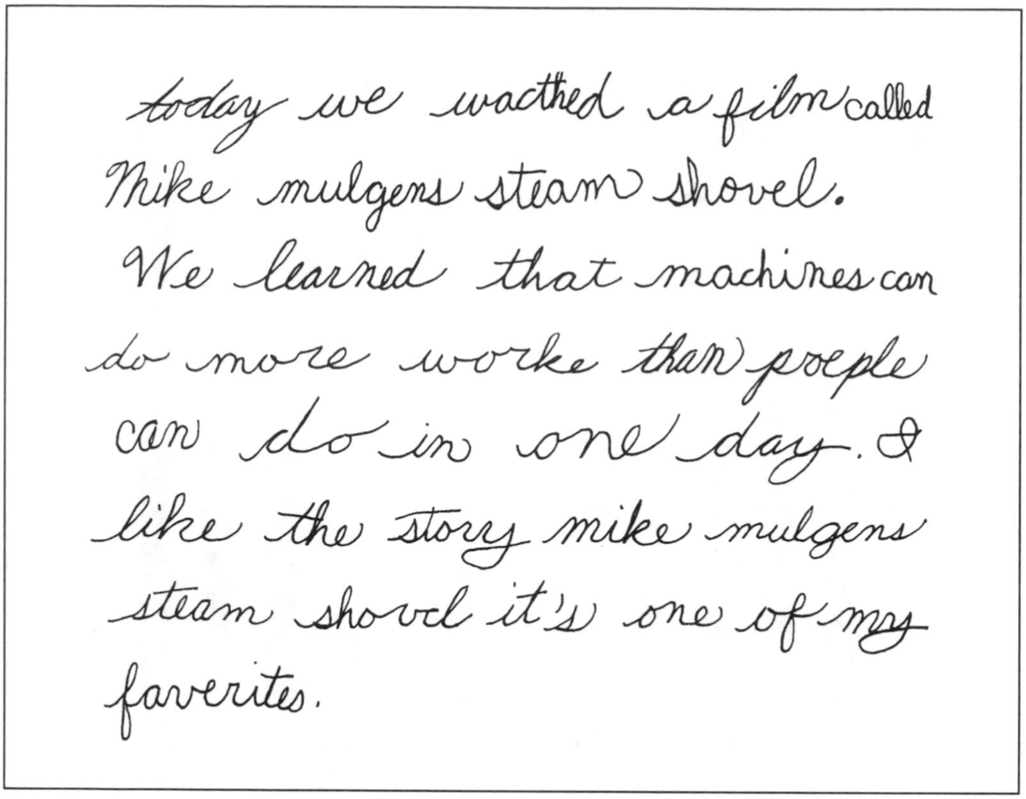

> today we wacthed a film called
> Mike mulgens steam shovel.
> We learned that machines can
> do more worke than poeple
> can do in one day. I
> like the story mike mulgens
> steam shovel it's one of my
> faverites.

Fig. 2.5. An Entry from Jayme's Journal

A second major writing activity for this unit is to have the children compose an alternative ending for the book. In the original story Mary Ann, the steam shovel, remains in the cellar to become the furnace for the town hall, while Mike assumes the role of janitor. To write an ending that would involve a workable solution to the problem of extricating the steam shovel from the cellar or to create another possible ending, students must show an understanding of concepts about machinery and work and devise ways to use simple or complex machines to solve the problem. The conclusion should be realistic and in keeping with the rest of the book. **Note:** This precludes the use of futuristic machines, robots, and so forth (see figure 2.6 for a sample alternative ending). Students can also draw a picture to further explain the proposed solution.

Students should be allowed to brainstorm ideas before they begin writing pieces other than their journals. In keeping with the writing process, teachers should conference with students during the writing time and allow students to read and conference about each other's work. Only after a piece has been rewritten and is ready to be "published" should attention be given to the mechanics of grammar and spelling for the final copy.

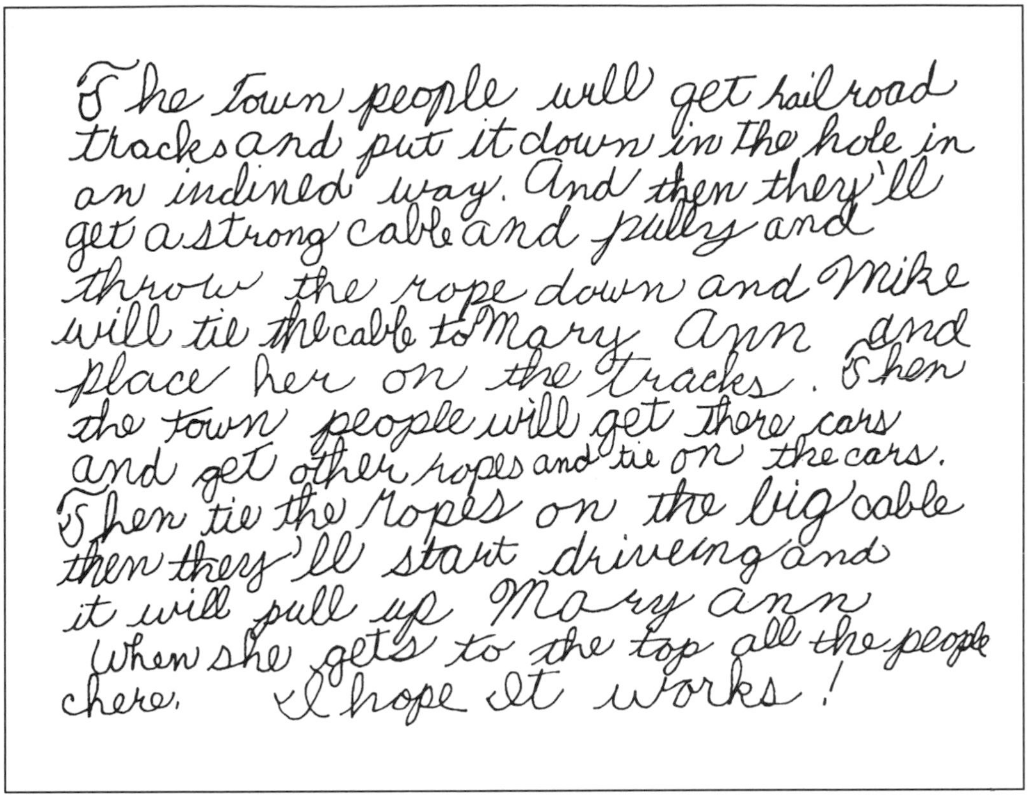

> The town people will get rail road tracks and put it down in the hole in an inclined way. And then they'll get a strong cable and pulley and throw the rope down and Mike will tie the cable to Mary Ann and place her on the tracks. Then the town people will get there cars and get other ropes and tie on the cars. Then tie the ropes on the big cable then they'll start driveing and it will pull up Mary ann When she gets to the top all the people cheer. I hope It works!

Fig. 2.6. Edward's Alternative Ending to *Mike Mulligan and His Steam Shovel*

Mike Mulligan and Change

A third area of study using this book is suggested by the sentence "Mike took such good care of Mary Ann she never grew old." This introduces the concepts of aging and change. Society is not constant; every human activity alters the environment and produces change. The only constant that does exist, therefore, is the fact that change will occur. We cannot control how change will take place. Instead we must examine whether it is an indication of progress and growth and decide if the new things are beneficial and acceptable. Students must cope with a world of change based on increasing knowledge and technological advances. Society values technology because it increases efficiency and lessens the effort we must make to accomplish desired tasks. These are assumed to be desirable traits because our economy is based on the idea that time is money.

Mike had to face the fact that even though Mary Ann was still beautiful and could do the necessary work, more efficient machines were being employed. Only when Mike claimed to be able to dig a cellar in one day was credibility given to an "old" machine, because, again, time is money. Despite Mike and Mary Ann's success, modern alternatives would still eliminate Mary Ann's usefulness as a steam shovel. Fortunately, the steam boiler that once provided mechanical energy (movement) to the shovel could be converted to produce heat energy in a furnace.

Several activities can help youngsters understand the role of change in their lives:

1. Have students study old photos of the community to see changes in transportation, housing, clothing, geographic features, and so forth. A walking tour of the downtown area might be arranged to view buildings of various ages and how they are used now.

2. Have the children interview older persons to learn how lifestyles have changed in areas such as schooling, occupations, recreation, church, and use of appliances.

3. Ask the students to bring in (or bring in yourself) examples of less technologically advanced objects such as an egg beater, a hand can opener, a manual adding machine, or a crystal radio set. Ask the children to identify how these items are similar to or different from more modern ones.

4. Assume your town has an old, run-down, but historic area. Developers wish to tear it down for a shopping mall. Ask the students to consider what options are available; for example, implementing the plan as is, revitalizing the area for business and shopping, or restoring only the historical buildings and building new ones in between. Different scenarios could be presented through debates, speeches, sketches, and so forth.

5. Ask students how people dispose of material objects that are no longer needed: yard sales, recycling, disposal. This might raise the issues of sanitary landfill, pollution, litter, and toxic wastes.

6. Ask the students to guess what life might be like at a certain time in the future and have them write descriptions of this society and design cities or machines that will be needed.

7. Have the children make a chart of items that have become obsolete in the last 50 years (for example, a scrub board, crank telephones, or an ice box) and items that they think will become obsolete in the next 50 years (for example, manual typewriters, glass bottles, coin and paper money, or libraries of books). A third column might include things that will become everyday necessities during this time (for example, non-fossil-fuel transportation devices, video telephones, and handheld computers).

8. Children's fiction at all levels is available on the topic of people aging. Examples are *Nana Upstairs and Nana Downstairs* by Tomie dePaola and *My Grandma's in a Nursing Home* by Judy Delton and Dorothy Tucker. Students can discuss these in relation to their own families.

9. Old photos of steam shovels can be found on the Internet. Have students use their favorite search engine on the Internet to locate such pictures. They should then compare the pictures to the illustration of Mary Ann in the book.

The Library Media Specialist

Working with the school library media specialist enhances the job of the classroom teacher. The specialist is trained in many areas: gathering and disseminating materials, facilitating small and large group instruction, working with individual needs, utilizing and producing audiovisual materials, and implementing the school computer literacy program.

Traditionally, science writing has been considered nonfictional in nature. As a result, scientific facts and concepts in a fictional piece of literature are often overlooked because people are not specifically looking for them in this genre or because their accuracy is suspect. The connection between fictional books and scientific facts and concepts must be established for the production of integrated units. The library media specialist is an excellent source for locating fictional books with scientific themes and related nonfiction sources.

When first working with the library media specialist, it is best for the teacher to share several fiction books being considered as the basis for integrated science units. This will give the teacher a chance to discuss the type of books that would be suitable for other units. If possible, the library media specialist should be given a broad range of topics so he or she can begin compiling a selection of potential works. This partnership will assist teachers in achieving maximum value from the available materials.

Once topics are selected, book clusters on similar topics may emerge. For example, *The Snowy Day* by Ezra Jack Keats, *The Big Snow* by Berta Hader and Elmer Hader, and *Katy and the Big Snow* by Virginia Lee Burton would be suitable as the basis of a lesson on snow

Interrelated topics are also useful. A reference to spiders in *Two Bad Ants* by Chris Van Allsburg might be followed by *The Very Busy Spider* by Eric Carle. Author clusters are a third possibility. Robert McCloskey and Barbara Cooney write of life along the Maine coast; Leo Lionni and Eric Carle explore scientific truths and human values through the fantasy animals they have created; Bill Peet and Dr. Seuss ponder the fate of humanity and the environment.

As more information is used to augment the original book, nonfiction books can be gathered together for sustained silent reading time, at-home reading, or classroom reference. Teachers or library media specialists may wish to assist students in performing searches on the Internet or locating Web sites. These sources are imperative if children wish to do further research on a topic or answer specific questions that have evolved from classroom discussions or activities. The library media specialist can address research skills in a teaching lesson, thereby emphasizing or reinforcing materials covered in the classroom and facilitating students' searches for additional information.

Although the use of books is of great importance in this integrated approach, many forms of media now exist that allow stories to be more easily seen and heard by large groups; they can also be used for individual or small group work. Films, filmstrip/tapes, book/records, book/tapes, and videos are available for many classic works of children's literature. Library media specialists have access to information about these materials and the expertise to preview and select those they consider both useful and of high quality. The library media specialist is often able to assist or train others in the production of videos, slides, tapes, "big books," and so forth.

Locating books for integrated units becomes an ongoing process for the teacher, as there are always additional units to be developed and new, exciting books to use. In addition to using the resources of the library media center and the library media specialist, teachers should visit book fairs, join children's book clubs, and go to children's bookstores. These stores often send out newsletters listing new books, author biographies, and activities at the store.

Networking is another means of locating books. At conferences, workshops, or meetings, teachers may meet others with similar interests and exchange bibliographies. Reading professional journal reviews, talking with friends and colleagues, browsing in the library, keeping abreast of award-winning books each year, reading publishers' catalogs, and watching educational television programs can all contribute to finding new books.

Selecting good works of fictional literature for reading to children is of paramount importance to the child's learning process. Through the use of stories, they are aided in understanding and interpreting the material being presented. Reading enables them to master the usage and nuances of their language. It is an invaluable tool in the learning of all other subjects.

Learning does not consist of lists to be read, memorized, and given back to the teacher on a test. Learning is the acquisition of knowledge. It is a change in behavior, an education for the present and for the future. Children can learn for the moment, but they must also develop the skills and strategies they will need for the future. This process is not restricted to isolated subjects, but integrates all the areas of the curriculum and enables the student to see relationships between them.

Bibliography

References Cited

Novak, Joseph, and D. Bob Gowan. *Learning How to Learn*. Cambridge, England: Cambridge University Press, 1984.

Science Activity Books

Abruscato, Joseph, and Jack Hassard. *The Earth People Activity Book: People, Places, Pleasures and Other Delights*. Glenview, IL: Scott, Foresman, 1978.

————. *The Whole Cosmos Catalog of Science Activities*. Glenview, IL: Scott, Foresman, 1978.

Bonnet, Robert L., and G. Daniel Keen. *Earth Science: 49 Science Fair Projects*. Blue Ridge Summit, PA: TAB Books, 1990.

————. *Environmental Science: 49 Science Fair Projects*. Blue Ridge Summit, PA: TAB Books, 1990.

————. *Space and Astronomy: 49 Science Fair Projects*. Blue Ridge Summit, PA: TAB Books, 1992.

Butzow, Carol, and John Butzow. *Exploring the Environment Through Children's Literature*. Englewood, CO: Libraries Unlimited, 1999.

————. *Intermediate Science Through Children's Literature*. Englewood, CO: Libraries Unlimited, 1994.

————. *More Science Through Children's Literature*. Englewood, CO: Libraries Unlimited, 1998.

————. *Science Through Children's Literature*. Englewood, CO: Libraries Unlimited, 1989.

Comstock, Anna B. *Handbook of Nature-Study*. Ithaca, NY: Cornell University Press, 1986.

Cornell, Joseph B. *Sharing Nature with Children*. Nevada City, CA: Dawn Publications, 1979.

Gardner, Martin. *Entertaining Science Experiments with Everyday Objects*. New York: Dover Publications, 1981.

Hanauer, Ethel. *Biology Experiments for Children*. New York: Dover Publications, 1968.

LeBruin, Jerry. *Creative, Hands-on Science Experiences.* Carthage, IL: Good Apple, 1986.

Lowery, Lawrence, and Carol Verbeeck. *Explorations in Earth Science.* Belmont, CA: David S. Lake, 1987.

——. *Explorations in Life Science.* Belmont, CA: David S. Lake, 1987.

——. *Explorations in Physical Science.* Belmont, CA: David S. Lake, 1987.

Mitchel, John, ed. *The Curious Naturalist.* Englewood, Cliffs, NJ: Prentice-Hall, 1980.

Mullin, Virginia L. *Chemistry Experiments for Children.* New York: Dover Publications, 1968.

Ontario Science Center. *Foodworks.* Reading, MA: Addison-Wesley, 1987.

——. *Sportworks.* Reading, MA: Addison-Wesley, 1989.

Outdoor Biology Instructional Strategies (OBIS). Nashua, NH: Delta Education, 1982.

Reuben, Gabriel. *Electricity Experiments for Children.* New York: Dover Publications, 1968.

Savan, Beth. *Earth Cycles and Ecosystems.* Toronto: Kids Can Press, 1991.

Vivian, Charles. *Science Experiments and Amusements for Children.* New York: Dover Publications, 1967.

Children's Literature

Burton, Virginia Lee. *Katy and the Big Snow.* Boston: Houghton Mifflin, 1943.

——. *Mike Mulligan and His Steam Shovel.* Boston: Houghton Mifflin, 1939.

Carle, Eric. *The Very Busy Spider.* New York: Putnam, 1985.

Cooney, Barbara. *Island Boy.* New York: Viking Kestrel, 1988.

Hader, Bertha, and Elmer Hader. *The Big Snow.* New York: Simon & Schuster Books for Young Children, 1967.

Keats, Ezra Jack. *The Snowy Day.* New York: Viking, 1962.

Lionni, Leo. *It's Mine.* New York: Alfred Knopf, 1986.

McCloskey, Robert. *One Morning in Maine.* New York: Viking, 1952.

Peet, Bill. *The Wump World.* Boston: Houghton Mifflin, 1970.

Seuss, Dr. (Theodore Geisel). *The Lorax.* New York: Random House, 1971.

Van Allsburgh, Chris. *Two Bad Ants.* Boston: Houghton Mifflin, 1988.

Professional Journals and Children's Magazines

Booklist. American Library Association. Chicago, IL. Published semi-monthly.

Chickadee. Young Naturalist Foundation. Des Moines, IA. Published 10 times a year.

Cricket: The Magazine for Children. Open Court. Boulder, CO. Published monthly.

Hornbook. Horn Book Inc. Boston, MA. Published 6 times a year.

Language Arts. National Council of Teachers of English. Urbana, IL. Published 7 times a year.

National Geographic World. National Geographic Society. Washington, DC Published monthly.

Owl, the Discovery Magazine for Children. Young Naturalist Foundation. Des Moines, IA. Published 10 times a year.

Ranger Rick. National Wildlife Foundation. Vienna, VA. Published monthly.

The Reading Teacher. International Reading Association. Newark, DE. Published 9 times a year.

Part II

Life Science

Introduction to
Parts II, III, and IV

The remainder of *Science Through Children's Literature: An Integrated Approach* provides activities for teachers to use in the classroom. Thirty-one children's books that are easily adapted to the integration of science, language arts, and other areas of the curriculum have been selected. They are divided into the three major categories of science—life science, earth and space science, and physical science—to coincide with the divisions of well-known science projects and text series.

Within each division, books that are easier to read and conceptually less complex are covered first. These may be most beneficial in lower grades. The following books are more difficult and may be of more use in the middle and upper elementary grades. However, many of these books can be used in any integrated classroom K-6, depending on the objectives that the teacher has determined for the unit and the particular activities selected for the lesson.

Each set of activities is written for children to perform under the supervision or facilitation of the teacher or another adult. However, it is the prerogative of each individual teacher to decide if the activity would best be carried out as a whole-class activity, in small groups, or by individuals. In many cases, such as corresponding with organizations, collecting specimens, gathering equipment, or choosing supplemental trade books for silent reading time, the teacher must be in charge of the process to ensure that materials are accessible for classroom work. However, it is desirable and most effective if the children are given the major responsibility for carrying out the tasks and are not just spectators.

The number of activities provided for any one book may exceed the amount of time that can be allotted to a single topic. The teacher must choose those activities that best suit the classroom situation and available resources. Also, activities may be used in conjunction with a text series, which would help identify the activities that would best correspond to the objectives of the school curriculum. Another major point to remember in selecting items is to choose a variety of activities that reflect the different content areas of the curriculum. Finally, books and references related to the activities are listed at the end of the appropriate activity.

Note: It is our intention to have students become familiar with various computer-based activities such as word processing, implementation of drawing programs, and the use of a Web browser. The use of the computer is not intended as an end in itself but rather as a facilitator to extend content learning. In making recommendations for the use of the Internet, we have supplied keywords for topics that we have found to be excellent for finding a number of Web sites. In other cases, we have furnished specific Web site addresses that contain material relevant to the activities of each unit. We have found that specific Web sites were sometimes altered while we worked on the revision of this book. These Web sites are up to date at this writing, and we hope they will be viable in the future.

Chapter 3

TREES

A Tree Is Nice
Janice May Udry
New York: HarperCollins, 1987

Summary

Living trees are very important to people and animals. They provide many items we need and are sources of comfort and recreation.

Science and Content Related Concepts

Uses of trees, parts and kinds of trees, tree growth, planting techniques

Content Related Words

Leaves, trunk, roots

Activities

1. Help the children make a chart or concept map showing the uses of trees (for example, recreation, food, buildings). Show both human and animal uses.

2. Botanists refer to trees as coniferous or deciduous. Ask the children what this means. Which kind are more common where the children live? Have the children gather fallen pieces from both kinds of trees, label them, and make a display for the classroom.

3. As a class, write a group letter to the state forest service asking for written materials about trees that grow in your state.

4. Have the children collect and learn to recognize leaves from five different trees native to the area. This could be done in conjunction with a nature walk near the school.

5. Do not let the children rely on leaf identification to recognize trees; this method is unusable during winter months. Make sure they can recognize the bark of five different species of trees indigenous to the area.

6. In a forested area, have students identify a section of trees by species. Ask the students if trees of the same species tend to exist in groups or are mixed randomly with trees of other species. Have the students measure the circumference of the trees to determine which are the largest and which are the smallest.

7. Ask the students to gather seeds from various types of trees. Ask them: How are they protected while they are on the tree? How do they fall? How are they dispersed?

8. Have the children use catalogs from a nursery to decide which species of tree would be best to plant in the schoolyard. Consider factors such as growth rate, climatic needs, and soil requirements. Get the children to raise money by selling cookies or candy, or through a similar activity, or ask a parent group to help purchase the tree. Consult a gardening book or the directions that come with the tree to help plant it properly. Assign students to water and care for the tree.

9. Small trees can be grown in the classroom if it is not possible to plant a tree outside (for example, a Norfolk Island pine). Ask the students to find out what care the tree must receive. Ask them: Where are trees found in the city (for example, parks, shopping malls)? What kind of trees are found? Why do people grow trees in indoor settings?

10. Have the students measure the temperature in the shade of a tree and in bright sunlight. They should do this at various times of the day for a week. Have them make a chart or graph for each reading and compare them. What accounts for the temperature variations?

11. Some trees are unique to certain areas (for example, the Joshua trees of southern California, the cypress trees of the Monterey peninsula). Ask the students why some trees grow only in certain areas.

12. Tree foliage often changes over the course of a calendar year. Have the children make drawings or collect pictures of trees at different times of the year. Ask them: Which trees change the most? Which change the least? Which trees are most common to the area where the students live?

13. Have the students look at a tree stump or a piece of firewood to observe the growth rings of the tree. Ask them to calculate how old the tree was when it was cut, if each ring equals one year. (Figure 3.1 shows a tree cross-section.)

14. A tree that is diseased or not growing properly must be treated or it will die. Have the students consult the yellow pages of the telephone book for a tree service or a county extension agent who can provide help for the tree. Ask the students: What diseases attack trees? Are there other problems common to trees? What types of treatments might be recommended to restore the trees to health?

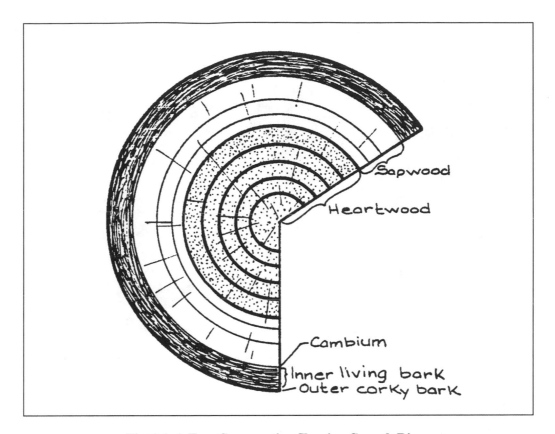

Fig. 3.1. A Tree Cross-section Showing Growth Rings

15. Have the children imagine a street lined with huge old oak trees, then role play a situation in which town officials feel these trees must be cut down so that the street can be widened to allow for more traffic. Have the children write letters voicing their opinions either for or against the proposal. They should give reasons, not just get emotional.

16. Ask the students: How have trees been important in history (for example, boundary markers, meeting places like Robin Hood's oak tree). Why do you think this is so?

17. Have the students make masks or paper bag costumes to represent the parts of a tree (roots, bark, branches, leaves, buds, and so forth). Ask them to present a short skit showing how these parts are important to the life of the whole tree.

18. Have the children imagine that they have been selected to design a new advertising campaign for the U.S. Forest Service. They are to write television commercials and design a bumper sticker about fire safety in the woods. Students may wish to incorporate Smokey the Bear in their work.

19. In the spring, have the students put twigs from trees into water and watch them blossom. Flowering trees and willows are good choices for this.

20. Have the students make a forest collage using tissue paper silhouettes of trees (see figure 3.2). They should overlap the trees to produce new shades that give the effect of the autumn color change.

Fig. 3.2. Shapes of Common Trees

21. Have the children use tree leaves, twigs, and fruit to make art projects such as mobiles, leaf rubbings, and apple prints. **Note:** Leaf rubbings are best when the veined side of the leaf is in contact with the paper and the side of the crayon is applied to the paper. For apple prints, students should cut the fruit in half crosswise, dip the pieces into ink, and press them on paper like a stamp pad.

22. Ask the students to create "tree" poems using text written in the form of a triangle to represent the tree.

23. In the biography section of the library media center, have the children look for books on Johnny Appleseed (Jonathan Chapman) and John Muir. Ask them to dramatize a scene from the lives of these persons. Ask the students: How were they important to the "tree population" of this country?

24. Have the class read *The Giving Tree* by Shel Silverstein. Ask them: What purpose does the tree serve? What are the tree's feelings? What is the reader's opinion of the boy in the story?

25. Have the students use a paintbrush program on the word processor to draw a picture to show how "a tree is nice."

26. Play music written about trees, such as "The Pines of Rome" by Ottorino Respighi.

Related Books and References

Cohen, Michael R., and Charles R. Barman. "Did You Notice the Color of the Trees in Spring?" *Science and Children* 31, no. 5 (February 1994): 20–22.

Findley, Rowe. "Will We Save Our Own?" *National Geographic* 178, no. 3 (September 1990): 106–136.

Fowler, Betty. "Take a Leaf from Our Book." *Science and Children* 34, no. 6 (May 1997): 20–21.

Graves, C. John. "Secondhand Trees, Firsthand Learning." *Science and Children* 28, no. 3 (November/December 1990): 22–24.

Moffett, Mark W. "Climbing an Ecological Frontier: Tree Giants of North America." *National Geographic* 191, no. 1 (January 1997): 44–61.

Respighi, Ottorino. "The Pines of Rome." The Philadelphia Orchestra, Ricardo Muti conducting.

Shelton, Marilyn. "Leaf Pals." *Science and Children* 32, no. 1 (September 1994): 37–39.

Silverstein, Shel. *The Giving Tree.* New York: Harpercrest, 1987.

Srulowitz, Frances. "Diary of a Tree." *Science and Children* 29, no. 5 (February 1992): 19–21.

Chapter 4

SEEDS

The Tiny Seed
Eric Carle
Natick, MA: Picture Book Studio, USA, 1987

Summary

Wind, weather, and water can prevent seeds from taking root and growing. But some seeds will overcome these problems and find the proper conditions to grow and flourish.

Science and Content Related Concepts

Seed distribution, conditions favorable to germination and growth, life cycle of a flowering plant

Content Related Words

Seed, dispersal, roots, stems, leaves

Activities

1. Have the students stuff an old sock or nylon stocking with crumpled paper and tie it shut with a yard of heavy string. They should then drag the sock through a field or along the forest floor. The sock will pick up seeds, which can be taken back to the classroom for examination. An alternate method for gathering seeds is to spread a sheet under a tree and gently shake the branches. Ripe seeds will fall onto the sheet.

2. Let the students observe seeds under a microscope or with a hand lens. They can use seeds gathered outdoors, packaged flower or vegetable seeds, or seeds from fresh fruits and vegetables (for example, tomatoes, snap beans, oranges). Have the students write descriptions of the seeds for others to identify from the clues.

3.   Have the children collect seeds and their seed pods in the fall of the year (for example, burdocks, milkweeds, thistles). After the seeds have been studied, the seed pod and stalk can be spray painted and used for a fall "flower" arrangement.

4.   Seeds are dispersed, or carried, by various means. They can float in water, glide on or be shot into the air, or latch onto animals and people. Have the students use a dried bean, pumpkin seed, or something similar and invent a new pod for the seed by attaching art scraps, cotton, or packing materials to it. Have the students write an adventure story about the seed telling how it is dispersed.

5.   Many seeds are used in cooking. These seeds are known as spices and can be used whole or ground. A display of these can be made by placing several seeds or the ground spice onto lengths of wide transparent tape, which can then be attached to posterboard and labeled.

6.   Have the students make a quick, easy snack that requires no baking, such as the following.

Crunchy Seed Candy

Mix together the following ingredients:
2 cups sunflower seeds (1 cup to be used for coating candy balls)
1 cup honey
1 cup peanut butter
1 cup cocoa powder
Shape into one inch balls. Spread 1 cup of sesame seeds on a sheet of waxed paper. Roll each piece of candy in the sesame seeds.

7.   Bread is a staple in the diet of almost every culture on earth. Bread is made from seeds: wheat, rye, oats, rice, and corn. In the library media center, have the children research "bread" and its various forms. They should include how the bread is made and used; for example, some bread is part of the religious ceremony for the culture. Have some of the various breads available for tasting (for example, pita, sourdough, potato). **Note:** Cookbooks from home may be very valuable when learning about bread from other cultures.

8.   Sprouted seeds, such as beans, radish, alfalfa, lentils, or mung seeds, are tasty additions to salads. These sprouts can be bought in a grocery store or sprouted in the classroom. To do the latter, have students place about 1 tablespoon of seeds in a clean glass jar, then cover the top with a piece of clean nylon stocking or several layers of nylon net held in place with a rubber band. The seeds should soak in warm water overnight. The students should then rinse and drain the seeds through the material. Each morning and evening the children need to run fresh warm water on the seeds and drain them. Sprouts should appear in a few days (see figure 4.1).

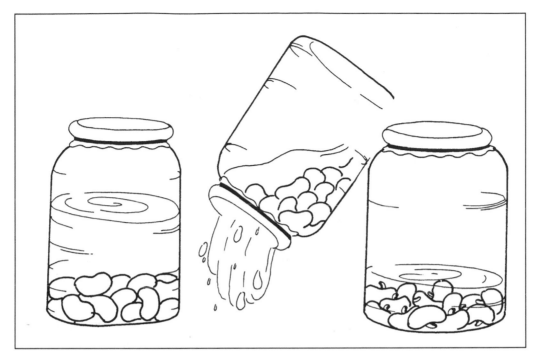

Fig. 4.1. Sprouting Seeds Indoors

9. Have the children soak dried bean seeds overnight in warm water, then gently break the seed open and look for the embryonic plant in the middle. The two halves contain stored food for plant growth.

10. Birdseed placed on a moist sponge will also sprout. Ask the students: How many kinds of plants are observed? Have them keep the sponge in a shallow dish and add water to the bottom of the dish without disturbing the sprouts.

11. Have the students grow fast-sprouting seeds (radish, carrot, mustard) in different media (for example, soil, vermiculite, sand, clay). Ask them: What effect did the medium have on the plant growth? In another experiment, have the students keep the medium constant but alter the growing conditions: amount of sunlight, amount of moisture, kind of water (tap, distilled, water with a bit of vinegar or lime added), and so forth. Have the students keep a daily log or make sketches to show the growth of the plants.

12. Some seeds and plants are poisonous to people or other animals (for example, poinsettias). Ask the students: What steps should be taken if a small child has eaten something that may be poisonous? Have them check the telephone book for a poison control center and learn what kind of information and services it provides.

13. Have the children decorate sticky labels with seeds, along with the telephone number of the poison control center or other information agency near you. These can be placed on home telephones or on the cover of the telephone book.

14. Have the children look through seed catalogs to choose three kinds of flowers to plant in a small garden (5-by-5-foot) at the entrance of the school. Select flowers that will all grow under the same natural conditions (for example, amount of sunlight and moisture needs). The flowers can be all the same color or coordinated shades and can represent different heights or be the same. Ask the students: How many seed packs will be needed? How much will this cost? To order the seeds after they are selected, children should fill out the order blank and envelope, or it may be possible to visit a hardware or garden store to purchase the seeds directly.

15. Ask the children to read the back of a flower or vegetable seed package and tell you what they learned about the plant from the information given there. Have them compare this information with an entry in a garden encyclopedia, then ask them which is more complete and helpful.

16. Ask the students: What basic gardening tools would you need to plant a small garden and keep it watered? Have them look in a newspaper ad or catalog from a hardware or garden supply store, then make a list of items they will need and decide how much this will cost.

17. Dig up clumps of several different weeds, leaving the roots intact. Mask the roots with bags so students can guess what the root will look like after seeing the plant. Ask the students: How do roots differ from one another? What is the job of the root?

18. The stem of a flower or plant carries water and food to the flower and leaves. This can be demonstrated by setting a stalk of celery in a jar of ink or colored water. Another method is to use a white carnation. Slit the stem lengthwise. Stand one section in plain water and the other in water tinted with food coloring. Ask the students what color the carnation will be after a few hours.

19. Raise some houseplants in the classroom. Select both flowering and nonflowering types. Have the students determine if the plants form seeds. Have them make a "care card" to accompany each plant, showing amount of sunlight and water needed, special fertilizer requirements, and so forth. Ask the students: How can you tell if the plant is getting improper care, has become infested with a disease, or needs to be repotted? What steps must be taken to cure these problems?

20. An avocado seed can often grow into a large houseplant. Have the children wash a seed in laundry bleach, then rinse and dry it thoroughly. They should then stick toothpicks into the seed at three different spots about one-third of the distance up from the pointed end. Have them suspend the seed in a cup of water with the toothpicks resting on the edge of the cup (see figure 4.2). Make sure the children change the water regularly. The rooted seed should be placed in a 6-inch flower pot that is partially filled with good potting soil. Then have the children add enough soil to barely cover the seed and press the soil down gently and continue to water as needed. Try the same activity using a potato that has well-developed "eyes."

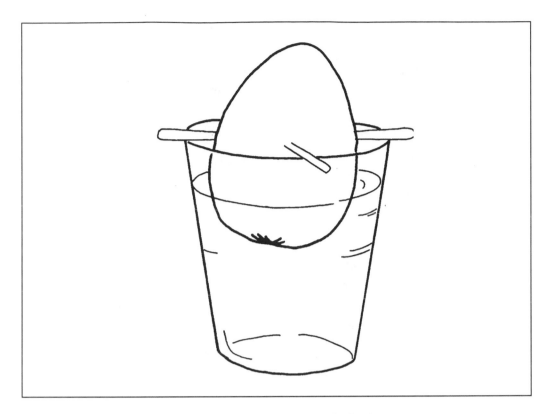

Fig. 4.2. Rooting an Avocado Seed

21. Have the children write poems, couplets, or descriptions of a flower, seed, or plant. These can be very serious or humorous in tone. If possible, have the poems word processed and printed with an accompanying picture.

22. Have the students make seed pictures or ornaments by spreading white glue thinly on a cardboard cutout, then arranging various seeds (dried peas, beans, lentils, peppercorns, sunflowers, pumpkins) on it to make an abstract design or actual scene. Seeds should be only one layer thick and can be sprayed with clear art varnish or painted with diluted white glue to keep them in place and add luster.

23. Teach the children songs about flowers, such as "Edelweiss" from *The Sound of Music* by Rodgers and Hammerstein.

24. Have the students take tunes they know and write their own words about a plant or flower. Ask them: Can you make up rhymes about dandelions? Crab grass? A cactus plant? Have them illustrate their work by using the drawing program on the word processor to make blooms.

25. Have the students read some legends or folklore about plants or flowers, such as *The Legend of the Bluebonnet* by Tomie dePaola.

26. Tissue-paper flowers can be made by cutting out six or eight circles, 6 inches in diameter. Tell students to place a pencil in the middle of the sheets, eraser end down, then gather up the sheets and tie a string or wind a wire around the pencil about half an inch from the end of the eraser. They should then remove the pencil and pull the string or wire tight. Wire or pipe cleaner stems and cut-out leaves can be added.

Related Books and References

Callison, Priscilla, and Emmett L. Wright. "Plants on Parade." *Science and Children* 29, no. 8 (May 1992): 12–14.

dePaola, Tomie. *The Legend of the Bluebonnet.* New York: Putnam, 1983.

Gerber, Brian. "These Plants Have Potential." *Science and Children* 33, no. 1 (September 1995): 32–34.

Kraus, Ruth. *The Carrot Seed.* New York: Harper & Row, 1945.

Martin, Alexander, Herbert Zim, and Rudolf Freund. *Flowers: A Guide to Familiar American Wildflowers: A Golden Guide.* New York: Golden Guide Press, 1987.

Rodgers, Richard, and Oscar Hammerstein II. *The Sound of Music.* The movie soundtrack.

Sisson, Edith A. "Seeds—Away They Go." *Science and Children* 27, no. 2 (October 1989): 16–17.

Van Scheik, William J. "Press and Preserve." *Science and Children* 29, no. 8 (May 1992): 15+.

Chapter 5

REPRODUCTION AND DEVELOPMENT

Everett Anderson's Nine Month Long
Lucille Clifton
New York: Henry Holt, 1978

Before You Were Born
Jennifer Davis
New York: Workman, 1997

Summary

Everett Anderson has mixed feelings about a baby in the family until his mother reassures him of her love. *Before You Were Born* explores the changes that occur during this period of waiting from a physical viewpoint as well as an emotional one.

Science and Content Related Concepts

Mammals, embryo genesis and development, pregnancy

Content Related Words

Reproduction, cell, sperm, egg, embryo, uterus, womb, prenatal care

Activities

1. Ask the students: What is the role of the sperm and the egg in the reproductive cycle? Where is the embryo nurtured during the gestation period? To help answer these questions, have students study a diagram or plastic model of a fetus in the womb. Ask them: What features can be seen? Why is there an umbilical cord? What must happen to the fetus before it is ready to be born?

2. Make a chart containing nine sections—one for each month of pregnancy. Have students use *Before You Were Born* as a guide to write down examples of the growth that occurs during each month, such as the baby sucking its thumb at three months.

3. Have the children draw their conception of the baby at each month of pregnancy. Sequence these pictures in a classroom display.

4. Some human babies receive nourishment from their mother after birth, while others get milk from a bottle. Get folders from a pediatrician explaining these two methods of feeding. Ask the students: What eating schedule do infants need? Have them read the labels from several different brands of baby formula, then ask them: What are the ingredients? Are the brands similar? How should bottles and formulas be prepared for a baby?

5. Ask the students: When can babies begin eating solid food? How is this food different from what you eat?

6. Human babies develop very slowly compared to most other creatures; for example, it is many months before they begin to have teeth. Have the students try making some teething biscuits (see below), then ask them why these are given to babies?

Teething Biscuits

Beat 2 eggs until creamy. Add 1 scant cup of sugar and stir with eggs. Gradually add 2 to 2 ½ cups flour until dough is stiff. Roll out between sheets of floured wax paper to ¾-inch thickness. Cut into shapes and let stand overnight on a greased cookie sheet. Bake at 325 degrees until brown. Makes 1 dozen biscuits.

7. Pregnancy involves physical as well as emotional changes for the mother. Ask the students: What changes did Everett Anderson see occurring in his mother? How did these changes affect him and his new step-dad? What fears did Everett confront at this time? How will everyone's lives change after the baby is born?

8. Have the students interview a teacher or parent who is expecting a baby. Some questions for the interview are: Can she share some of the experiences of her pregnancy and answer questions from the students? What tests, such as sonograms, has she had? What information can the parents find out about their baby before it is born? **Note:** Sonogram images can be printed out and shared with the class.

9. Invite parents of students to bring baby brothers or sisters to class. Ask the students: How are small babies held and fed? Do they sleep a lot? What can babies do for themselves as they become toddlers? Point out to the students the babies' ability to move, communicate, express emotion and desires, and so forth. Have the children write out the observations they made, including what impressed them most about the babies.

10. Parents usually buy many items before their baby is born. Have the students make a checklist of necessities that an infant will need (for example, a crib, diapers, infant seat, toys). Then have them use a catalog from a department or discount store to list these items and total the cost. Have the children work in small groups to make up their shopping lists. Are there "luxury" items on the list too?

11. Survey the class to see where the children were born. On a large map, indicate the city and date of birth of each class member. How many states are represented? Are there any foreign countries? Were children born in hospitals, at home, or elsewhere?

12. Have the children (and other teachers) bring in baby photos and make an anonymous display. Challenge the class to match the photos and the students (teachers).

13. Parents or other caregivers often sing lullabies to babies to help them go to sleep. Many songs originated in other countries; for example, Brahms's "Lullaby" is German, "All Through the Night" is Welsh, and "Hush, Little Baby" is English. Have the music specialist help find other lullabies.

14. Have the children write down their thoughts about a baby that is expected. After the child arrives, have the students design a "Welcome Home" greeting card for the newborn or newly adopted child, using the thoughts they had before the birth as part of the greeting. **Note:** Greeting cards are easy to produce using programs on the word processor.

15. Naming a child can be a difficult decision. A dictionary of names contains many ideas. These books may also give the definition of the children's names. Have the children examine these books for name suggestions and to see if their own names are defined.

16. Adoption is an important part of the lives of many children. Have the library media specialist gather books on adoption to share in class. Two examples are *Abby* by Jeannette Caines and *Tell Me Again About the Night I Was Born* by Jamie Lee Curtis.

Related Books and References

Caines, Jeannette. *Abby*. New York: Harper & Row, 1974.

Curtis, Jamie Lee. *Tell Me Again About the Night I Was Born*. New York: HarperCollins, 1998.

Kapp, Richard, ed. *Lullabies: An Illustrated Songbook*. New York: Harcourt Brace, 1997.

Matthews, Catherine E., and Helen Cook. "Oh, Baby, What a Science Lesson." *Science and Children* 33, no. 8 (May 1996): 18–21.

Chapter 6

DUCKS AND OTHER BIRDS

Make Way for Ducklings
Robert McCloskey
New York: Viking, 1941

Summary

Mr. and Mrs. Mallard determine that the proper environment for raising their ducklings can be in the middle of a crowded city. Despite the obstacles involved, Boston's Public Gardens are a suitable habitat for these wild ducks.

Science and Content Related Concepts

Ducks, birds (in general), physical characteristics of birds, behavior, habitat, survival instinct, reproductive instinct

Content Related Words

Instinct, habitat, environment, waddle, predator

Activities

1. Have the students examine a feather with a hand lens or microscope. Ask them: What do you observe? Are all the feathers on a duck identical in size, color, texture, purpose? What is the reason for any differences?

2. Have the children look in a field guide on birds. Ask them: What color are mallards? Are males and females the same? Why or why not? Have them make colored drawings of the adult ducks (see figure 6.1).

Fig. 6.1. Mr. and Mrs. Mallard

3. Ducks are colored white on their undersides so they cannot be seen by predators that swim in the water beneath them. To demonstrate this, paint potatoes a variety of colors or cut circles from an array of colored papers. Hang these from the ceiling or overhead hooks. Ask the students: Which would be the easiest for a predator to see? Which would be the hardest to see?

4. Have the students plan an imaginary trip to Boston, Massachusetts. Locate Boston within the United States and on a map of Massachusetts. A map of the city of Boston, obtainable from an automobile club or the Chamber of Commerce of Boston, would also be very helpful. Students may wish to use the Internet as a source of information.

5. On a city map of Boston, have the students locate the Boston Commons, the Public Gardens, Beacon Hill, Beacon Street, Louisburg Square, and Mt. Vernon Street. What bodies of water lie in and around Boston? Locate famous buildings or other places the children have studied in social studies, such as Paul Revere's house, the Old North Church, the Boston Tea Party site, and Old Ironsides. Ask the children: Are there other historical and cultural points of interest (for example, the Freedom Trail)? What sports teams play in the area? **Note:** Mark the spot where Mr. and Mrs. Mallard have chosen to live.

6. Have the class pretend that a large radio station in Boston has heard that a family of ducks is seeking a home. Ask them: What qualities must the home possess? What types of places must be avoided? Have the children write an appeal to the people of Boston to help find a home. Use these appeals as class presentations to practice information-gathering and speaking skills.

7. Have the students design a "Duck Crossing" sign to assist Officer Clancy as he directs traffic.

8. Mr. and Mrs. Mallard love Boston so much they write to many of their relatives inviting them to visit. As a group, decide what this letter would say and copy it on a flip chart or poster.

9. Many birds migrate for the winter. If this unit is being done during the fall or spring, watch for flocks of birds flying overhead. Ask the students: What kind are they? In which direction are they flying? How many appear to travel together? Do they fly in formation? For a couple of weeks, have the students record this information along with the time of day you see the birds. Ask the library media specialist to recommend an atlas or other reference book that would contain a map of common flyways used by birds. Do the children live near any of these flyways?

10. Birds are a distinct group of animals that have feathers, wings, beaks, and scaly feet. But birds also differ from each other; for example, the penguin has a strong wing that aids it in swimming; the ostrich cannot fly. In the library media center, have students research characteristics that distinguish one group of birds from another. Have them work in pairs or small groups to create specific information cards about the following birds: 1) penguin, 2) robin, 3) pigeon, 4) woodpecker, 5) owl, 6) parakeet, 7) hummingbird, 8) parrot, 9) eagle, and 10) ostrich. Students should include on the cards facts about size, habitat, geographic location, nesting habits, food, migratory habits, and so forth. Use these cards in a bulletin board display.

11. In figure 6.2, the birds are shown adult size. Have the students arrange the birds from largest to smallest. Have them use cash register tape as a visual indicator for a display area; for example, cut a piece of register tape 4 feet long to represent the 4-foot high penguin.

12. Ducks are characterized by their webbed feet, which are an aid in swimming. Humans use swim fins and paddles and oars to accomplish what the webbed foot does. Have students bring in examples of these implements and discuss how they work. To simulate the webbed foot, have students wrap one outstretched hand in plastic wrap or a baggie, then sweep the hand through a pan of water. Ask them: How is this different from sweeping the unwrapped hand through the water?

13. The Mallards gave their children names that rhymed with "quack." Ask students to think of other sets of eight rhyming names that could have been used for the ducklings (for example, Tim, Slim, Jim).

Fig. 6.2. Scale Comparison of Commonly Known Birds

14. Wild ducks are often hunted by sportsmen. Ask the students: What are the rules and regulations concerning this sport in your state regarding such things as dates and length of season, type of weapons to be used, necessity of obtaining a license, and so forth?

15. Ask the students: What is a bird sanctuary or wildlife refuge? Why do they exist? Who provides support for them? How are they administered? Have the children locate and learn about a nearby refuge, then if possible make a visit. **Note:** Refuges are often listed on a state highway or recreation map or on the Internet. Use the key words "bird sanctuary" or "wildlife refuge."

16. The duck is an important character in the musical story "Peter and the Wolf" by Serge Prokofiev. Ask the students: What instrument represents the duck? Why do you think it was chosen? What other implements are used to imitate the sound of a duck?

Related Books and References

Carlson, Nancy, trans. *Peter and the Wolf.* New York: Viking Penguin/Puffin Books, 1986.

Flack, Marjorie. *The Story About Ping.* New York: Viking, 1933 (Reprint: Turtleback, 1999).

Peterson, Roger Tory, and Virginia Peterson. *A Completely New Guide to All the Birds of Eastern and Central North America.* Boston: Houghton Mifflin, 1998.

———. *A Field Guide to the Birds.* Boston: Houghton Mifflin, 1947.

———. *A Field Guide to Western Birds: A Completely New Guide for Field Marks of All Species Found in North America West of the 100th Meridian.* Boston: Houghton Mifflin, 1998.

Potter, Beatrix. "The Tale of Jemima Puddleduck," in *The Complete Tales.* London: Frederick Warne, 1997.

Prokofiev, Serge. *Prokofiev's Music for Children.* New London Orchestra, Ronald Corps, conducting.

Tafuri, Nancy. *Have You Seen My Duckling?* New York: Greenwillow, 1984.

Chapter 7

ANTS AND OTHER INSECTS

Two Bad Ants
Chris Van Allsburg
Boston: Houghton Mifflin, 1988

Summary

The quest for a mysterious, sweet-tasting crystal leads to near disaster for two curious ants. They persevere to overcome the trials and tribulations of the outside world before returning to the safety of the ant colony.

Science and Content Related Concepts

Insects, the life of an ant, physical and social qualities of the ant world, predator-prey relationships, the ant in the human's world, household safety, magnification, the senses

Content Related Words

Crystal, scout, queen, insect, antennae, colony

Activities

1. During a walk outside, have students look for ant hills and ant trails. Have them trace the movement of the ants. Ask the students: What are the dangers for the ants as they move about?

2. Have the children observe the kinds of food that ants seek in nature. Ask them: What methods do the ants utilize to transport food back to their home?

3. Have a snack outside with the class and see which foods attract ants. Include items that represent the four basic tastes: sweet, sour, bitter, and salty.

4. Keep an ant farm in the classroom to study these insects.

5. Have the children observe ants moving on a clear tray that has been placed on the overhead projector. Ask the students: How do the ants move and react? As a class, create a list of words or phrases to describe their actions.

6. Ask the students: Why are ants considered to be insects? What characteristics distinguish them? What common insects are found in your locale? Are insects generally welcomed or considered to be pests?

7. Have the students build an ant out of pipe cleaners and modeling clay. **Note:** A Cootie game can help students recall the parts of the ant's body.

8. This book is written so that the reader can see the world through the eyes of the ant. Have the students use a hand lens or microscope to magnify other objects around their kitchens (for example, bread, onion skins, oatmeal, salt, peppercorns, tea, oregano, crackers, cereal, raisins). Have them write descriptions of how these would appear to an ant. In class, pass out baggies containing samples of these items. Can the children describe the contents of their baggie well enough for others to guess the identity?

9. Many objects in nature are made of crystals. Have the children grow salt or sugar crystals on a string. For salt crystals, put 8 to 10 teaspoons of plain table salt into 1 cup of water and stir until it dissolves. Tie a string around a pencil. Place the pencil across the cup and let it rest there. Submerge the string in the water but do not let the string touch the bottom of the cup. Allow the water to evaporate. Crystals will form on the string (see figure 7.1). Have the children observe the crystals through a hand lens or microscope, then draw pictures of the shapes observed. Follow the same procedures for sugar crystals, using $\frac{1}{2}$ cup water and 26 level teaspoons of white sugar.

10. Duplicate the paper templates in figure 7.2 for common crystal shapes such as four- or six- or twelve-sided solids. Have the students fold these into the crystal forms and glue the tabs to secure the crystal. Explore the ways the sides appear to change after folding. Have the students make mobiles from the completed solids and compare them to the crystals seen under the hand lens in Activity 9.

11. Have the children write a language experience story in which they are an ant. The ants may be at a picnic, in the kitchen cupboards, in a sugar bowl, in the garden, climbing a jungle gym, and so forth. Make sure they include factual information about the ants as part of the story.

12. Have the children pretend to see the world through the eyes of an ant and write a journal about the ant's life for several days. **Note:** More research on ants and insects may need to be done to provide enough background material; for example, Do ants carry disease? Are ants destructive? Can ants inflict harm on humans? Ask the library media specialist to locate both fiction and nonfiction materials about ants.

13. Have the students create a newspaper published by the ant colony, reporting on the problems encountered by the "two bad ants" in the world of humans.

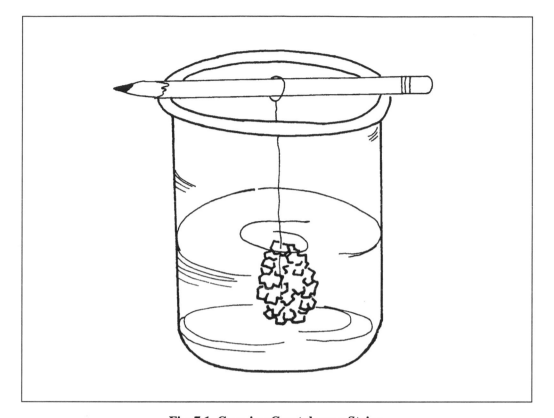

Fig. 7.1. Growing Crystals on a String

14. Have the children interview an ant, taking turns being the ant who is questioned by others in the class. Questions can be written down before the interviews begin. **Note:** The "ant" may wish to use notes to help answer questions.

15. Have the students add and subtract numbers of ants for math class. For example, if four more ants joined the two bad ants, how many ants would there be? If three ants stayed behind in the house, how many ants would return to the colony? **Note:** Cuisenaire rods can help students determine the answers and write additional questions of their own.

16. Household appliances can also pose problems for humans. Have students make a safety list for small children for such items as a toaster, a microwave, or an electrical socket.

17. Have students read the instruction papers provided with new household appliances. Review the safety features and hints for safe operation with the children.

18. Have the students write and act out a classroom drama about safe operation of appliances.

19. Read the instructions on an ant trap to the students without opening the outside covering. Then ask them: How should it be used? In what ways can these traps be dangerous for people?

20. The National Pest Control Association, Inc., which can be reached at http://www. pestworld.org, has much information on insects. Have students try this Web site, and also http://fumeapest.com.

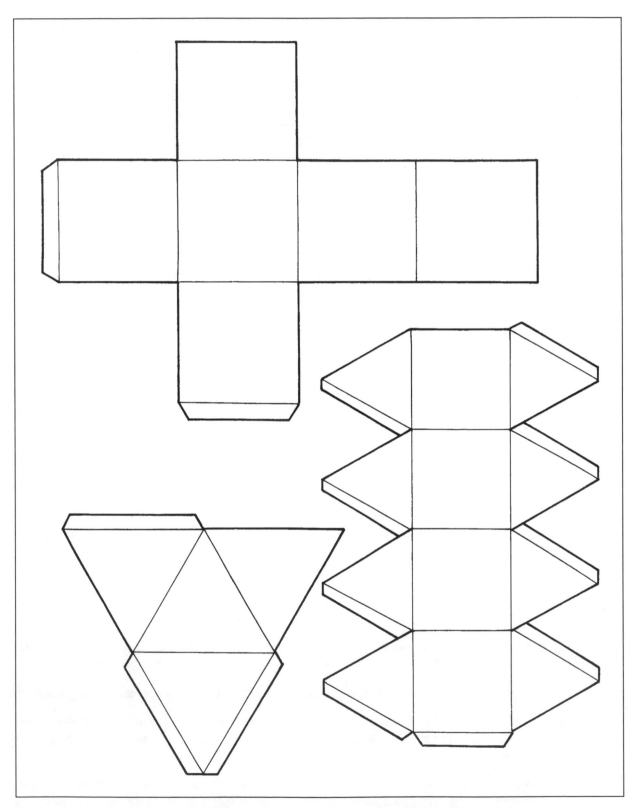

Fig. 7.2. Paper Templates to Make Three-dimensional Crystal Shapes

Related Books and References

Cottam, Clarence, and James Gordon Irving. *Insects: A Guide to Familiar American Insects: A Golden Guide.* New York: Golden Guide Press, 1987.

Glanville, Liana. "Bug Buddies." *Science and Children* 35, no. 7 (April 1998): 22–25.

Lobel, Arnold. *Grasshopper on the Road.* New York: Harper & Row, 1978.

Moffett, Mark W. "Leafcutters: Gardeners of the Ant World." *National Geographic* 188, no. 1 (July 1995): 98–111.

Palapodi, Marie, and Philip T. Matsekes. "How My Class Caught the Bug." *Science and Children* 32, no. 8 (May 1995): 33–36.

Chapter 8

SPIDERS

The Very Busy Spider
Eric Carle
New York: Putnam, 1985

Summary

All day long, various animals attempt to keep the spider from completing her web. However, at day's end the exhausted spider has completed her task and woven a beautiful web.

Science and Content Related Concepts

Daily activities of a spider, predatory behavior

Content Related Words

Web, predator, prey

Activities

1. Have the students search for spider webs around the school. They should use clean spray bottles filled with water as misters and spray water on webs to make them easier to see and study. Dark places like corners of basements or unused areas are ideal locations to look for webs. They may need to use flashlights in these places. Ask them: How does the spider react when a light is aimed at its web?

2. Spiders spin different sized threads, depending on the part of the web they are making. Ask a parent who sews to show samples of different kinds of thread and explain their purposes—for example, carpet thread, quilting thread, monofilament nylon, polyester thread, cotton thread. Have the students test the strength of the fibers by trying to break them.

3. Ask the students what they want to learn about spiders; for example, Are spiders helpful or harmful to the environment? Are they helpful to people or are they destructive? Are there poisonous spiders? How do spiders kill their prey after trapping it? Have them answer these and other questions using information found in the library media center.

4. Conduct a "spider interview." Questions can be made up ahead by groups of children after doing research in the library media center.

5. Keep a spider and its web in a terrarium or large jar for a short time. Have the children study the spider and write a series of observations on what they see. Someone will need to capture insects to feed the spider until its release.

6. Have the children observe spiders with a hand lens to see how they react and move. They can also be seen on the overhead projector if they are first placed in a clear plastic tray that is set on the machine. Cover the tray with a film of plastic wrap. Make a list of action or descriptive words to relate what the children see, such as gliding, dropping, or weaving.

7. Have the children make a model using yarn pom-poms or modeling clay, showing that spiders have two distinct body parts and eight legs (see figure 8.1).

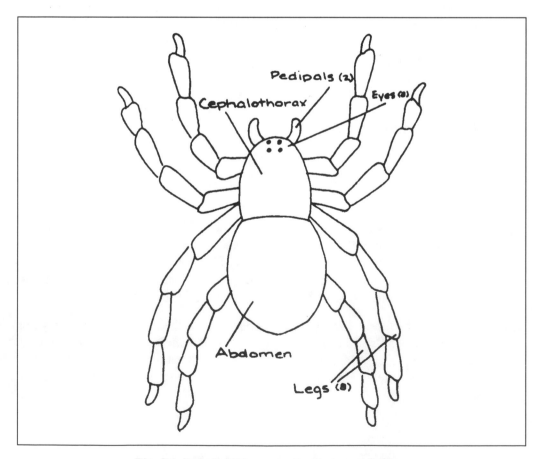

Fig. 8.1. Labeled Diagram of a Common Spider

8. Webs can also be made of pipe cleaners wound together. Have the children paint them with thin school glue and sprinkle them with glitter for holiday ornaments.

9. Have the students use string to make webs. Nails can be driven into a fiberboard base as a framework. The string is wound around one nail, taken to the next nail, and wrapped around it. This continues until the pattern of the entire web is completed. A large web made on a bulletin board can be used to hold the children's spider models (see figure 8.2). **Note:** Students should not use heavy hammers which cannot be easily manipulated. Exercise caution when setting the nail into place, as well as when hammering the object.

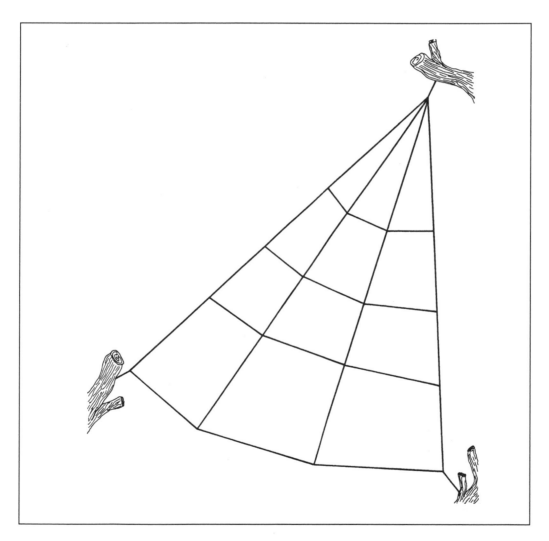

Fig. 8.2. A Spider Web Pattern

10. Ask the students: What geometric shapes can be found in the picture of the spider web that appears in this book? Are there additional geometric shapes in the webs you made?

11. Have the children edit a newspaper for spiders. They should report on events of the spider community. There might also be a handyman's column on the best shapes for building webs or a gourmet cooking section on tasty insects that spiders would enjoy. Remind the students that the spider itself is not an insect.

12. Use *The Very Busy Spider* as a source for choral reading. A drum or other percussive accompaniment can emphasize the rhythmic language of the book.

13. Have the class read other animal books by Eric Carle (for example, *The Grouchy Ladybug* and *The Very Quiet Cricket*).

14. Read poems about spiders. Have the children write poems such as couplets (two lines that are rhyming stanzas).
     Look at the spider.
     There's a bug inside her.

15. *Charlotte's Web* by E. B. White is the classic story of a spider named Charlotte and her farmyard friends. Read a chapter or two each day to the class as they study spiders. Finish the unit with a video or film of the story.

16. Ask if anyone knows any songs about spiders. Ask the school music specialist to find more examples. Are these songs factual or are they just silly? Have the children make up words about a spider to fit a tune they know. Share these songs.

17. Ask the students: Is there a spider plant in the classroom? Why is it called that? What are the "baby spiders," and what is their purpose?

Related Books and References

Beck, Charles R. "Are You As Clever As a Spider?" *Science Scope* 16, no. 2 (October 1992): 12-16.

Carle, Eric. *The Grouchy Ladybug*. New York: Thomas Y. Crowell, 1977.

———. *The Very Quiet Cricket*. New York: Putnam, 1997.

Conniff, Richard. "Tarantulas." *National Geographic* 190, no. 3 (September 1996): 99–115

Jackson, Robert R. "Portia Spider: Mistress of Deception." *National Geographic* 190, no. 5 (November 1996): 104–115.

McDermott, Gerald. *Anansi the Spider*. New York: Holt, Rinehart & Winston, 1975. (Reprint: Henry Holt, 1988).

McNulty, Faith. *The Lady and the Spider*. New York: Harper & Row, 1986.

Moffett, Mark W. "All Eyes on Jumping Spiders." *National Geographic* 180, no. 3 (September 1991): 43–63.

Nabors, Martha L., Linda C. Edwards, and Virginia Bartel. "Webbing with Spiders." *Science and Children* 31, no. 8 (May 1994): 33.

White, E. B. *Charlotte's Web*. New York: Harper & Row, 1952. (Reprint: Harper Trophy, 1974.)

Chapter 9

LADYBUGS

The Grouchy Ladybug
Eric Carle
New York: Thomas Y. Crowell, 1977

Summary

The "grouchy" ladybug refuses to share the aphids on the leaves with the other ladybugs. Instead, she spends her day antagonizing different animals, all of which have their own particular protective adaptations to defend themselves. At the end of a very humbling and tiring day, a much wiser ladybug returns home, willing to share with others.

Science and Content Related Concepts

Protective adaptation, food chain, time, rotation of the earth, animal characteristics, sequencing

Content Related Words

Aphid, ladybug (ladybird), adaptation

Activities

1. Before finishing the book (after the whale page), have the children predict the ending. Compare their endings with that written by Mr. Carle.

2. Have the children study the picture of a ladybug. Make patterns from felt or paper pieces. These can be used to construct a large ladybug on a flannel board. (Use the example shown in figure 9.1.) Make sure they include the head, thorax, abdomen, wings, legs, and antennae. The number of spots will vary with different species. Have the children make a similar cutout of an aphid. Ask the children: How are these insects alike and how are they different?

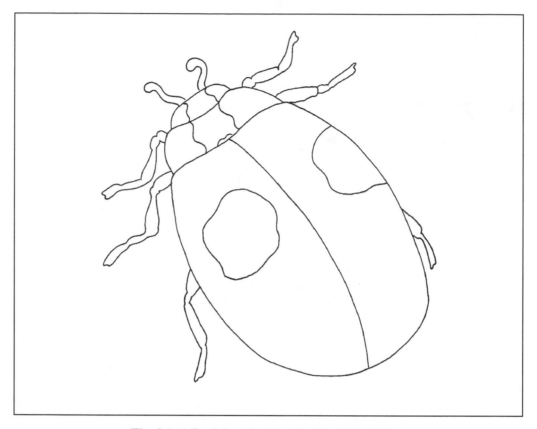

Fig. 9.1. A Ladybug Outline for Craft Activities

3.   Have the students make thumbprint ladybugs or "pet rock" ladybugs.

4.   Use a clear plastic box with no top to make a bug house (see figure 9.2) for holding in-sects collected through sweep netting a field or lawn. Cover the box with a nylon stock-ing to contain the insects. This will allow air to enter the box. Study these insects in class and release them promptly. **Note:** See activity 1 of *The Tiny Seed*.

5.   Have the children make a chart of the animals in the book. They can find information on some of the following topics in the library media center:

   a.   classification of animal (mammal, insect, and so forth)

   b.   natural habitat

   c.   size of animal

   d.   type of food eaten

   e.   use by humans

   f.   destructive qualities

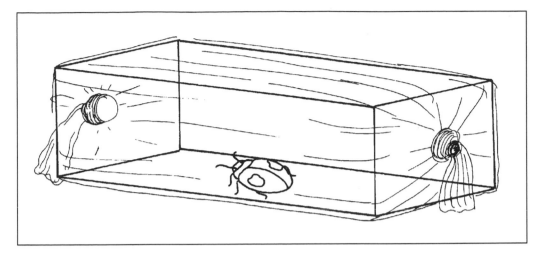

Fig. 9.2. "Bug House" for Observing Insects

6. From the chart above, select two characteristics for each animal. Write each characteristic on a separate card. There are 12 animals, so there should be 24 cards when you are done. Do not list the names of the animal on the cards. Give each child one card. Then have them walk around the room comparing cards and looking for someone who has a card bearing another characteristic of the same animal. The students must find two cards that describe the same animal and decide which animal it is. If the group of students is larger, more cards can be made for each animal (for example, three characteristics for 12 animals equals 36 cards total). Examples of characteristics of some of the 12 animals in the book follow. **Note:** A children's encyclopedia will provide excellent ideas for animal descriptions.

Yellow Jacket

Despite my average length of one inch, my protective defense can cause great discomfort, or even death, to humans.

I do not have two or four legs and am very essential to the reproduction of many species of the plant kingdom.

Boa Constrictor

There are 40 to 60 species of this animal found mainly in warm regions. They depend on neither legs nor feet for locomotion.

The young are born alive, not from eggs, and can grow to a length of 25 feet.

Skunk

I am a member of the weasel family and prefer to eat rodents, rats, and birds, although I will eat plant material.

To defend myself, I emit a foul odor that can reach up to 20 feet.

Lobster

My flipper tail helps me navigate as I scavenge dead matter. I also feed on seaweed and live animals.

My visibility is good because my eyes are located at the end of movable stalks.

7.   Have the children list the different words the author uses for "meet." Instruct them to look in a thesaurus for more words that mean "encounter."

8.   Have the students practice the proper form of introducing people. Have them write out these introductions to show proper use of quotation marks.

9.   Have the children write poems about the grouchy ladybug and the nice ladybug, using contrasting adjectives and figurative language such as similes.

10.   Ask the students to write a paragraph explaining why they think the ladybug changed her attitude.

11.   The ladybug is also known as a ladybird beetle. Ask the students: What famous nursery rhyme does this bring to mind? Can you change the words of that tale and fit in some adventures of this ladybug? They should try to keep the same rhythm.

12.   Ask the students: How many hours does the book cover? Is that a whole day? Which hours are A.M. and which are P.M.? Set up a sundial on the playground and mark the shadow length to correspond to the clock faces in the book. **Note:** See activity 6 of *Shadow*.

13.   Have the children make their own personal time lines showing where they are or what they are doing at each time shown on the clocks in the book. They should make one list of activities for a school day and another for a vacation day.

14.   Using a clock with moveable hands, work with simple fractions: half hour, quarter hour, and so forth. The amount of time represented by these fractions might be explained in terms of class length, recess time, or a television program.

15.   Ask the children to select an animal from the book and pantomime how it protects itself.

16.   Animals sometimes protect themselves through the use of camouflage. Have the children design a yet undiscovered animal with very special adaptations for survival. Animals can be drawn or painted, or created from odd bits of cloth, wood, colored paper, and packing materials glued to a stiff sheet of paper. Use the adaptations listed below, or have the children invent ones of their own. For example, invent a "grouchy animal" that:

   a.   rips its food apart before swallowing it

   b.   squeezes its enemies to death

   c.   can hide anywhere without being seen

   d.   lives in the cracks of sidewalks

   e.   has skin "harder than nails"

   f.   poisons its enemies in a blink of its eye

   g.   uses beauty to lure its enemies

   h.   can change the size of its mouth to fit its prey

17. To demonstrate the comparative size of the animals, find other objects that are about the same size as each animal in the book; for example, a ladybug is the size of a dried pea. For the larger animals, have the children make outlines on the playground to show relative size. Back in the classroom, have the children make a mobile of the various animals using drawings or silhouettes or origami (see figure 9.3). Try to get them to make these to relative scale; for example, each inch represents one foot of the animal's size.

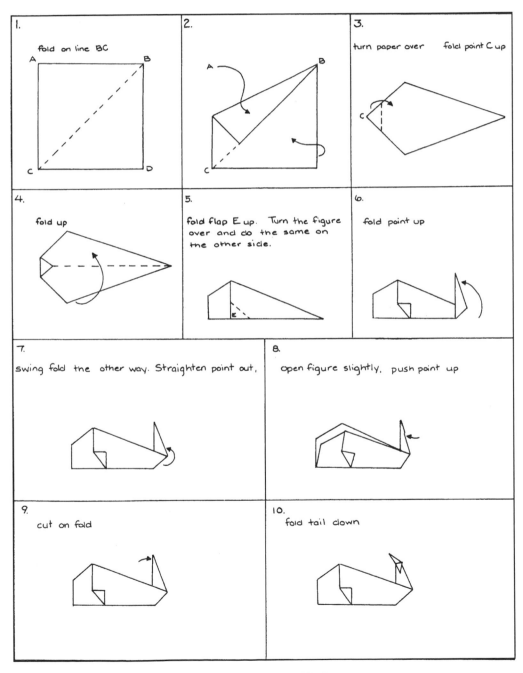

Fig. 9.3. An Origami Whale

18. Play recordings about animals, such as "Carnival of the Animals" by Camille Saint-Saens. Have the children do some creative movements to these selections. Ask them to try to imitate the sounds and movements of other animals in the book.

19. On a world map, have the students locate and mark the natural habitats of the animals that the ladybug visited. Ask them: Is a journey like this possible in a day?

20. Ask the students to name some wild animals native to their country. Ask them: How do they protect themselves from predators? In what way are some animals protected by the national government?

21. Ask the library media specialist to obtain films or videos on topics such as the balance of nature, endangered species of animals, or wildlife refuge centers.

22. The whale was the "hero" of the story. Have the children use the directions in Figure 9.3 to make an origami whale. Notice how many geometric shapes are used.

23. Have the children use the keyword "Ladybug" to locate many interesting Web sites about ladybugs or ladybird beetles.

Related Books and References

Ayture-Schule, Zulal. *The Great Origami Book.* New York: Sterling, 1987.

Cottam, Clarence, and James Gordon Irving. *Insects: A Familiar Guide to American Insects: A Golden Guide.* New York: Golden Books, 1987.

Hechtman, Judi. "Ladybug, Ladybug, Come to Class." *Science and Children* 32, no. 6 (March 1995): 33–35

Saint-Saens, Camille. "The Carnival of the Animals." Pittsburgh Symphony Orchestra, Andre Previn, conducting.

Chapter 10

FISH

Swimmy
Leo Lionni
New York: Pantheon Books (Random House), 1963

Summary

A tuna swallows an entire school of fish, except for Swimmy. Sad and lonely, the little black fish explores the wonders of the ocean until he becomes part of a school of red fish. Here, in the middle of these new friends, he feels safe.

Science and Content Related Concepts

Schooling behavior of fish, predator-prey relationships, varieties of fish, marine life

Content Related Words

Schooling (of fish), protection, behavior (biological meaning)

Activities

1. Before reading the story, discuss the saying "There is safety in numbers." Does the saying have an additional or different meaning after reading the story?

2. Ask the children: What are the characteristics that make a fish unique? Have them make a chart comparing fish and humans; for example, fish breathe through gills but people breathe through their lungs.

3. Photographic stores have glass slide mounts. Place a few scales from a fish between the layers of glass and project them using a slide projector or examine them under a microscope. Each scale has a series of rings on it. Have the children count the rings to determine the age of the fish (see figure 10.1).

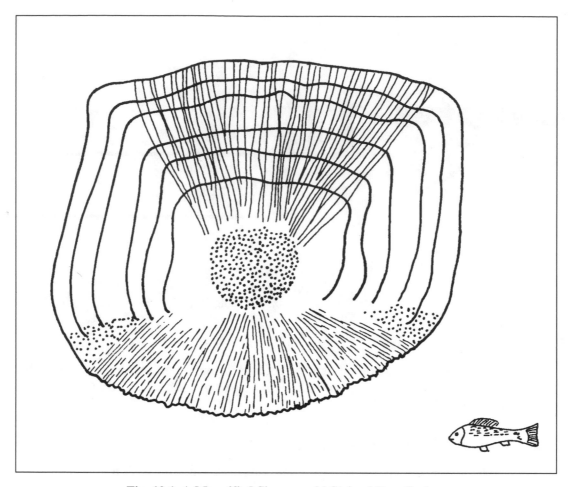

Fig. 10.1. A Magnified Six-year-old Striped Bass Scale

4.   Fish exist in a variety of sizes and shapes and live at different depths in the ocean. This placement is called the *water column*. Following is a list of water column depths and the fish that are found in them:

    a.   Surface area: small fish, floating algae, and plankton

    b.   Middle depths: quick-moving fish, fish with streamlined body shapes, predatory fish

    c.   Bottom/floor area: slow-moving fish, fish that hide on or blend in with the ocean bottom, flat fish, sea creatures that eat food that collects on the ocean floor.

Have the students use this information in the following craft projects:

   a.   Make silhouettes of several unique fish (see figure 10.2) and attach them to a wall display that depicts an underwater environment. Colored tissue paper and watercolors make efficient and realistic backgrounds for ocean scenes.

   b.   Glue pictures of fish onto Styrofoam meat trays along with cutouts of underwater plants. Cover the entire scene with blue plastic wrap.

   c.   Using geoboards and rubber bands, create a fish. Transfer the outline to one inch graph paper so that the fish can be colored and displayed.

5.   Have the students identify the sea creatures in the story that are not fish. Ask them to look up some important characteristics that make each of those animals unique. They should include the means of protection each animal uses.

6.   Make a set of "Sea Creature Rummy" cards based on the animals in the book. Have four cards for each creature. Have the students play rummy with this deck. When it is time to lay down groups of four similar cards, the student must also give a fact about the animal. Pictures can be from nature or sporting magazines, or hand sketched. Commercially made cards can be used to play "Go Fish." Ask the children to find out some facts about the fish portrayed on the cards. **Note:** Making 13 sets of cards would equal the number of cards in a regulation-sized deck.

7.   Have the students dramatize the story of Swimmy. They should include additional details on Swimmy's enemies, how fish protect themselves, why they travel in "schools," where they live, and what they eat. The terms "predator-prey relationship" and "protective adaptation" can be used here.

8.   Fish are part of the food chain. Small fish are eaten by bigger fish, which are eaten by even bigger fish, and so forth. Some fish are eaten by people. Discuss the food chain and the various means by which people can catch fish (fishing poles, nets, spears, and so forth). Include both recreational and commercial fishing in the discussion. Ask the students: Is deep-sea fishing similar to fresh water fishing?

9.   If there is an aquarium in the area, arrange a field trip for the children to visit it. Sometimes a staff member will come to class before the visit to discuss what the children will see.

Fig. 10.2. Representative Silhouettes of Saltwater Fish

10. A saltwater or fresh-water aquarium can be set up and maintained in the classroom. A pet store can supply a list of necessary items and also advise the class on the choice and care of fish. Have the children help with all stages of setting up the aquarium and getting the water ready. Try to have the fish delivered while students are in class.

11. Assemble a class book about the aquarium. Ask each child to contribute a story and an illustration about setting up or maintaining the aquarium.

12. Each state publishes a handbook of rules and regulations about sport fishing. Get a copy of these rules and have the students compare them to the regulations governing fishing near their homes—the need for a license, the time of year fishing is permitted, and so forth.

13. Have the children visit a fish market or grocery store to see the different sea animals that can be purchased in their area. Ask the children to find out: Where do the various creatures originate (for example, Alaskan king crab, Maine lobster)? What are the prices per pound for different seafood? Which seafood is most popular in this area? If the entire class cannot go, a list of questions might be written for a video visit, a telephone interview, or a guest appearance by the person from the fish market; for example, Where does the store buy the seafood? How long does it stay fresh in the store?

14. Some restaurants that specialize in seafood conduct school tours, followed by a sampling of their products. Find out if there is such a restaurant nearby and arrange to take your class to it.

15. Ask the students: What are the advantages of fish and other seafood as a food group for human beings? What do industries do with the remains of these animals after they have been processed for market?

16. Have the children use the *World Almanac* or other sources in the library media center to identify the countries that engage in commercial fishing. Have them list the top ten nations in order. Ask them: Where is the United States ranked? What can be learned about the fishing industry from the encyclopedia or the Internet? Where are U.S. fisheries located? What marine animals are commercially marketed?

17. We speak of a "school of fish." Other groupings of animals are referred to by unique names, such as a den of lions or a flock of geese (or a gaggle if they're not in flight). How many of these collective nouns can the students list? Have them ask at home for ideas.

18. Swimmy was accepted and liked because his color was different from the other fish. How do we treat people who are "different" because of their color, religion, background, or physical impairment? Have a group discussion on "being different" and "fitting in."

19. Ask the children what method of illustration is used in this story. Have them use this method to create a picture, placemat, bookmark, or book cover. They should use clear adhesive film to seal and strengthen the piece.

20. Fish are often portrayed in artwork. *Gyotaku* is the process of Japanese fish printing. As a demonstration, use a very flat fish that has been washed with soap and water and dried. Place the fish on several layers of newspaper and be sure the fins and tail are spread open. With a small brush, cover the fish with a water-based ink or acrylic paint, working against the grain of the scales, then smoothing them out. The print may be transferred to rice paper, a clean, plain T-shirt, or a piece of cloth. Place the cloth or paper onto the inked fish and rub firmly, but gently. Peel the paper or cloth off slowly to avoid smudging. **Note:** If a T-shirt is used, put several layers of newspaper inside the shirt so that the ink does not bleed through to the back.

21. Have the children make and fly Japanese fish kites (see figure 10.3).

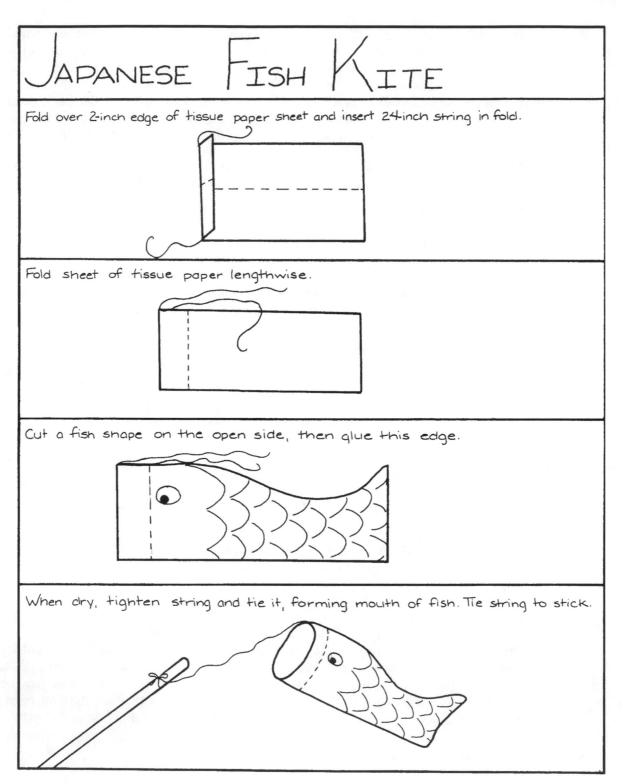

Fig. 10.3. Making a Japanese Fish Kite

22. Play the orchestral composition "La Mer" by Claude Debussy. Ask the children what images of the ocean it creates for them.

23. Have the children learn about fish and the ocean from materials available from the New England Aquarium at http://www.neaq.org, which contains resources for both teacher and student.

Related Books and References

Cole, Joanna. *The Magic School Bus on the Ocean Floor.* New York: Scholastic, 1992.

Debussy, Claude. "La Mer" in *Great Orchestral Works.* Cleveland Orchestra, Michael Tillson Thomas, conducting.

Lionni, Leo. *Fish Is Fish.* New York: Alfred A. Knopf, 1987.

Zim, Herbert, and Hurst Shoemaker. *Fishes: A Guide to Familiar American Species: A Golden Guide.* New York: Golden Press, 1987.

Chapter 11

REPTILES

Verdi
Janell Cannon
New York: Harcourt Brace, 1997

Summary

Verdi is proud of his yellow skin and does not want to mature into an adult green snake. Moreover, he thinks adults are lazy, boring, and rude. In time, Verdi learns to accept his fate as well as the other snakes around him.

Science and Content Related Concepts

Ecosystem, population control

Content Related Words

Constrictor, shed, camouflage, hatchling

Activities

1. To begin this unit, have each child administer a true-false survey about reptiles to an adult. Each statement is either "True" or "False."

    a. All snakes are slimy.
    b. All snakes shed their skin by rubbing against rough surfaces.
    c. All snakes live in trees, on the earth or in water.
    d. All snakes are helpful to the environment because they eat insects.
    e. All snakes swallow their food whole.
    f. All snakes are poisonous.
    g. All snakes are hatched from eggs.
    h. All snakes bask in the sun to absorb energy.

(See appendix for answers.) Score the surveys and rank the participants: 7–8 correct = excellent; 5–6 correct = good; 3–4 correct = fair; 1–2 correct = poor. Construct a bar graph showing the number who scored in each of the four ranges.

2. Divide the class into groups that will research the topic of snakes. Assign a topic to each group of children. Topics include a) description of snakes, b) body temperature, c) housing the snake as a pet, d) feeding, e) skin shedding, f) disease, and g) reproduction. **Note:** There are many facts about pythons in *Verdi*. Have the children integrate these with the results of their research in the library media center.

3. For information on reptiles, have the students access http://www.thesnake.org.

4. Each research group should make a display poster that shows the snake and its habitat and shares the information they collected. **Note:** Students may wish to use the text of *Verdi* as well as the end pages of the book as a source of information.

5. Many people harbor prejudices against snakes because they do not know much about these creatures. As part of the ongoing research on snakes, have the children list the ways in which snakes are helpful to the environment. Ask them to use these facts to write an article for the school newspaper on why snakes should not be destroyed.

6. Reptiles can be categorized into four groups: 1) snakes, 2) lizards, 3) turtles and 4) crocodilians. Ask the students to use a book such as Herbert Zim and Hobart Smith's *Reptiles and Amphibians* to list the animals in each category.

7. Ask the students: What are the characteristics of a reptile? Why were dinosaurs once considered to be reptiles?

8. Snakes can be very good pets if they are cared for properly. If the class is to keep a pet snake, have a worker from the pet store establish the snake's environment and provide information on its care and feeding.

9. Keeping a snake in the classroom might not be possible. Arrange for a visit from a pet store owner or zoo worker who can bring in a snake for a lecture-demonstration.

10. Ask the children to invent and draw a snake and the environment in which it lives. Remind them to be sure the snake is able to camouflage itself in this environment. They can include other facts about the snake on a card, which can be part of a bulletin board display.

11. Snakes live in every part of the world except the polar regions, Ireland, Iceland, New Zealand, and several small Pacific Islands. Tropical countries are most noted for their abundance of snakes. Ask the students to locate all of these areas on the globe.

12. Snakes come in many sizes—from a few inches to several feet. Compare the length of the following snakes to a length of rope representing concrete objects that the children know, such as a bicycle, a car, a dog, a person, a horse, a telephone pole, a classroom, a semi-truck, a house, and a gymnasium:

hognose snake (3 feet)

rattlesnake (5 feet)

boa constrictor (12 feet)

python (20 feet)

coral snake (3 feet)

copperhead (4 feet)

garter snake (1 foot)

kingsnake (4 feet)

cobra (4 feet)

cottonmouth (4 feet)

bullsnake (6 feet)

Note: Lengths are taken from the Zim and Smith book on reptiles.

Related Books and References

Hilke, Eileen. "A Snake in the Class." *Science and Children* 25, no. 6 (March 1988): 34-35

Lange, Karen. "Hunting the Mighty Python." *National Geographic* 191, no. 5 (May 1997): 110–117.

McNulty, Faith. *A Snake in the House.* New York: Scholastic, 1994.

Palotta, Jerry. *The Yucky Reptile Alphabet Book.* New York: Trumpet Club, 1989.

Ryder, Joanne. *Lizard in the Sun.* New York: Mulberry Paperback Book, 1990.

Smith, Hobart M. "Snakes As Pets." *Science and Children* 25, no. 6 (March 1988): 36.

Zim, Herbert S., and Hobart M. Smith. *Reptiles and Amphibians: A Golden Guide.* New York: Golden Books, 1987.

Chapter 12

AIR POLLUTION

Michael Bird-Boy
Tomie dePaola
Englewood Cliffs, NJ: Prentice-Hall, 1975

Summary

A large black cloud causes many changes in the environment of a young boy, Michael. When he locates the factory that is producing the pollution, he helps to solve the problem.

Science and Content Related Concepts

Air pollution and its effects, pollution control, weather, seasons of the year, bee keeping, manufacturing

Content Related Words

Pollution, environment, assembly line, sequence, factory

Activities

1. Ask the students: What is pollution? How is it harmful to people and the environment? Does the local newspaper or television station monitor weather pollution and report an index to their viewers? If so, ask students to record this information on a line graph and see how the pollution amounts change over a certain number of days. Ask them: What does this mean to humans as well as the environment?

2. Select one student in the class to "run for office" on the position that pollution must be contained. How many different arguments can the students find to support this cause? Assign small groups of children to act as speech writers to develop short television spots dealing with the various issues. Others can make posters or bumper stickers to rally constituents around the cause. Still others may stage a short interview with people who are greatly affected by air pollution, such as those with respiratory diseases or older citizens.

3. There are several different types of pollution. Ask students to find out: Which kinds exist in the local community? Are efforts being made to eliminate these problems? What still needs to be accomplished? How are these projects reported by the local media?

4. Young people can fight solid waste pollution by participating in litter cleanup programs and gathering empty bottles for recycling or refunds. Make your class a part of a project of these efforts.

5. Ask the students: What can adults do to help lessen pollution? What can politicians or factory owners do? How could you let your views about pollution be known by persons in power or the media? How can these suggestions be implemented?

6. This book shows how plants and animals are affected by air pollution. Are objects also affected?

    a. Divide the class into groups and assign them to various outside sections of the school building. Do they see dirt and discoloration or other signs of pollution? Mark the areas with colored stickers, then have the class as a whole examine the various sites and discuss the problem.

    b. Visit an old cemetery to see how tombstones are affected by pollution and weathering. Have the children list the death dates that appear on the most severely affected stones.

    c. Hang a white cloth out of a school window. Ask the children to examine it after a few days for evidence of pollution. **Note:** Rain will ruin the effect of this investigation. Plan to do this when no rain is predicted.

    d. Melt snow, then pour it through filter paper or a clean cloth. Ask the children what they see.

    e. Ask the children to help someone wash a car, then report on what it looks like after sitting outside for a day or so.

7. Michael Bird-Boy loved nature and did not want it ruined by pollution. Have the children select something they enjoy about nature that could be adversely affected by pollution and then write about how pollution could hurt it; for example, toxic chemicals damaging a favorite fishing stream.

8. If possible, invite a beekeeper to explain about raising bees: kinds of bees, division of labor within the bee colony, types of hives, use of beeswax and honeycombs, honey production, and so forth. Or have small groups of students research these topics in the library media center and share their findings with the class.

9. Use honey in a baking project:

Michael Bird-Boy's Honey Cake

1 cup honey
1 cup quick-cooking oats
1 ½ cups flour
pinch of salt
1 teaspoon ginger
½ cup shortening

1 cup boiling water
1 teaspoon soda
1 teaspoon cinnamon
¼ teaspoon cloves
¾ cup sugar
2 eggs

Pour boiling water over the oats; let stand covered for 20 minutes. Cream shortening and sugar; beat in honey. Stir in eggs and oatmeal. Sift in all dry ingredients and mix well. Bake at 350 degrees for 60 to 65 minutes in a well-greased and floured 13-by-9-by-2-inch pan. Leave in pan and frost.

Boss Lady's Honey Frosting

¼ cup butter or margarine (softened)
⅓ cup honey
½ cup flaked coconut
¼ cup chopped pecans or walnuts

Cream honey and butter until light and fluffy. Stir in coconut and nuts. Use to frost cooled cake. Have a celebration!

10. A grocery store sells three different brands of honey. The honey is in glass containers of different sizes. Have the students calculate which jar of honey is the best value, using the number of ounces and cost per ounce.

Brand A

12 oz. $2.29

16 oz. $2.79

40 oz. $5.39

Brand B

    12 oz. $2.49

    16 oz. $2.99

    40 oz. $5.99

Brand C

    16 oz. $2.55

    32 oz. $4.89

    64 oz. $9.69

11. Bee stings can cause allergic reactions or even death for some humans. Ask students to find out what they would do for an allergic classmate if someone were stung at school. They can ask parents or other adults what home remedies they use for bee stings (assuming no allergy is involved); for example, some people make a paste of meat tenderizer and water.

12. Killer bees can be very harmful for any human. Ask the students to watch for news items or magazine articles about these bees or surf the Internet using the keywords "killer bees" to locate Web sites.

13. Gather various kinds of flowers or find cross-sectional diagrams of flowers for the class to examine (see figure 12.1). Ask the students: Where is the nectar located? How does the bee get to it? Does this harm the flower? What is done with the nectar?

14. Boss Lady's factory is efficient because it is automated. Set up an assembly line in the classroom to make pipe cleaner bees. Each child or team will have one task to perform before passing the item on for the next step. Supplies include yellow and black 12-inch pipe cleaners, rulers, scissors, and small boxes for packing. **Note:** Each bee requires one yellow and two black pipe cleaners. Scissors with rounded tips can be used, as well as wire cutters. Exercise caution if using sharp-tipped scissors. (See figure 12.2.)

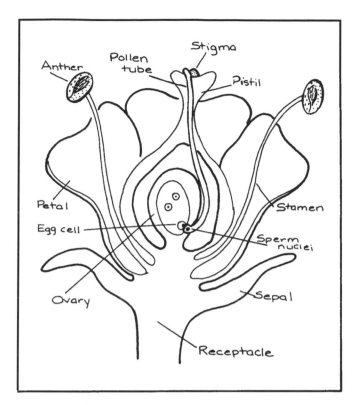

Fig. 12.1. Cross-section of a Flower

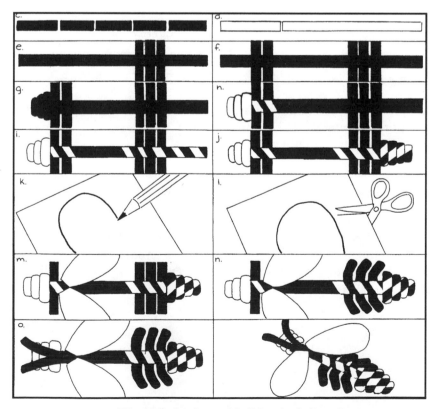

Fig. 12.2. An Assembly Line Activity

Organize the workers into the following roles:

    a.   The Boss: starts, regulates, and stops work rate, for example, if a breakdown occurs in the assembly line.

    b.   Unpackers: give out black and yellow pipe cleaners.

    c.   Cutters I: cut half of the black pipe cleaners into five equal pieces; cut the others into two equal pieces.

    d.   Cutters II: cut yellow cleaners into two sections, 4-inch and 8-inch.

    e.   Loopers: tie three short pieces of black pipe cleaner to half of a black pipe cleaner, 4 inches from one end.

    f.   Loopers: tie two pieces of black pipe cleaner to a whole pipe cleaner, 2 inches from the other end to form wing and antennae ends.

    g.   Headers: twist front end of long black pipe cleaner into a head.

    h.   Wrappers: wrap the 4-inch yellow piece around the head.

    i.   Twisters: twist the 8-inch yellow piece around the tail and leg sections.

    j.   Coilers: coil the tail end to form the abdomen.

    k.   Tracers: trace wings onto a transparent sheet.

    1.   Wing Cutters: cut wing sections out of the transparent sheet.

    m.   Gluers: glue wings onto wing holders.

    n.   Leggers: bend legs into shape.

    o.   Shapers: bend antennae into shape.

    p.   Inspector: checks completed bees for quality.

    q.   Disassemblers: take apart defective bees for remanufacture.

    r.   Packers: pack completed bees for "shipping" or "storage."

15. Bees and honey are mentioned in many common sayings, such as "busy as a bee" and "sweeter than honey." Ask adults and others to share sayings they know with the class. Post these on the bulletin board.

16. Ask the students: If you could interview a bee, flower, or another animal, what might it have to say about pollution? Have them write a story from the animal or plant's point of view.

17. Music has been written about bees (for example, "The Flight of the Bumblebee" by Nikolai Rimsky-Korsakov). Play this piece or another one for the students and then ask them: What picture does the composer want you to visualize? How does he achieve this?

Related Books and References

D'Augustino, Jo Beth, Maryanne Kalin, Diane Schiller, and Stephen Freedman. "Dancing for Food: The Language of Honeybees." *Science and Children* 31, no. 8 (May 1994): 14–17.

Domel, Rue. "You Can Teach About Acid Rain." *Science and Children* 31, no. 2 (October 1993): 25–28.

Harris, Mary, and Sandra Van Natta. "A Classroom of Polymer Factories." *Science and Children* 35, no. 5 (February 1998): 18–21.

Marston, Alan. "America's Beekeepers: Hives for Hire." *National Geographic* 183, no. 5 (May 1993): 73–93.

Peet, Bill. *The Wump World.* Boston: Houghton Mifflin, 1970.

Rimsky-Korsakov, Nikolai. "The Flight of the Bumblebee," from *The Tale of Tsar Sultana Suite.* Philadelphia Orchestra, Joseph Ormandy, conducting.

Van Allsburg, Chris. *Just a Dream.* Boston: Houghton Mifflin, 1990.

Chapter 13

ADAPTATIONS OF ANIMALS

Chipmunk Song
Joanne Ryder
New York: E. P. Dutton, 1987

Summary

This story portrays the life of a chipmunk as it deals with the challenges of the changing seasons. These include food gathering, ways to keep warm or cool, and avoiding predators. The reader's imagination is aided by illustrations showing a young boy simulating the chipmunk's activities.

Science and Content Related Concepts

Animal adaptations, protective behavior, communication, seasons, life cycle of the chipmunk, food gathering, winter survival

Content Related Words

Camouflage, hibernation, predator, prey, insulation

Activities

1. Chipmunks are able to hide from predators because of their protective coloration and patterned pelt. Invent "imaginary critters" that can be camouflaged and hidden in the classroom or school yard. Have a scavenger hunt for students to find these "animals." Which are hardest to find? Which are easiest to find? Have the children write descriptions of their "critters" and the environment in which they can hide best.

2. People can wear special clothing to camouflage themselves. Ask the students: What clothing would best help people go unnoticed? When or where would this most likely be used?

3. In nature, larger animals often eat smaller animals, which in turn eat even smaller animals. Have the students locate all the animals and plants pictured in the book and decide where these animals would fit into the food chain. Some animals eat only plants but can still be eaten by other animals. What different plant food sources do the students see? **Note:** Children should locate the following: ferns, grasses, flowers, nectar, blackberries, acorns, red berries, roots, thistle seeds, turtles, starlings, evening grosbeaks, blackbirds, butterflies, deer, moles, weasels, toads, mice, hawks, chipmunks, worms, and grubs.

4. After the animals and plants have been listed, have the children write these names on large cards and distribute the cards among the children. To demonstrate how the food chain works, place the children in a semicircle. Ask each represented animal what plant or animal it would eat. Attach a string or length of yarn between the "animal" and the food source (see figure 13.1). Discuss the interrelationships between the plants and animals. After the discussion, cut one of the strings. What effect will it have on the balance of nature? Cut another string. How long before there is no food for any animal?

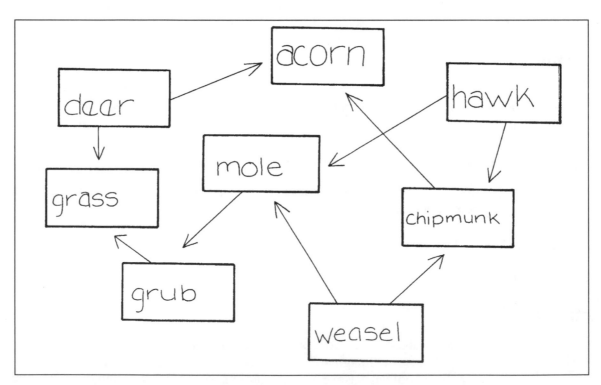

Fig. 13.1. A Forest Food Chain

5. Chipmunks belong to the group of animals known as rodents. Have the children work in the library media center to find information about other rodents, such as chipmunks, rabbits, mice, beavers, woodchucks, squirrels, moles, voles, shrews, and rats. Ask them to find out: What attitudes do people have about these animals? Are they useful to people? **Note:** Rodents have teeth that grow continually, making it necessary for them to gnaw objects.

6. Self-protection is a major concern of animals. Ask the students: What dangers does the chipmunk face? How does he avoid them? Have the children discuss the dangers they might encounter at home, school, or play, and how these can be avoided. Have them make safety posters to illustrate these ideas.

7. Using string or yarn, mark off an area 1 square yard in size. Scatter colored toothpicks in the area. Give a student a specific number of seconds to pick up a certain color toothpick. Repeat this for the other colors. When all have been picked up, discuss these questions with the children: How many of each color are chosen? What can you conclude about the color of the toothpicks and the background? What color is the easiest to see? Which is the most difficult to see?

8. Take the class to visit an outdoor site where a shallow hole can be dug or where an existing hole in the ground exposes soil vertically. Make sketches of the area and take samples of each soil layer to form a profile. If the soil is dry, a profile can be collected in one piece by applying a sheet of clear adhesive paper to the side of the soil cut. With the class, compare the kinds of soil and the objects found in each layer.

9. This book shows many wildflowers and plants. Gather examples of these and have the children observe the flowers, leaves, and stems. A local garden club or extension service agent may be able to provide an identification guide or a general field guide to wildflowers for help naming the specimens.

10. Have an outdoor "animal food hunt." Have the children list the foods that can be found outside (acorns, berries, and so forth). Ask the children where these foods are found.

11. In some locales, forest animals come into peoples' yards and gardens. Ask the students: Why is this so? What types of food do these forest animals eat (for example, lettuce from gardens, seed from bird feeders)?

12. Have each student examine an acorn. Can the nut be opened without implements? Which ones can be peeled? What is the inside part like? What can the student conclude about the chipmunk from these observations?

13. Bring in different types of nuts from the grocery store. Identify and categorize both the outside shells and the inside nuts. The students should be able to match the shell and the nutmeat and describe them; for example, almond shells are smooth, porous, and easily broken, but the rust-colored nut inside has tiny ridges on it. How does the shell act as a protective device for the nuts? Cut the nuts in half and have the students examine the inside, observing the texture, coloring, and so forth. Rub the nut on blotter paper. Ask the students: Why does it leave a spot?

14. The chipmunk's heart beats faster as it flees its predators. A child's heartbeat also increases with activity. Check pulse rates before and after walking or running. Record these scores and use them to calculate averages or make graphs.

15. To observe a student's pulse, push a flat-headed thumbtack into the bottom of a wooden kitchen match and place it on the child's wrist, over the pulse beat. Be sure the arm is resting on a table (see figure 13.2). The match will vibrate as the heart beats. Have the children do this with each other.

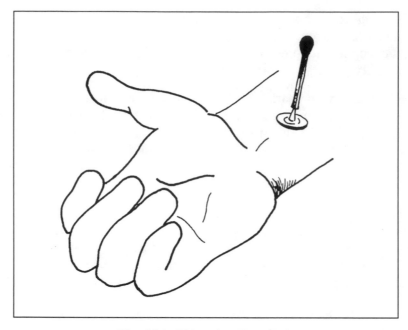

Fig. 13.2. Observing Your Pulse

16. The chipmunk lives underground to keep cool or warm, depending on the season. Ask the students: How do people control the temperature of their rooms? How does the temperature of our rooms change from floor to ceiling or from inside wall to outside wall? **Note:** Thermistor strips simplify temperature measurement.

17. Ask the children: How do people prepare their houses, lawns, gardens, cars, and themselves for the winter (for example, by bringing in lawn furniture, checking storm windows). Have them ask their grandparents what this preparation involved when the grandparents were younger. What activities were involved (for example, canning fruits and vegetables)?

18. "The Chipmunk's Song" by Randall Jarrell also tells of the chipmunk's winter preparation. Have the children read this, then ask them: How is his account similar to Ryder's? How is the environment of the chipmunk different in the two works?

19. The tunnels made by the chipmunk resemble a maze. Have the children use the Maze Maker Home page to create mazes or access www.flint.umich.edu/departments/ITS/crac/maze.forum.html for assistance.

Related Books and References

Ehlert, Lois. *Nuts to You.* New York: Harcourt Brace, 1993.

Jarrell, Randall. "The Chipmunk's Song." In *Piping Down the Valleys Wild: Poetry for the Young of All Ages,* edited by Nancy Larrick. New York: Delacorte Press, 1985.

McCloskey, Robert. *Blueberries for Sal.* New York: Viking, 1987.

Morean, Roger. *Jungle Mazes.* New York: Scholastic, 1998.

Ryder, Joanne. *The Snail's Spell.* New York: Puffin Books, 1988.

Chapter 14

NUTRITION

Gregory, the Terrible Eater
Mitchell Sharmat
New York: Scholastic, 1980 (Reprint: Turtleback, 1985)

Summary

Gregory, the goat, had no taste for boxes and cans and only wanted food such as vegetables and eggs. His parents worried about Gregory's bizarre tastes but a compromise eventually resulted in a balanced diet for everyone concerned.

Science and Content Related Concepts

Nutrition, balanced diet, food requirements (the food pyramid)

Content Related Words

Nutrition, calories, protein, carbohydrates, fats, vitamins, minerals

Activities

1. "Junk food" has different meanings for different people. How does this concept differ for the children and their parents, and Gregory and his parents?

2. Select several food items that the class agrees are "junk food" and several that are considered "good for you." Compare these items by looking at the nutritional information on the packaging.

3. Have the students keep a journal of the snack foods they eat during a week. Are they really "junk foods"? What snacks would be considered more nutritional?

4. Take a survey of class favorites: favorite fruit, vegetable, main course, dessert, after-school snack, and so forth. Also survey the students' least favorite food. Make a bar graph of two or three winners in each category. Compare the list of most and least favorites. Try the same survey with a group of adults, such as parents and teachers. Do you find more similarities or differences? Which group has the most nutritious list?

5. Have the children check labels on common items like baby food, peanut butter, fruit punch, cereal, canned vegetables, and bread to learn what additives have been included during the processing of this food. Ask them: Do these additives enhance nutritional value? Do they help preserve the item? Do they make it look more attractive (waxing cucumbers, dying oranges)?

6. A vitamin pill bottle lists several vitamins and minerals that people need in their diets. Assign each student a vitamin or mineral to research. They should answer these questions: Why is this vitamin or mineral necessary? In what foods is it found? What is the difference in vitamins for infants, children, adults and seniors? Record the information on a large chart.

7. Have a cafeteria worker talk to the class about how the food service staff plans meals to be both nutritious and appealing. Analyze the menu from the school cafeteria for one week and see if each meal contains food from the major food groups. Which meals are most popular? Are they nutritious?

8. Access information on the Internet for the topic "The Food Pyramid." Several different Web sites will appear. The pyramid is divided into these sections:

    a. fats, oils, and sweets: use sparingly

    b. milk, yogurt and cheese: 2–3 servings a day

    c. meat, poultry, fish, dry beans, eggs: 2–3 servings a day

    d. fruit: 2–4 servings a day

    e. vegetables: 3–5 servings a day

    f. bread, cereal, pasta, and rice: 6–11 servings a day

9. After accessing a Web site that will indicate exactly what makes up a "single serving," have the children plan daily menus and include at least the minimum amount suggested for each category. For example, one serving is a cup of milk or yogurt, a slice of bread, or a medium apple.

10. Children may also wish to search for additional information at http://kidshealth.org.

11. Make a simple cookie recipe following the standard directions. Make another batch using three-fourths of the normal amount of sugar, and a third batch using one-half the sugar. Have the students taste the cookies and ask them: Is there a taste difference? What can you infer from this?

12. Grind peanuts in a blender to make peanut butter or buy all natural peanut butter. Have the students compare the taste to a processed commercial peanut butter. Ask them: What ingredients are added to the processed item? Why is this done? Is it necessary?

13. Adults sometimes use various devices to get children to eat. Have the students write or tell about how someone disguised food or played a game to get them to eat. Perhaps the food was arranged in a particular way to make it fun to eat, such as pancakes with Mickey Mouse ears and chocolate chips for a face.

14. Have the children invent a food arrangement, such as a salad, that resembles a particular object. Then have them write down a recipe for that item, including a list of ingredients and the way they are to be cut and arranged. **Note:** Illustrations can add to the effectiveness of this activity.

15. Some of us no longer like a food we once loved. Ask the students to write a story that explains what happened (for example, "Too Many Green Peppers Can Make You Green"). Sometimes we learn to like a food we once disliked. Have the children invent slogans for these (for example, "Don't Squash Squash," "Spinach Is Special").

16. Proper exercise is needed along with proper eating. Have the physical education teacher demonstrate exercises that are beneficial to staying in shape. What are some that would help young people who have a weight problem? Which are best for keeping muscles toned?

17. Ask the students: How many different books on diets can you find in your local bookstore? How many diet aids are available in the local drug store? What promises do they make? Are these products safe?

18. Have the children write and perform a television commercial for a new super-nutritional food. What is the food and how does the company claim it will be beneficial? How do you convince people that they want to buy this product?

19. Discuss anorexia and bulimia—the differences between them, why they occur, what the results can be, and so forth. If possible, interview someone who has overcome an eating disorder or have the school nurse give you details on it.

20. Have the children make a collage of pictures titled "I Am What I Eat." Have them include favorite foods and other items to reflect their personalities.

21. Have the children imagine that it is the twenty-first century. A pill has been invented that contains all the nutrients needed by people. Eating, as we know it, will become obsolete because it will be possible to take a pill instead. Have the children write or discuss their reactions to this. Is taking a food pill preferable or are there reasons for retaining the concept of food that must be prepared and then eaten?

22. "Food for Thought." Have the students ask various people why they think Americans spend so much money on nutritious pet food and worry about what their animals eat, when they themselves often eat non-nutritious "junk food."

23. Are there children's cookbooks in the library media center? Copy recipes for children to try at home.

Related Books and References

dePaola, Tomie. *Pancakes for Breakfast.* New York: Harcourt Brace, 1978.

Ehlert, Lois. *Eating the Alphabet: Fruits and Vegetables from A to Z.* New York: Trumpet Club, 1989.

Hoban, Russell, and Lillian Hoban. *Bread and Jam for Frances.* New York: Scholastic, 1964 (Revised 1993).

Rhoades, Robert E. "The World's Food Supply at Risk." *National Geographic* 179, no. 4 (April 1991): 75–105.

Riley, Linnea. *Mouse Mess.* New York: Scholastic, 1997.

Seuss, Dr. (Theodore Geisel). *Green Eggs and Ham.* New York: Random House, 1960.

Chapter 15

THE EAR AND HEARING

I Have a Sister, My Sister Is Deaf
Jeanne Whitehouse Peterson
New York: Harper & Row, 1984

Summary

A young girl expresses her love for her hearing-impaired younger sister as she describes her sister's many capabilities, as well as her limitations. Family life, recreation, and school are particularly emphasized as we see how a deaf child learns to communicate in a world of hearing people.

Science and Content Related Concepts

Sound, hearing, hearing loss, communication, characteristic sounds

Content Related Words

Vibration, hearing-impaired

Activities

1. Objects must vibrate to produce sound. Have the children observe and describe what happens when they do the following:

    a. Strike a tuning fork and dip it in water.
    b. Sprinkle cereal flakes on a drum, then tap the top.
    c. Stretch a rubber band between their fingers and have someone pluck it; stretch the elastic farther and pluck it again.
    d. Place a hand on the top of a radio that is playing.

2. What materials conduct sound best? Visit the music room and have the students test the different percussion instruments—wood blocks, plastic blocks, a wooden xylophone, a metal xylophone, glasses (empty), glasses (filled with water), plastic drum heads, leather or hide drum heads, metal triangles. The loudest, clearest tone indicates the best conductor of sound. **Note:** Glasses can be filled to varying depths, to produce the notes in a scale.

3. Have the children make a tin can telephone using two empty tin/aluminum cans. They need to remove one end of the can and punch a hole in the other end, then connect the cans with at least 15 feet of string that has been threaded through the hole and knotted inside the can so that it cannot slip out. Let them experiment with the length of the string and how well it conducts sound. Ask them to dictate something over their phones for a friend to copy; was it heard correctly?

4. To encourage students to become aware of the sounds that surround them that they ordinarily might not notice, observe five minutes of silence in class, then ask the students: What sounds are heard? Which ones would probably be blocked out by the normal class activities? Were any of the sounds so loud they would have interrupted a regular class? Did the sounds you make change during the five minutes? Have the children write out their impressions of this time and how they felt. Discuss afterwards how people felt, how much was accomplished, how they could communicate during the silent time.

5. Conduct a class in which no spoken words or sounds are used. **Note:** Write out only those directions that would normally be put on the board.

6. Have two groups of students alternate wearing earplugs for a certain length of time during the day. Ask them: How did you feel when you couldn't hear? What was it like when others couldn't hear? Follow up this experience by listing various ways that students with hearing problems can be accommodated in the regular classroom.

7. Have the children watch a complete television program with the sound turned off. Then have them write down what they think the story was about. Don't let them look in the TV guide for clues or watch a repeat of a show already seen. Have the students compare these impressions with someone who watched and heard the same show. Reverse roles the next day with another show.

8. Ask the students: Would it change the enjoyment of a movie if there were no sound effects or music in the background? Which is more important? What different kinds of music are used in various situations?

9. Have the students study a plastic model or diagram of the ear to see the many parts it contains and trace how the sound travels from the outside environment to the brain. Ask the students: What can happen to impair or destroy the hearing of a person? How can you tell if a baby has a hearing problem?

10. There are many types of hearing problems, which can be diagnosed by various tests. Does the school do a simple, routine hearing check on all students? Discuss these different types of tests. Where else might children go for further testing?

11. Get a pamphlet from an audiology center or ear doctor on the proper care of the ears. Discuss this in class and have the class make posters for a hall display to indicate proper ear care and safety.

12. Have an audiologist demonstrate various kinds of hearing aids and how they work.

13. Discuss with the class: If a child has a serious hearing impairment, could he or she attend special classes locally? Where is the nearest school for the deaf? Is it a boarding school? Which subjects does the school teach?

14. Deaf or hearing-impaired persons can learn to communicate by reading lips, through sign language, and with actual speech. Figure 15.1 shows the signs for two very common phrases. Try to find someone to teach the class other common phrases.

Fig. 15.1. Examples of Sign Language

15. Learn, and teach the children, to sign the numbers from one to twenty, as well as the signs for "plus," "minus," "times," "divided by," and "equals." Have them sign and answer math problems with a partner.

16. There are many organizations that assist the hearing impaired. Search the Internet for such groups and become familiar with their services. Use the keywords "hearing impaired services" or check the Web site at Gaulladet College for the Deaf at http://www.gallaudet.edu/~nicd/184.html.

17.   Play sections of Ludwig von Beethoven's "Symphony No. 9 in D Minor" (the Choral Symphony), which was written after the composer was totally deaf. Ask the students how they think Beethoven was able to do this.

18.   Read a book to the class about Helen Keller, who had multiple physical impairments, including deafness.

Related Books and References

Beethoven, Ludwig von. "Symphony No. 9 in D Minor." Chicago Symphony Orchestra, Sir George Solti, conducting.

Bove, Linda, Thomas Cooke, and Anita Shevitt. *Sign Language ABC with Linda Bove.* New York: Random House, 1985.

Huetinck, Linda. "Physics to Beat the Band." *Science and Children* 32, no. 3 (November/December 1994): 27–30.

Lundell, Marge, and Irene Trivas. *A Girl Named Helen Keller.* Minneapolis, MN: Cartwheel Books, 1995.

Sabin, Francene. *The Courage of Helen Keller.* Mahwah, NJ: Troll Associates, 1998.

Thompson, Stan. "Sizing Up Ears." *Science and Children* 32, no. 8 (May 1995): 19–21.

Wheatley, Jack, and Bonnie Wheatley. "This Science Is Sound." *Science and Children* 33, no. 6 (March 1996): 28–31.

Part III

Earth and Space Science

Chapter 16

TERRITORIAL AND ENVIRONMENTAL OWNERSHIP

It's Mine
Leo Lionni
New York: Alfred A. Knopf, 1986 (Reprint: Turtleback, 1996)

Summary

Three frogs pass the time of day quibbling over who owns the earth, the air, and the water. A natural disaster makes them realize their foolishness and leads to a better understanding of their world.

Science and Content Related Concepts

Ownership of the environment, defense of personal territory, competition for space, air, water, food

Content Related Words

Ecology, environment, territory, competition, cooperation

Activities

1. Frogs belong to a class of animals known as amphibians. Ask the students: What does this word mean? How do amphibians differ from mammals, birds, reptiles, fish, and insects?

2. Divide the class into six groups, one group for each class of animals. Have the children determine what makes their animal group unique. What advantages do their animals have over others? What are their disadvantages? How do the animals move and find food? Do the animals go through stages in becoming adults? **Note:** Have the students use trade books in the library media center as well as encyclopedias for information gathering.

3. Have the students make segmented frogs (see figure 16.1) using construction paper and brass fasteners. Demonstrate how these animals move by manipulating the pieces.

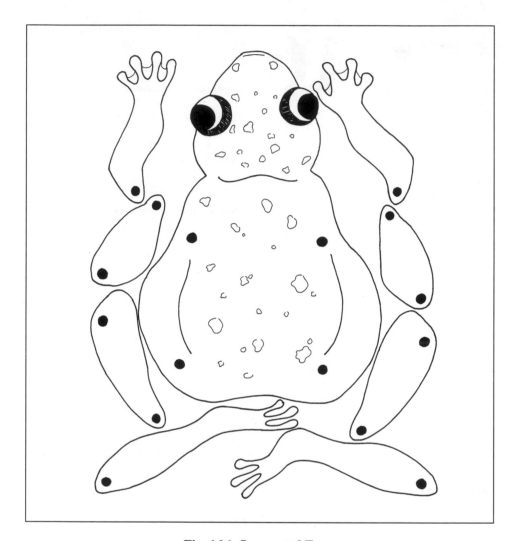

Fig. 16.1. Segmented Frog

4. Have the students dramatize this story by attaching sticks or straws to the backs of the frogs and producing a puppet show. They can make a large mural of a pond environment to serve as the backdrop.

5. Create a wall collage of a beach scene. Have the students make leaves by folding paper in half and cutting shapes; they can also cut them freehand. Compare the symmetry of these two methods. Ask the students: Which is more authentic looking? Do the same with rocks, flowers, butterflies, and so forth. Wallpaper samples and tissue boxes often have excellent designs to use.

6. Have the students make origami frogs using Karen J. Meyer's "Folding Frogs." Ask them to name the different geometric shapes that are utilized as each frog is created. Use these frogs in the beach scene above.

7. Ask the children: What events in the book indicated that a storm was coming? List these in proper sequence. What kinds of storms are most common where we live? What are the consequences of a bad storm?

8. There are many kinds of beaches in the world (sandy, rocky, pebbly, swampy, mangrove). Ask the children to describe the differences between these beaches. How are they used by people? The library media specialist may be able to find pictures of various beaches for a display.

9. Divide the room into three groups of children and give each group one unique item to "control"—the water fountain, the art supplies, the reading corner. Have the children role play the characters in the book who refused to share. Discuss the problems that arise from this "monopoly" of items and how children feel about the situation.

10. Have the children write a sequel to the book. The frogs have learned to stop arguing and know they must share the environment. How do they spend their time now? What values do they have?

11. As a class, debate who "owns" outer space or the ocean floor. How is it decided which nation can build a space station, or who can fish in the St. George's Banks? Have the children represent various countries—the superpowers, developing nations, poor countries with large populations, small technologically advanced nations. What conclusions can be drawn? What is the basis for these decisions?

12. It is not possible to "buy" the air or the water, but people can buy land. Have the library media specialist save copies of the classified section of several newspapers to see what kind of land can be purchased (house lots, farm acreage, shore property, and so forth). Do the children live in an area where one can buy an island? How do the ads indicate the size of the piece of land? How much does one acre of land cost in the city? In the country? At a beach?

13. States have areas that are protected by law from being developed (for example, state forest lands). Display the tourist map published by your state and ask the children to locate the various kinds of protected areas. Why are these areas protected? What activities can take place there? Have the class visit an area or invite someone in to talk about a nearby preserve.

14. Have the children invent an island and indicate its geographical features. Ask them to determine: What resources must exist to support human or animal life? Could inhabitants be self-sufficient? How would the island change as the population grew? **Note:** *Rotten Island* by William Steig portrays the problem of overpopulation of an island.

15. Play "King of the Mountain" during recess. How does this relate to the story?

16. Ask the children: How big was the frogs' island? As large as the gymnasium? The school? The local mall? To measure the area of a room in square feet, have the children multiply the length of the room by the width. They can check their answers using calculators. Have them measure other rooms in the school or calculate the size of outside areas. Areas larger than 43,560 square feet are measured in acres.

17. The frogs learned to share the land, the water, and the air. This sharing is part of the philosophy of the Nature Conservancy. Have students learn about this group on the Internet at http://www.tnc.org.

18. Have the children pantomime some of the action words from the story—croak, defy, subside, huddle, recognize, tremble, argue, quarrel, quibble, yell, shout, scream, bicker, hop, cry, rumble, cling, disappear.

19. See if the library media center has any of the Frog and Toad series by Arnold Lobel. These are tales of friendship and show a different relationship between the animals.

Related Books and References

Czerniak, Charlene M., and Linda D. Penn. "Crossing the Curriculum with Frogs." *Science and Children* 33, no. 5 (February 1996): 28–31.

Lobel, Arnold. *Frog and Toad.* New York: Harper Trophy, 1979.

MacDonald, Golden. *The Little Island.* New York: Doubleday, 1946 (Reprint: Turtleback, 1993).

Meyer, Karen J. "Folding Frogs." *Science and Children* 30, no. 5 (February 1991): 27–29.

Steig William. *Rotten Island.* Boston: Godine, 1969.

Zim, Herbert S., and Hobart M. Smith. *Reptiles and Amphibians: A Golden Guide.* New York: Golden Press, 1987.

Chapter 17

VOLCANOES

Hill of Fire
Thomas P. Lewis
New York: Harper & Row, 1971 (Reprint: Turtleback, 1983)

Summary

Life in the small Mexican village was quiet and peaceful until the day Pablo's father's plow sank into a hole in the cornfield. Smoke and fire rose from the earth and soon a mountain-sized volcano had been formed. Hot lava and ash poured forth, destroying the tiny village and forcing the peasants to seek safety away from El Monstruo.

Science and Content Related Concepts

Volcanic eruptions, Mexican village life and technology, multiculturalism

Content Related Words

Eruption, lava, ash, magma, crater, amigo, fiesta, El Monstruo, continental drift, reconstruction

Activities

1. *Eruptions of Mount St. Helens: Past, Present and Future* is an excellent pamphlet available from the Superintendent of Documents, U.S. Government Printing Office, Mail Stop SSOP, Washington, DC 20402-9328, or call the USGS Information Services at 303-202-4700. Several weeks before beginning the unit, have children arrange to receive this reference.

2. Have students make a list of active volcanoes using the *World Almanac*. Tally these by country. A color-coded bar graph can be used to visualize this information.

3. A list of major volcanic eruptions over hundreds of years can be found in the *World Almanac.* Have the students arrange these events in descending order from most destructive to least destructive (that is, in terms of number of casualties). Ask the students to find out: When and where did these eruptions occur? Are any U.S. volcanoes named? Is Paricutin on the list?

4. Indicate the location of these volcanoes with pushpins or sticky dots on a world map. Many of the volcanoes exist around the Pacific Rim and are often referred to as the "Ring of Fire." Ask the students: What does this mean? How do scientists describe the land near these volcanoes?

5. The earth's continents were once joined. Have the students make silhouette cutouts of the continents and see how they probably fit together in the past. Ask them: Why are they separate now? What effect did the movement have on animals and plants? What is the meaning of the term "continental drift?" **Note:** The edges of the earth's plates are thinner than the rest of the area of the plate. Volcanoes can emerge more easily. This is responsible for the "Ring of Fire" surrounding the Pacific Ocean.

6. Make a display of pictures of famous volcanoes such as Mount Fuji in Japan and Mount Baker in Washington State. Many Pacific islands are the tops of inactive volcanoes. Ask the students: What characteristic features do these volcanoes have in common? **Note:** Check the library media center for photos from calendars, travel magazines, and so forth.

7. The most recent major volcanic eruption in the continental United States was Mount St. Helens on May 18, 1980. Locate news articles about this event in newspapers and magazines in the library media center or through interlibrary loan. Compare these to *National Geographic* articles written the year after the eruption and discuss the differences with the children.

8. Have the students locate and research Paricutin volcano in the Mexican state of Michoacan. **Note:** The *Seattle Times* published a story about Paricutin called "Once Upon a Volcano." Access this at http://archives.seattletimes.com/cgi-bin/texis/web/vortex/display?storyID=386a420a16+query=Paricutin.

9. Show a film or video of a volcanic eruption. Identify the important parts of the volcano (see figure 17.1). Ask the students: What materials come forth from the volcano? What is their ultimate source? When a volcano erupts, what is the major cause of destruction to property, and to human and animal life? **Note:** For free educational catalogs listing videos on this topic, access National Geographic's Web site at http://www.ngstore.com/ngstore/ngsstore.htm. Another reference source on volcanoes is http://www.usgs.gov/education/learnweb/volcano/htm.

10. Have the students make a bulletin board display showing a cutout section of the earth, from the surface to the core. They should label the different layers (see figure 17.2) and describe them (for example, solid, hot).

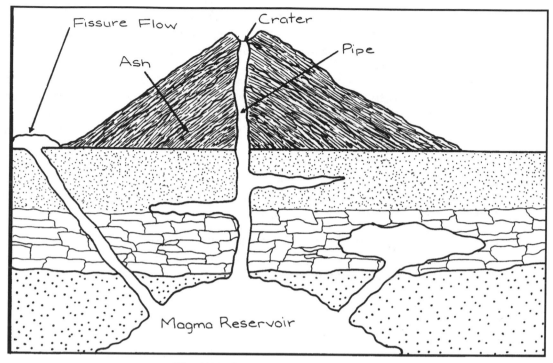

Fig. 17.1. Cross-section of a Volcano

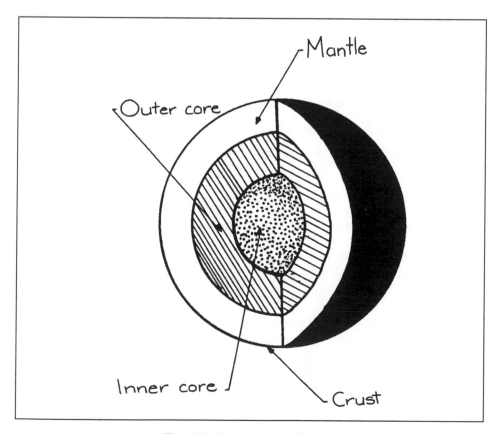

Fig. 17.2. Layers of the Earth

11.   Many volcanic eruptions can be predicted. Have the students investigate the work and tools of a seismologist. Ask them: What is the Richter scale? What is a fault? Can you give an example of a fault in the United States?

12.   Have the children draw a series of pictures showing the formation of the volcano in *Hill of Fire* as it progressed from a hole in the field until the eruption was over. They should label and sequence these events. Or have each child make a series of drawings of the changing volcano on small paper, staple them, then flip the pages fast like a cartoon. Does the volcano appear to grow?

13.   Have the children use the school database or the card catalog in the library media center to locate books on rural life in Mexico. Compare life in the Mexican village to life in the United States. This can be done using a comparison word chart or by using drawings.

14.   Have the children pretend that they are visiting this Mexican town before the explosion. Have them write a postcard telling what they like best about life in the town and what is most difficult or unfamiliar to them.

15.   Have a breakfast similar to that which the people in the story had.

Soft Tortillas

1 ½ cups milk	1 teaspoon salt
3 eggs	1 cup cornmeal (white or yellow)
1 cup regular flour	2 tablespoons melted butter or margarine

Beat milk and eggs together in bowl. Sift in flour and salt; stir in cornmeal and melted butter. Beat until smooth. Pour into a hot, greased 7-inch frying pan, using ¼ cup batter for each tortilla. Tip the pan so batter spreads evenly; fry until top appears dry, then flip and brown on other side. Makes 12 tortillas.

---

16.   Have the children pretend to be on-the-spot reporters for the "Nightly News." They are at the site of the volcanic explosion. Have them write out news stories, feature stories, and interviews that might be sent back to the network.

17.   Have the children try to write acrostics using an important word from the story (such as the following) as a base.

Violent	Cone-shaped	Ominous
Overflowing	Ashes	
Lava	Noise	

The following acrostic uses phrases about the explosion and its aftermath.

Every day it grew
Lava came from the earth
Molten rock shot into the air
Overflowing the village
Nothing was spared
Smoke and ashes everywhere
Thunderous shaking
Rumbling inside the earth
Until the village was gone
Only the hill of fire remained

18. Visit the local music store to obtain works that could be heard at a Mexican festival. What sights and activities do the students imagine as they listen to this music?

19. Play George Frederic Handel's "Music for the Royal Fireworks" to give the students an impression of how music conveys the concept of explosion.

Related Books and References

Cole, Joanna. *The Magic School Bus Blows Its Top.* New York: Scholastic, 1996.

———. *The Magic School Bus Inside the Earth.* New York: Scholastic, 1988.

DuBois, William Pene. *The Twenty-One Balloons.* New York: Dell, 1984. (Chapter 10 describes the explosion of Krakatoa.)

Findley, Rowe. "Mount St. Helens." *National Geographic* 159, no. 1 (January 1981): 640–653.

———. "Mount St. Helens Aftermath." *National Geographic* 160, no. 6 (December 1981): 713–733.

Grove, Noel. "Volcanoes: Crucibles of Creation." *National Geographic* 182, no. 6 (December 1992): 5–41.

Handel, George Frederic. "Music for the Royal Fireworks." The English Consort, Trevor Pinnock, conducting.

Lauber, Patricia. *Volcano: The Eruption and Healing of Mount St. Helens.* New York: Bradbury Press, 1986.

Thompson, Susan A., and Keith S. Thompson. "Volcanos in the Classroom—An Explosive Learning Experience." *Science and Children* 33, no. 6 (March 1996): 16–19.

Chapter 18

ROCKS

Everybody Needs a Rock
Byrd Baylor
New York: Charles Scribner, 1974 (Reprint: Turtleback, 1987)

Summary

No matter who you are, you need a rock. However, there are ten rules to follow in finding the one that is perfect for you.

Science and Content Related Concepts

Categories of rocks, characteristics of rocks, uses of rocks, landforms

Content Related Words

Category, characteristic, texture, crystal, rock cut, erosion, glacier, fossil

Activities

1. Discuss the tools and procedures students would use to make a detailed observation of a rock.

2. Bring in rocks and pebbles of varying sizes, shapes, and colors. Spread them on a large table and have the children classify them. Don't give any specific directions; see what characteristics they discover (size, geometric shape, color, texture, and so forth). Mix the rocks around and have the students perform the same task one or two more times. Have the rocks been shifted to other categories? What criterion was used to decide each time?

3. Dip the rocks into water. Ask the students: How does this change the qualities that were observed? Do the rocks have an odor?

4. Have children bring in rocks that they have collected from their local area or from other places they have visited. Repeat the preceding activities.

5. Have the students observe the rocks using a hand lens. Ask them: How do the descriptive qualities change? Are there more possible categories for comparison?

6. Have each child choose one rock and describe its characteristics so that a friend could select it from an array of rocks. Emphasize using terms from the classification exercises above.

7. Have each student select and adopt a favorite "pet" rock from the rocks studied in class, then write a description of all the outstanding qualities this rock possesses and determine its purpose (for example, doorstop, paperweight). The rock may be decorated as an animate or inanimate object.

8. Select rocks with cracks in them. Freeze them in water, then break them with a hammer. Ask the students what they observe. Do the rocks all break easily and evenly? Ask the students: What does this tell you about the effects of natural forces on rocks? **Note:** Rocks should be wrapped in a heavy bag before striking them and safety goggles must be worn by the person in charge.

9. Ask the children: In what other ways does nature change rocks (for example, erosion, glaciers)? Are there examples of these forces in the local vicinity? Are pictures available that show the results of these forces?

10. *Lapidary* refers to how rocks can be cut and polished to make jewelry. Have the students use a rock tumbler and note how the appearance of the rock changes. What additional characteristics are seen? Locate lapidary supply houses such as the one at http://www.acelapidary.com.

11. Rocks serve many purposes for both people and animals (for example, hiding places for animals, fences, building materials). Have the children make a chart indicating these uses and bring in magazine pictures to illustrate them.

12. Have the children look at the school and other large buildings in the area. Ask the children: Were they built from stone? How many different kinds of stone were used? Was stone used for a purpose other than decoration? Are there fossils in the stone?

13. Early cultures used stones as tools and weapons. If possible, visit a museum display that illustrates this.

14. Have students work in pairs to make a stone artifact (see figure 18.1). They should first decide the purpose for the implement and the materials required to make it, then select a stone and construct the actual item. Do not let them use modern technology. **Note:** It might be necessary to substitute items such as twine for leather strips, if the original materials are not available.

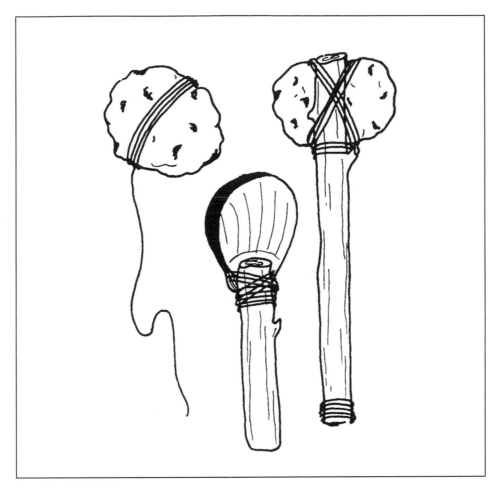

Fig. 18.1. Stone Artifacts

15.   Study a rock cut near the school, at a building site, or in a photo (see figure 18.2). What do the students observe? What do they think the layers indicate? Why are some layers tipped or broken?

16.   Are there fossils in the local area? Borrow or buy some samples and bring them into class. Ask the students: What is a fossil? What objects can be fossilized? What do fossils tell about an area? **Note:** A book on the geology of the state may be obtained from the local bookstore or from the library media center to serve as a reference guide.

17.   The United States is a land of varied landforms—mesas, buttes, mountains, and many others. These are different rock formations. Show a video or film that illustrates different areas of the country. Compare the landforms. Ask the students which are most common in your local area. **Note:** You can get videos of this type from the National Geographic Society; the Society's Web site for catalogs is http://www.ngstore.com/ngstore/ngstore.htm.

18.   Find photos of famous natural and carved rocks, such as the Natural Bridge (Virginia), Mount Rushmore (South Dakota), and Half Dome (California). United States travel books or atlases may also include photos of these formations. The library media center may have a file of pictures that can be borrowed for a bulletin board display.

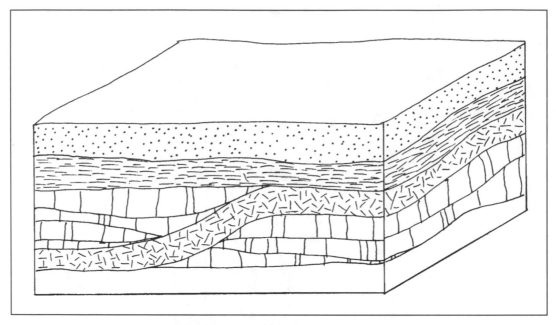

Fig. 18.2. Rock Types and Layering

19. Measure the volume of a rock using a procedure called displacement of water. Fill a glass measuring container with a specific amount of water. Immerse the rock in the water and note the change in the level of the liquid. The difference between the first and second water-level readings will indicate the volume of water displaced by the rock. Explain to the students that this method can be of use around the home to measure the volume of other solid objects such as vegetable shortening. **Note:** The principle of water displacement can be used to explain how water can be conserved by putting a brick in the toilet tank.

Related Books and References

Baylor, Byrd. *If You Are a Hunter of Fossils.* New York: Aladdin Paperbacks, 1984.

Carlson, Kenneth W. "Pieces of the Past." *Science Scope* 17, no. 5 (February 1994): 38–39.

Cole, Joanna. *The Magic School Bus Inside the Earth.* New York: Scholastic, 1986.

Shaw, Edward J., Betty Crocker, and Barb Reed. "Chipping Away at Fossils." *Science Scope* 14, no.2 (October 1990): 30–32.

Shewell, John. "Focus on the Rock." *Science and Children* 31, no. 6 (March 1994): 28–29.

Thompson, Ada. *National Aubudon Society Field Guide to North American Fossils.* New York: Alfred A. Knopf, 1982.

Chapter 19

SOIL

The Gift of the Tree
Alvin Tresselt
New York: Lothrop, Lee & Shepard, 1972

(Originally published as *The Dead Tree*. New York: Parents' Magazine Press, 1972.)

Summary

The life cycle of the oak tree is examined as the tree decomposes over many seasons. Still, the tree remains as a home for animals and becomes a source of new soil.

Science and Content Related Concepts

Forest ecology, soil composition, soil properties, seasons, animal homes, life cycle of the tree

Content Related Words

Erosion, decomposition, weathering, loam, fungus, mold

Activities

1. Ask the students: What is "the gift of the tree?" To whom is this gift valuable? What is the value that it has? Have the children produce a skit telling the story of the oak tree:

    Part I, The Healthy Tree: description of the tree, the animals that live in it, how the tree helps the forest creatures

    Part II, The Aging Tree: description of the tree, forces of nature, the animals that live in the tree

    Part III, The Renewing Tree: description of the "tree," decomposition process, the animals that live in the "tree," the great oak returns to the earth.

2. Obtain several soil samples (about 2 cups each) from various locations around your town. Also buy a small amount of potting soil, sand, topsoil, and peat moss. Put a sample of each on a plate and have the students compare their color, odor, texture, moisture, presence of other particles, and so forth. Have the children observe each sample with a hand lens or under a microscope. What other materials do they see in the soil?

3. Have students write descriptions of each soil sample. Compare these observations. Are there differences within each sample? Leave a small portion of each sample out in the air. What happens? Contrast this to the samples that have been put back into a sealed container or bag.

4. Soil is porous; that is, water will run through it. Line several funnels with a piece of coffee filter paper and put a different kind of soil in each one. Add the same amount of water to each sample and see which one allows the water to penetrate first. Which is last? Make a chart indicating the time needed for the water to filter through each sample, and put them in order by type. **Note:** Make a funnel by cutting the open end off a 2- or 3-liter soda pop bottle. (See figure 19.1.)

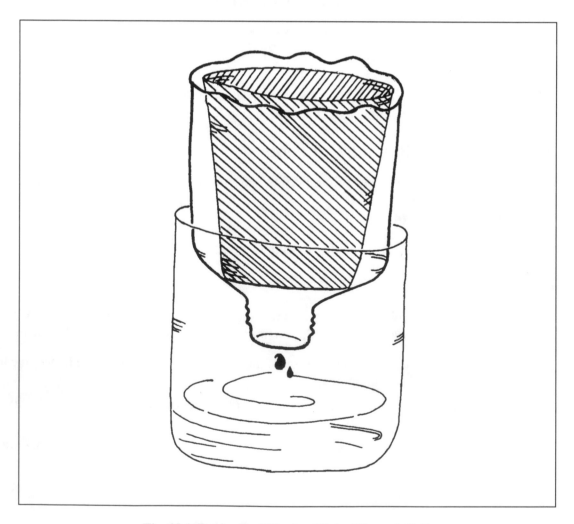

Fig. 19.1. Device for Filtering Water Through Soil

5. Mix several different soil samples with various sized stones or pebbles in a quart jar of water and shake it. Ask the students to predict which objects will be at the bottom of the jar when the materials settle. Ask them: Which items will be in each of the other layers? What does this tell us about the samples?

6. Find a place where the earth has been cut exposing several layers of soil, or dig down a couple of feet and observe the layers. Point out to the students the changes in color, texture, content, and thickness of layers. Soil samples can be preserved by scattering them onto small glue-lined containers such as plastic lids from food containers. Have the students do this with a sample from every layer and mount them in order on posterboard to make a soil profile. Have them label the soil type and characteristics of each sample.

7. Have the students study a chart or overhead transparency of a soil profile (see figure 19.2). Ask them: What types of things are found under the ground? How do these change with increasing depth? How do living plants and animals contribute to the composition of the soil? Compare the profile in the book to the one made by the students in item 6. **Note:** The soil profile is also depicted in Joanne Ryder's *Chipmunk Song*.

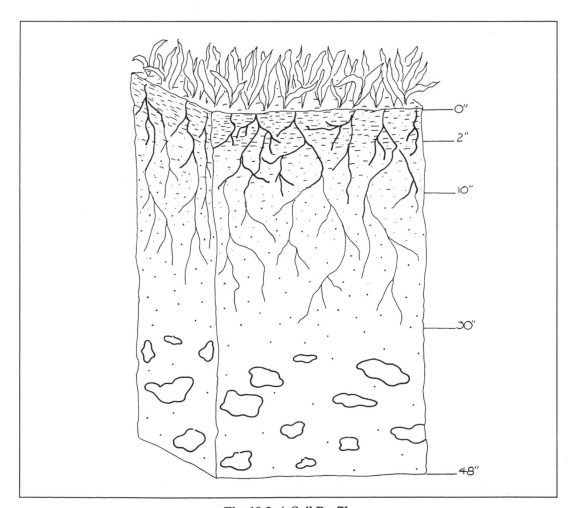

Fig. 19.2. A Soil Profile

8. Have the children write to friends in other parts of the country asking them for a small sample of a typical soil from their area, such as red clay from Georgia, sandy soil from Florida, or topsoil from Iowa. Have the students compare the physical qualities of the samples to the local soil and try to predict what effects differences have on the lives of the people, such as which crops can be grown or the type of drainage provided by the soil.

9. Soil loses its nutrients after a period of use. Ask the students: How do farmers renew the nutrients in their fields? How are home flower gardens renewed? If possible, arrange for a farmer or a home gardener to share his or her experiences with the class.

10. The tree in the book is an oak tree. There are many other trees commonly found in the United States. Have each child select a tree and find out two or three interesting facts about that tree. These can be compiled into a bulletin board display. Possibilities include maple, birch, linden, ash, sycamore, chestnut, tulip, beech, cherry, apple, magnolia, dogwood, willow, aspen, elm, poplar, walnut, locust, hickory, flowering crab, and gum. Ask the students what varieties of trees are located near the school or the nearest park area.

11. Animals live under the soil or in trees during winter because these places have insulating qualities to keep the animals warm. To simulate this activity, make a "Warm Fuzzy" to use in the following insulation experiment. The objective of the activity is to make a home that will keep the "Fuzzy" as warm as possible. Use a thermometer to measure the temperature in the "home." The insulating qualities are tested by measuring the temperature inside the container on a cold day. In warmer climates the activity is reversed, using insulation to keep the "Fuzzy" cool. Use plastic, paper, Styrofoam, ceramics, stoneware, wool, cotton, aluminum foil, plastic wrap, and so forth. **Note:** A "Warm Fuzzy" is a pom-pom with two moveable plastic eyes attached to it. These materials can be found in a craft shop.

12. Have the children apply their acquired knowledge of insulation to their own lives. Ask them: Which material keeps a cup of coffee or hot chocolate warm for the longest time? How do we insulate our homes against the cold or the heat? How do we insulate ourselves to go out on a cold day? How do we guard against the food in the picnic basket spoiling in the heat? Discuss other situations in which items must be kept cool or warm.

13. Bring in a large shovelful of the covering of the forest floor. What items do students find? Are there any living organisms? What does this indicate about soil formation?

14. Soil can be made in the classroom. Place a large scoop of rotting tree matter, wet leaves, and soil into a box about 1 foot square in size. Biodegradable materials such as grasses, plants, twigs, acorns, berries, worms, small insects, fungi, mold, and apple pieces may be added. Have the students mix the items, then place the box in a warm corner of the room and keep the mixture moist. Be sure to have the students add earthworms or night crawlers. These animals will digest the organic matter in the box and it will pass through their bodies to become an element of the soil. After several weeks, check the decomposition process. What is taking place in the box? Is there evidence of "new" soil being made?

15. To learn more about soil, have the students access the National Resources Conservation Service, which is part of the U.S. Department of Agriculture. The Web site is http://www2.NRCS.USDA.gov/default.htm.

16. A situation parallel to that in *The Gift of the Tree* occurs in *Cactus Hotel* by Brenda Guiberson. A giant saguaro cactus is home to many animals, but eventually it ages, falls to the ground, and is returned to the soil. Have the class compare these two books.

17. Alvin Tresselt is the author of many books on nature, including *Hide and Seek Fog*. Have the students read some of his other books and compare the texts. **Note:** Mr. Tresselt does not illustrate his books.

Related Books and References

Fields, Shirley Ellis. "Life in a Teaspoon of Soil." *Science Scope* 16, no. 5 (February 1993): 16–18.

Guiberson, Brenda. *Cactus Hotel.* New York: Henry Holt, 1991.

Romanova, Natalia. *Once There Was a Tree.* New York: Dial Books, 1985.

Ryder, Joanne. *Chipmunk Song.* New York: E. P. Dutton, 1987.

Tresselt, Alvin. *Hide and Seek Fog.* New York: Lothrop, Lee & Shepard, 1965 (Reprint: William Morrow, 1987).

Udry, Janice. *A Tree Is Nice.* New York: Harper & Row, 1956.

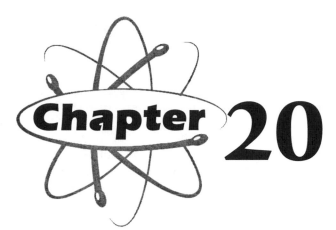

Chapter 20

LIGHTHOUSES AND OCEANS

Keep the Lights Burning, Abbie
Peter and Connie Roop
Minneapolis, Carolrhoda Books, 1985 (Reprint: Turtleback, 1987)

(Originally published as *Abby Burgess: Lighthouse Heroine* by Dorothy Jones and
Ruth Sargent. Camden, Maine: Down East Press, 1969.)

Summary

When her father goes ashore for supplies, Abbie is left in charge of her family and the lighthouse on Matinicus Rock, Maine. Her determination, dedication, and hard work enable her to keep the lamps lit throughout a storm that rages for nearly a month. **Note:** This event took place in January 1856 and is recorded in Abbie's own journals and elsewhere.

Science and Content Related Concepts

Physical oceanography, lighthouses, tides, storms, navigation

Content Related Words

Lighthouse, wicks, oil lamp, concave lens, hurricane, puffin

Activities

1. Have the students locate Matinicus Rock and Matinicus Island off the coast of Maine. Ask them: What body of water surrounds them? Why is there a lighthouse there? What are the nearest mainland towns? How many miles away are they? **Note:** Contact the Maine Publicity Bureau at 207-636-0363 for materials about this area.

2. Have the children make a list of essential items that Papa would need to bring back from town. Remind them that this is a solid rock island, so everything must be carried in on a boat. Only chickens can be kept on the island.

3. Have the students compare the pictures of Abbie's room and her clothes to the items found in their rooms and the way they dress. What everyday essentials in their lives were unknown to Abbie?

4. A lightkeeper's family stayed on the lighthouse rock or island for months at a time. Discuss with the students how they would feel if their houses were suddenly surrounded by miles of open ocean and they were to be confined there for six months. Also assume that they will no longer have electricity, running water, and other modern conveniences. What would life be like?

5. The cutaway diagram of Abbie's lighthouse (see figure 20.1) shows both work rooms and living areas. Have the children build a model lighthouse using paper tubing, shoeboxes, cardboard, and the like. **Note:** Lighthouses can be located on a rock, on a small island, or on the shore near the ocean.

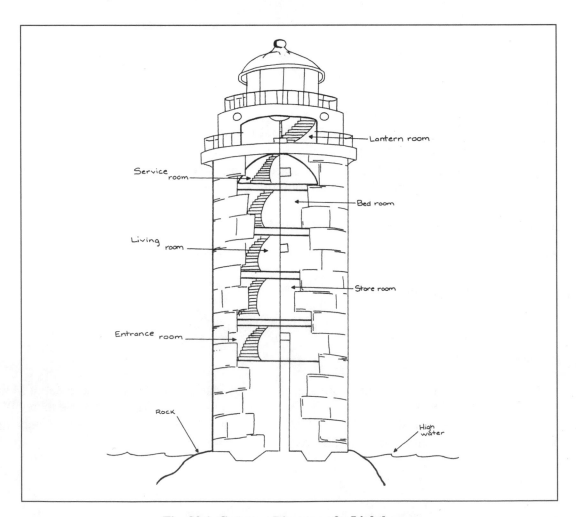

Fig. 20.1. Cutaway Diagram of a Lighthouse

6. To show the effect of the ocean tides on land and objects, place a lighthouse model on rocks piled in a large wash basin. Add water to show that the land disappears from view as the tide comes in. Scoop out water to simulate the tide going out. Tie a small toy boat close to the lighthouse. Ask the students: What happens as the tide comes in and goes out? How do tides affect the lives of the people on these small islands?

7. Abbie tended lamps that burned whale oil. Ask the students what would happen to the oil as the temperature dropped. To simulate this situation, put small amounts of every-day oil (for example, motor oil, salad oil, or lamp oil) into a refrigerator and some into a freezer. What do the students observe when these are examined? Ask them how this would complicate the process of filling the lamps. How could Abbie solve the problem?

8. Bring in a kerosene lantern or decorative oil lamp for the students to examine. Ask them: What parts does it have? What is the difference in brightness when you place the glass chimney over the burning wick? What happens to the chimney after several hours of burning? How can you restore the brightness?

9. To increase the effectiveness of the lighthouse lamps, a concave lens was placed be-hind the lamps to reflect light. Place a magnifying makeup mirror behind a burning candle or lamp. Ask the students what the result is. **Note:** Use a darkened room to heighten the effect.

10. The force of the wind at sea is measured in knots. A knot, or 1 nautical mile per hour, is about 6,000 feet, which is slightly longer than a land mile. The following chart shows the wind speeds triggering various storm advisories by the National Weather Bureau:

18-33 knots	Hazardous wind and wave conditions
34-47 knots	Gale-force winds
over 48 knots	Storm conditions
over 64 knots	Hurricane conditions

    Have the students compare these speeds to driving speeds such as 25 mph city traffic, 55 mph highway speed, and 65 mph limited-access highway speed. Are there any other speeds they could use for comparison?

11. The sea water froze on the windows of the lighthouse. Have the students figure out how cold it may have been on Matinicus Rock, using the freezing point for this water and the speed of the hurricane wind. A wind chill chart in the *World Almanac* will assist them. **Note:** Sea water freezes at about 10 degrees Fahrenheit.

12. Have the children pretend that they are Abbie. Ask them to write journal entries from various times during the story, such as soon after Papa leaves, when the storm begins, when Abbie lights the lamps for the first time and saves the chickens, when the sup-plies are nearly gone and she begins to despair, and when Papa returns. Ask the library media specialist to get a copy of the original Jones and Sargent book about Abbie or some of her actual journal writings through interlibrary loan. **Note:** One account of Abbie's life is in *Women Who Kept the Lights* by Mary Louise Clifford and J. Candace Clifford.

13. If there had been an award for heroism in 1856, Abbie would have been an excellent candidate. Ask the children to write an essay or speech nominating her for this honor. Remind them to be sure to explain what she did and why they think she deserves to win.

14. Ask the students: If the weather bureau predicted that a very bad storm would hit your town during the night, what precautions would you take? How would you cope with an interruption in electrical or water service? In what part of the house is it best to stay? What supplies would you keep on hand?

15. Papa's boat was called *The Puffin*. The puffin is a rare bird that lives in only a few places, one being Matinicus Island, Maine. Have the students look up "puffins" in the library media center and learn about this nearly extinct species of bird. They may also access the Internet at http://www.aqua.org/animals/species/seepuffin.html.

16. Have the students design a T-shirt, bumper sticker, or banner to publicize the need to protect puffins because their existence is endangered.

17. Information on lighthouses can be obtained from the Lighthouse Preservation Society, 4 Middle Street, Newburyport, MA 01950, 1-800-727 BEAM, or from the following Web site: http://www.maine.com/lights/lps.htm. Have the students acquire this information for reference.

18. There are still many lighthouses in Maine. On a road map, locate some of the most popular:

> West Quoddy Head Light—Lubec
> Bass Harbor Light—Mt. Desert Island
> Rockland Breakwater Light—Rockland
> Owls Head Light—Rockland
> Pemaquid Point—Pemaquid Point
> Portland Head Light—Portland
> Cape Elizabeth (Two Lights)—Cape Elizabeth
> Nubble Light—Cape Neddick
> Matinicus Rock Light—Matinicus Rock
> Monhegan Island Light—Monhegan Island

These are just some of the working lights in Maine. Ask the students: Why are there so many? How are modern lighthouses different from those of nineteenth-century Maine in terms of equipment, personnel, the physical shape of the building, and so forth? Other areas of the country have working lighthouses (for example the Great Lakes and Florida). Ask the students: How are these like the Maine lighthouses? How are they different?

19. Have the students find pictures of lighthouses in magazine ads, photography ads, and calendars and make a display of them. Ask them to identify the similarities and differences between the lighthouses. **Note:** A very well-known light is the Portland Head Light in Maine, which was commissioned by George Washington as the first lighthouse in the United States.

20. To pass the long hours, Abbie's family probably sang songs of the sea and its sailors. Check the library media center for books or records of sailing songs or sea chanteys.

Related Books and References

Clifford, Mary Louise, and J. Candace Clifford. *Women Who Kept the Lights.* Williamsburg, VA: Cypress Communications, 1993.

Maine Publicity Bureau, 97 Winthrop Street, Hallowell, ME 04347. 207-623-0363.

McCloskey, Robert. *Time of Wonder.* New York: Viking, 1957 (Reprint: Turtleback, 1989).

Oleszewski, Wes. *Great Lakes Lighthouses: American and Canadian.* Gwinn, MI: Avery Color Studios, 1998.

Tresselt, Alvin. *Hide and Seek Fog.* New York: Lothrop, Lee & Shepard, 1965 (Reprint: William Morrow, 1987).

Chapter 21

MUSSELS AND ARCTIC LIFE

The Very Last First Time
Jan Andrews
New York: Macmillan, 1986

Summary

Eva was very excited, yet apprehensive, about her first experience walking alone under the ice on the bottom of the sea. She had never gathered mussels without her mother's help, but she overcame many difficulties and problems to return with a full pan of food.

Science and Content Related Concepts

Arctic life, oceans, tides, length of day, sea life

Content Related Words

Mussels, Arctic, tide, tundra, Inuit

Activities

1. Illustrations are a very important part of children's books. Before reading this book, have students study the cover. What predictions can they make about the life and environment of this little girl?

2. Eva's way of life is portrayed through the illustrations as well as through the words. Assign a small group of students to each of the first four pictures in the book. List all the inferences they can make about Eva's way of life from these illustrations.

3. Have the groups present their findings. As items are listed, put them on a chart indicating what is similar to modern U.S. life (Cornflakes) and what is generally unfamiliar (an animal skin drying in the yard).

4. In *The Very Last First Time,* several sea animals are pictured on the ocean floor. Have the students identify them and learn if they are edible. Ask them what other shellfish people eat. Have the students look at a fish store display or consult a cookbook from the library media center for more information.

5. Obtain some blue mussels from a seafood store, preferably while they are still held together by bissell threads. After the children have examined the outside of the mussels, scrub them under running water using a small utility brush. Pull off any remaining threads. Throw away any open shells, unless they close as you tap them. Put the mussels in a pan with a small amount of water, cover, and steam them for five or six minutes. Drain and remove the mussels from the shells. Serve them to the students with melted butter, if desired. Mussels can also be dipped in batter and deep-fried or made into chowder.

6. Have the students examine the blue mussel shell. Ask them: What makes it unique? How is it similar to or different from other shells you have seen? Have the children compare it with other shells if possible.

7. Mussels can be grown commercially in contained areas near the shoreline of the ocean. For more information on this project, have some students write to the Marine Advisory Service, Coburn Hall, University of Maine, Orono, ME 04469.

8. Mussel shells can be used in art projects. Drill small holes in them to make mobiles. Have the children paint pictures on them or scratch designs on them in the manner of scrimshaw art, which was once done on whalebone. After the design has been scratched in, the students may paint the area with India ink. They should leave the ink on for a minute, then wipe it off.

9. Eva is an Inuit. These people live in the Arctic regions of the North American continent. Ask the students to identify which countries, provinces, territories, and states this includes? **Note:** Inuits were formerly known as Eskimos.

10. Have the students find words from the story that fit the blanks next to Eva's name in figure 21.1. (Answer key is in appendix.)

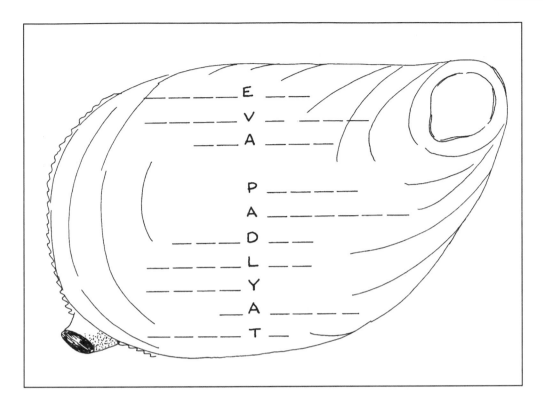

Fig. 21.1. Mussel Word Ladder

Clues:

    a.   These people live in an isolated area near the Arctic Circle.

    b.   These edible sea creatures have blue-black shells and attach themselves to rocks on the ocean floor.

    c.   Eva's only means of light came from this source.

    d.   These sea animals look more like beautiful moving flowers.

    e.   This heavy jacket provides warmth in a cold climate.

    f.   This country is one of the largest in size, but very small in population.

    g.   Eva walked under the ice of this body of water.

    h.   The ocean water would have this taste.

    i.   The soil is frozen most of the year in this vast, treeless area.

    j.   Many forms of marine plants and animals can be found here.

11.   Eva has many different emotions throughout the book. Ask the children to think of adjectives to describe her (excited, scared, clumsy). Have them write Eva's name vertically as in the puzzle, then try to fit these words around the letters of her name. Or have them think of words that begin with the 10 letters of her name so that they all fit on one side of her name.

12. Have the students find the province of Quebec in northeastern Canada on the globe. Also have them locate Ungava Bay (south of Baffin Island), then find the Arctic Circle and the North Pole. Ask them: How far is Eva's home from the Arctic Circle? From the North Pole? What is the climate like in that part of the world?

13. Ask the students: What U.S. state is nearest Eva's home? What is the approximate distance from Ungava Bay to your home? How far is it to the nearest major Canadian city? Which forms of transportation could be used to get there—ship, commercial airplane, truck, auto, railroad?

14. Eva's home lies about 60 degrees of latitude north of the equator. On a globe, have the students locate on the globe cities that are at approximately the same degree of latitude. Which one is in the United States?

15. This area is known as the tundra. The soil temperature is below freezing for most of that year. Have the students dig down about a foot near their homes or the school and measure the temperature of the soil. Ask them: How would this compare to the tundra? Can there be any agriculture near Eva's home?

16. Ask the children to observe the number of bodies of water, towns, and roads in the area of Ungava Bay. What does this tell them about life there: buying goods, getting food to eat, the cost of items, availability of modern conveniences, and so forth?

17. Eva went down to gather mussels shortly after the sun came up. By the time she was finished, the moon was out. Ask the students: What inferences can be drawn from this? Remember how far north they are. Can you figure out what time of year this is?

18. Ungava Bay empties into Hudson Strait and then into the Atlantic Ocean. This strait is frozen for half the year, and there are icebergs in it the remainder of the year. Ask the students: If you planned to sail into Ungava Bay, what information would you need to have?

19. The major part of an iceberg is below the surface of the water. This is very hazardous to ships. Have the students make their own icebergs by filling an 8 ounce plastic cup with water and letting it freeze solid. They should then run warm water over the outside of the cup to loosen it and put the block of ice into a deep bowl of water. How much of the "iceberg" can they see? Ocean water is salty. Have students repeat the iceberg activity but with the water in the bowl containing several spoonfuls of salt. Is the "iceberg" more or less visible than it was in the unsalted water?

20. Ocean depth is measured in fathoms instead of feet. A map of Ungava Bay shows depth readings ranging from 5 to 84 fathoms. Ask the students: What would this be in feet? How does this relate to the story? **Note:** A fathom equals six feet.

21. Eva's candles went out while she was under the ice because they were dropped and because they burned down. Candles also need air or oxygen to burn. Place identical burning candles in holders and cover them with clear glass containers that measure a specific volume: a pint, a quart, a half gallon, a gallon. Ask the students to predict how long each candle will burn and which will go out first. Time how long each candle burns and make a chart. Try the experiment again with candles of varying thickness but identical length. Do they all burn out at the same time? **Note:** Glass canning jars work well for this.

22. The Inuit homeland is known as the newly formed territory of Nunavat. A newspaper serving this community can be seen on the Internet at http://www.nunatsiaq.com. **Note:** Since this is an adult newspaper, teachers may wish to choose the articles that will be given to the children.

Related Books and References

Joosse, Barbara. *Mama Do You Love Me?* San Francisco: Chronicle Books, 1991.

Nanogak, Agnes. *More Tales from the Igloo.* Edmonton, Alberta: Hurtig Publishers, 1986.

National Geographic Atlas of the World. 7th ed. Washington, DC: National Geographic Society, 1999.

Chapter 22

ASTRONOMY AND OUTER SPACE

The Magic School Bus Lost in the Solar System
Joanna Cole
New York: Scholastic, 1990

Summary

Everyone in Ms. Frizzle's class was planning to go to the planetarium. Instead, they got to take a trip through the solar system.

Science and Content Related Concepts

Outer space, heavenly bodies, gravity

Content Related Words

Planetarium, moon, sun, planets, asteroids, orbits, craters

Activities

General

1. A visit to a planetarium or museum outer space display is an excellent way to introduce or wrap up the unit. If this cannot be done, obtain some of the excellent videos on outer space. **Note:** See the Web sites listed at the end of the section for more information.

2. Have students locate newspaper and magazine articles about discoveries or exploration in outer space, the U.S. space program, and celestial occurrences, such as eclipses, comets, or meteor showers. The library media specialist should have resources about this topic.

3. Keep track of technical words from this unit and use them to make a crossword puzzle. **Note:** Students may wish to refer to an astronomy book for names of other celestial bodies that do not appear in this book, such as comets, constellations, black holes, and satellites. These can be topics for individual research projects.

4. Have the students design a rocket or other means of transportation that could be used in outer space. Paper cups, plates, tubes, and the like make excellent construction materials.

5. In outer space, a person's weight would change according to the gravitational pull of the heavenly body. Have the students determine their weight on:

   a. the moon (one-fifth your Earth weight)

   b. the sun (30 times your Earth weight)

   c. Venus (three-fourths your Earth weight)

   d. Mars (one-third your Earth weight)

   e. Jupiter (two and one-half times your Earth weight)

6. Have students access information about the U.S. space program at http://www.nasa.gov.

7. Have students access the National Air and Space Museum Web site at http://www.nasm.edu.

The Moon

1. Have students use a detailed map of the moon as a guide to draw the face of the moon, complete with craters and seas. Ask them how place names were chosen?

2. Have the students observe the moon each night for one month and keep a log. Ask them to make sketches of how the moon looks, along with a brief written description. On some nights, they should observe the moon several times. Ask them: How does its relative size and color appear to change? Is it ever visible during the day? What time does the moon "rise"? Are there nights you cannot see the moon? Why?

3. Shine a flashlight or slide projector on a large ball. One side of the ball will be illuminated, like a full moon (see figure 22.1). As children move to the side of the ball, less of the light will be seen and the moon will appear to become a crescent. By moving from one side of the ball, across the front of it to the other side, it is possible to observe the phases of the moon. Discuss why this is so.

The Planets

1. Have the students make a solar system on a bulletin board display or use various sized spheres to make a free-hanging solar system across the room. They should arrange the planets in the proper order, starting with those closest to the sun. Commercially made planet mobiles are also available in educational supply stores or from mail order houses.

Fig. 22.1. Phases of the Moon Simulation

2. Have the children stand on the playground according to the distance of the planets from the sun. Let 1-inch equal 1 million miles. Mercury is 36 million miles from the sun, so that student would stand 36 inches from the sun. Other distances are:

Mars, 41 million miles

Venus, 62 million miles

Earth, 93 million miles

Jupiter, 482 million miles

Saturn, 856 million miles

Uranus, 1,721 million miles

Neptune, 2,656 million miles

Pluto, 3,660 million miles

Also, sequence the children by the size of the planet each represents.

3. Divide the class into eight groups, one for each planet except Earth. Have the children research facts about each planet, then invent a creature that could live there. A written and visual description should accompany the drawing.

4. "The Planets" by Gustav Holst is an exciting symphonic description of seven of the planets. Play it for the children and ask them to note how the composer differentiates between the planets. **Note:** Pluto had not been discovered when this piece was written and Earth was not included.

The Sun

1. Show a film or video of the sun. One source of videos is the National Geographic educational store, which can be accessed at http://ngsstore.nationalgeographic.com.

2. For students to observe the sun safely, have them make pinhole cameras (see figure 22.2). They can make a camera by cutting a piece 2 inches square from the end of a large box, taping aluminum foil over the opening, then making a small pinhole in the center of the foil. The students then should tape an index card inside the box, opposite the foil end. Outdoors, have them place their boxes over their heads with the pinhole towards the bright sun. Warn them not to look at the pinhole; they should carefully observe the image of the sun on the index card. They should see the colors of the sun and possibly even solar flares. Ask them to describe in writing and through visual arts what they have seen. **Note:** Under no conditions should anyone look directly at the sun. The pinhole camera allows the children to safely see a reflection of the sun and its activity.

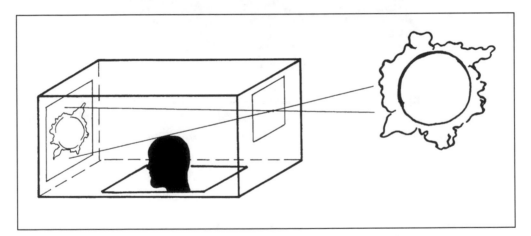

Fig. 22.2. Pinhole Camera

3. Solar flares shoot out from the edge of the sun. Have the children create their own flares using yellow and red finger paints or watercolors.

4. Make "sun tea." Place four tea bags and one quart of water in a clear, closed container. Place the bottle in the sun for several hours until the tea has brewed. Serve the tea over ice with lemon, if desired.

5. The sun is the source of energy for growth and life, but it can also cause harm. Have the students read the labels on various suntan lotions and sunscreen products in the drug store. Ask them what ingredients are most commonly found in these products. Each container should bear a number to indicate its protective qualities. Ask the students: What do these numbers represent? Which products should give the best protection?

Asteroids

1. Ask the students: How are asteroids formed? Where are they found? What keeps them in orbit? Do asteroids have names? What do their names represent?

2. Have the children design an asteroid using a potato that is painted and decorated. Suspend the potato from the ceiling along with the solar system.

3. "Avoid the Asteroid!" In the gymnasium or on the playground, have the children crouch down and pretend to be asteroids. They are allowed to move their bodies, but cannot actually walk around. Select several students to "navigate" from one end of the room to the other without being "hit" by an asteroid.

Related Books and References

Abbott, David, Holly Hultgen, Gail Olson, Melody Randall, and Randy Sachter. "Make Space for Space Science." *Science and Children* 33, no. 5 (February 1996): 20–22.

Cronin, Jim "Teaching Astronomy with Multicultural Mythology." *Science Scope* 20, no. 3 (November/December 1996): 15–17.

Edgett, Ken. "The Legend of Joe the Martian." *Science and Children* 35, no. 5 (February 1998): 14-17.

Hirst, Robin, and Sally Hirst. *My Place in Space.* New York: Orchard, 1988.

Holst Gustav. "The Planets." The Boston Symphony Orchestra, Seiji Ozawa, conducting.

Lebofsky, Nancy R., and Larry A. Lebofsky. "Celestial Storytelling." *Science Scope* 20, no. 3 (November/December 1996): 18–21.

Mann-Lewis, Melanie. "Playing with Planets." *Science and Children* 26, no. 5 (February 1989): 34–37.

National Geographic Atlas of the World. 7th ed. Washington, DC: National Geographic Society, 1999.

Newcott, William R. "The Hubble Telescope." *National Geographic* 191, no. 4 (April 1997): 2–17.

Ressmeyer, Roger H. "The Great Eclipse." *National Geographic* 181, no. 5 (May 1992): 30–51.

Smith, Bradford A. "New Eyes on the Universe." *National Geographic* 185, no. 1 (January 1994): 2–41.

Tomlinson, Gary, and Adela Beckman. "Count Your Lucky Stars." *Science and Children* 28, no. 5 (February 1991): 21–23.

Zim, Herbert, and Robert Baker. *Stars: A Guide to the Constellations, Sun, Moon, Planets and Other Features of the Heavens. A Golden Guide.* New York: Golden Press, 1956.

Part IV

Physical Science

Chapter 23

WEATHER AND SEASONS

The Big Snow
Berta Hader and Elmer Hader
New York: Simon & Schuster Books for Young Readers, 1967

Summary

Each of the animals prepared for the winter in its own way. But for those who chose to stay close to home, the big snow made it impossible to find food until they were helped by the old couple.

Science and Content Related Concepts

Weather, seasons of the year, preparation for winter, winter survival

Content Related Words

Migration, icicles, hibernate, animal tracks

Activities

1. Have the students list the animals in the book. Ask them: Will they migrate to the south, spend the winter sleeping, or adjust to the winter climate? How are animals protected from the harsh, winter environment?

2. Discuss how humans get ready for winter (for example, by buying winter jackets and putting on snow tires). **Note:** Many people who live in northern climates go south to live during the winter months. They are sometimes called "snow birds."

3. Set up a bird feeder for the winter months. Have the students consult books in the library media center to determine the type of food to be set out. Ask the students what animals they think will be attracted to this site? **Note:** The feeder should be maintained for the entire season because animals will become dependent on the feeder.

4. As the snow is falling, have the students catch snowflakes on pieces of dark construction paper and quickly observe them with a hand lens or magnifying glass, looking for the patterns that are formed. Have the children draw or cut out snowflakes from this observation. **Note:** Remind the children that snowflakes are six-sided.

5. After a snowfall, have the children walk around the school yard and find the places where the amount of snow is the greatest. Where is it the smallest? Make a chart indicating the locations and amounts of snow. Do they know what causes the variation in depth? Measure the same places in a few days. What do they think has happened to produce different measurements? Make a line graph using both sets of numbers and compare them.

6. Patterns of light and shadow will appear on the snowy school yard. Snow will melt faster in sunny places and more slowly in shadowy areas. Have the students map these areas of sun and shadow and use thermometers to check the actual temperature of the places. They should repeat the measurement at different times of the day. Ask the students: Do the shadows remain in the same place? What happens to the temperature?

7. The wind blows snow around the school yard and small snow dunes are formed. Ask the students how fences, walls, and other standing objects affect the formation of these dunes.

8. Icicles form at the edges of roofs when the sun turns snow to water. This water refreezes into icicles. Ask the children: Do icicles always form on the same side of the building? Are they uniform in appearance? **Note:** Icicles will form on the side of the building that receives the most sunlight.

9. A glassful of snow will melt inside the classroom, but the container will no longer be full. Place similar glasses of snow in various parts of the classroom, for example, next to the windows, near a heat source, or in a dark closet. Have the students check on these and tell you which container of snow melts first, which last, and why. Ask them what the melted snow has become and what happens if this liquid is heated in a tea kettle.

10. The drawing in figure 23.1 shows the tracks of three common animals. Have the children compare each animal's front paws to its hind prints. The smaller figures represent a short trail made by each animal. The position of the prints represents the way in which the animal moves. Ask the students: Which animal is fastest? Which is slowest? Have them compare the three sets of tracks and make hypotheses and observations about these animals. Also have them make prints of their own hands and feet. What do they think are the most distinguishing characteristics of human prints?

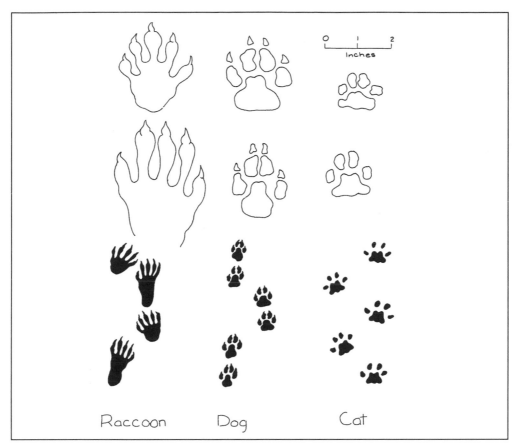

Fig. 23.1. Animal Tracks

11.   Make sets of tracks on index cards, one animal per card. Put the names of the animals on another set of cards. Have children try to match the animals to the tracks.

12.   Have the students use these identification cards as a guide to draw track variations, such as an animal hopping then running or one animal being pursued by another. Can others guess what event is occurring?

13.   Have the children draw a foot track on half a raw potato, then carefully cut away the excess potato until the track protrudes about ¼ inch. They then wipe the potato dry and ink the track. The stamp can be used for making stationery, wrapping paper, and the like. **Note:** Before starting this activity, children should be instructed in the safe use of a knife.

14.   Take a walk on a snowy day and have the children list words to describe the many characteristics of snow. Use these words to help write simple poetry such as a cinquain or "Five Liner" following these instructions:

Line 1: Write down a noun such as "snow."

Line 2: Write two adjectives that describe the noun.

Line 3: Write three verbs further describing what the noun does. Use a participle form (words ending in "ing" or "ed").

Line 4: Write a thought about the noun using a short phrase.

Line 5: Repeat line 1 or use a synonym for that word.

Icicle
Sharp, cold
Melting, dripping, growing
Clinging to the roof
Stalactite

Note: All words, except those in the phrase, should be separated by commas. With very young children, avoid grammatical terms and substitute "describing words" and "action words" to elicit a response. This can be done as a group activity until children are comfortable with the process.

15. Have children write or tape stories about an experience they have had in the snow. Work on good beginnings and endings, details, and proper sequencing of events. You might begin by reading from *On the Banks of Plum Creek* by Laura Ingalls Wilder, in which Pa becomes lost in the snow on the way home from town and survives by eating Christmas candy. **Note:** Children living in areas where there is no snow may use experiences with other types of storms.

16. Collect pictures of winter scenes from calendars, greeting cards, or magazines. Have the children write captions or poems to accompany them. Make a room or hall display of the work.

17. Have the children sing songs about snow. Children are probably familiar with several, such as "Winter Wonderland," "Let it Snow," and "Frosty the Snowman."

18. If a child were going to live in a snowy climate for the first time, he or she would need heavy clothing. What essential items would that include? Have the students look in a department store or sporting goods catalog to find styles and costs. Have them do some comparison shopping among items to ensure that the selection is practical and affordable. Have the children practice filling out the order forms.

19. Have the children solve these problems by reading the graph on snowfall in figure 23.2. (Answers are in the appendix.)

    a. Children could make lots of snow figures if they lived in these cities.

    b. It would probably be impossible to make a snow figure in this city.

    c. Which cities had more than 30 inches of snow in 1997?

    d. Was there more snow in Pittsburgh, Pennsylvania, or in Philadelphia, Pennsylvania?

    e. Alaska is the northernmost state in the United States. Does that mean that Fairbanks, Alaska, is the snowiest city?

    f. What else does this graph tell you about snowfall in 1997? The cities in figure 23.2 are: 1) Pittsburgh, Pennsylvania; 2) Fairbanks, Alaska; 3) Grand Rapids, Michigan; 4) Philadelphia, Pennsylvania; 5) Buffalo, New York; 6) Dallas, Texas.

Find other snowfall amounts in the *World Almanac* and have the children make up similar questions.

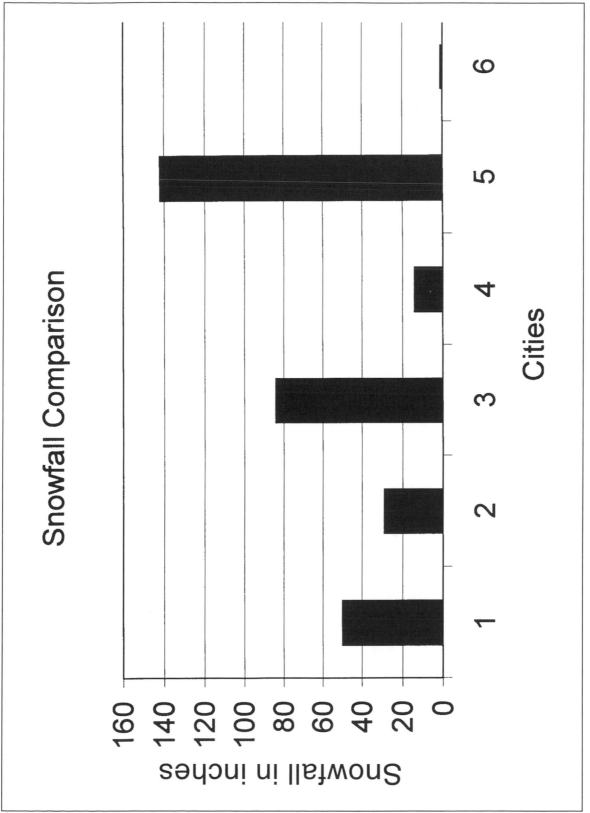

Fig. 23.2. Snowfall Comparison, Selected U.S. Cities, 1997

20.   Have the children learn more about weather and storms by accessing UM Weather's *USA Weather* page at http://cirrus.sprl.umich.edu/wxnet/states/states.html.

21.   *The Big Snow* ends with a reference to Groundhog Day. Have the children check the following Web site to find out about the "real" groundhog in Punxsutawney, Pennsylvania: http://www.groundhog.org.

Related Books and References

Burton, Virginia Lee. *Katy and the Big Snow.* Boston: Houghton Mifflin, 1943.

Graves, Larry R. "How Can We Save Frosty?" *Science Scope* 20, no. 4 (January 1997): 12–15.

Keats, Ezra Jack. *The Snowy Day.* New York: Viking Press, 1962.

Kroll, Steven. *It's Groundhog Day!* New York: Holiday House, 1987.

Murie, Olaus. *A Field Guide to Animal Tracks.* Boston: Houghton Mifflin, 1998.

Scarnati, James. "Tracks Revisited." *Science and Children* 30, no. 6 (March 1993): 23–25.

Wilder, Laura Ingalls. *On the Banks of Plum Creek.* New York: Harper & Row, 1971.

Woelfel, Kay D. "Make An Impression—Find Snowflakes Twins." *Science and Children* 29, no. 4 (January 1992): 26–27.

Chapter 24

THE EYE, VISION, AND OPTICS

Arthur's Eyes
Marc Brown
Boston: Little, Brown, 1979

Summary

Arthur just couldn't see very well, so his parents took him to the optometrist. Dr. Iris said that Arthur needed glasses but Arthur was not happy. Soon he found out that other people need to wear eyeglasses too, and that made him feel much better.

Science and Content Related Concepts

The eye, vision, corrective lenses, eye examinations, visually impaired

Content Related Words

Eye glasses, contact lenses, prescription, optician, optometrist, ophthalmologist

Activities

1. Have the students put a few drops of water on a sandwich bag or a small piece of plastic wrap, lay the plastic wrap on some printed material, and gently move the plastic wrap around. Ask them: What happens to the words? If the drops run together, is there a change?

2. Mix a packet of unflavored gelatin with ½ cup water. Put the mixture into two or three plastic sandwich bags and fasten them tightly. Let the gelatin congeal. As a demonstration for the class, place the bag on any printed material such as words in a book. The clear gelatin will change shape as the lens in the human eye does, and it will magnify the item underneath it. **Note:** Use one bag inside the other for added strength. Do not use fold-over sandwich bags.

3. Have the children look at a set of eyeglass lenses. Ask them to examine the thickness, the shape, and the color of the lens, then hold them 12 to 18 inches in front of them. If objects are magnified, the lens is convex, to correct farsightedness. If objects seem smaller, the lens is concave, to correct nearsightedness. Correction for astigmatism is evident if objects change shape when the lens is rotated.

4. Have a person who wears contact lenses explain how they are different from regular eye glasses: comfort level, care of lenses, cost advantages, disadvantages, and so forth. Ask the children if they know what the advantages or disadvantages of regular glass and plastic lenses are?

5. Have the students compare a plastic or paper eye model to a camera and its parts. Ask them: How are they similar? How are they different? Have the class take a few snapshots around the school and get them developed to post on the bulletin board.

6. Have the school nurse give vision exams to the students. Contact parents of any children who have problems and arrange a follow-up appointment.

7. Take a field trip to the optometrist, ophthalmologist, or optician, or visit the office and have an assistant show the students the equipment and facilities. Have the students write a language experience story about the visit. **Note:** Explain to the children the difference between these three caregivers.

8. Discuss good eye care and list examples of how to protect the eye, such as the use of protective gear in sports, playground safety, and avoidance of dangerous toys and pointed objects.

9. Have the students use magnifying glasses, magnification boxes, or Fresnel lenses to look at items around the classroom or outside the school. Insects, small plants, and soil can be especially interesting.

10. A grandparent or older person who has had cataracts removed might explain why the operation is necessary and how it is done. Children can make up interview questions before the visit.

11. Design an eye chart for younger children using little pictures or symbols to be identified as a means of indicating whether they can see at a distance.

12. Have the children sit through a class blindfolded. Also, have them try maneuvering around the classroom in this manner. Ask them to write about the experience. What problems did the children have? In what ways did they compensate for the lack of sight? How would this help them to assist a visually impaired classmate?

13. When light beams pass through bottles of water or a prism, the eye sees a rainbow. (Follow the example in figure 24.1 to create a rainbow in the classroom.) Ask the children: What are the colors of the rainbow or spectrum? How are rainbows produced in nature? What stories are associated with rainbows?

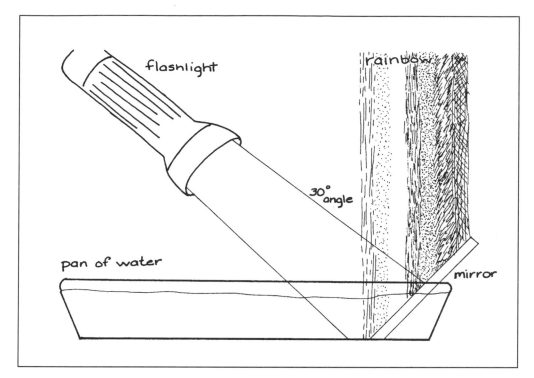

Fig. 24.1. A Rainbow or Spectrum Produced Indoors

14. After studying about rainbows, teach the children some rainbow songs, such as "Over the Rainbow" from *The Wizard of Oz* and "The Rainbow Connection" from *The Muppet Movie.*

15. Have the children write haiku poems about the sights of nature and the world. You may begin the lesson by reading poems that are intense in their visual imagery.

16. Use magazine photos from the library media center or home to make a display showing people wearing glasses. Ask the children: Why do people wear glasses? What image do these people give? Are there famous people who wear glasses? Who wears them around the school?

17. Make a mystery box. In the box, place an unknown item that will make a distinctive sound when the box is manipulated (for example, a pine cone or some rice). Let each child shake the box but not look into the bag. Record the guesses made about the identity of the object. Don't reveal the name of the object until all have had a chance to guess. A different version of this activity is to let children touch the object with their hands to help them identify it. In both cases, children are not allowed to see the object.

18. Have the students use the Internet to locate information about services for the visually impaired. They may find directories of services very helpful. What services and educational opportunities can they find for those who are visually impaired or blind (for example, special schools, guide dogs, talking books, or home-delivered meals)?

19. Have the children design eyeglass frames and cut them out of thin cardboard. The designs should vary and be humorous, intelligent, glamorous, and so forth.

20. Have the art teacher demonstrate ways of drawing pictures that have dimension. Or have the students make three-dimensional objects, such as cardboard castles from paper towel rolls, empty tissue boxes, or cereal cartons.

21. Make a cutout section about 8 inches square in paper grocery bags. Cover the opening with waxed paper or colored cellophane and secure it with masking tape (see figure 24.2). Place the bags over the students' heads to enable them to see how their perceptions of the world can be changed. **Note:** Do not allow students to put plastic bags near their faces.

22. Play tag or have a scavenger hunt while the children are wearing these paper bags. What problems do the children have? This activity also simulates the poor vision that many animals have and shows how difficult it is for them to find food. Ask the children to write language experience stories about the simulation.

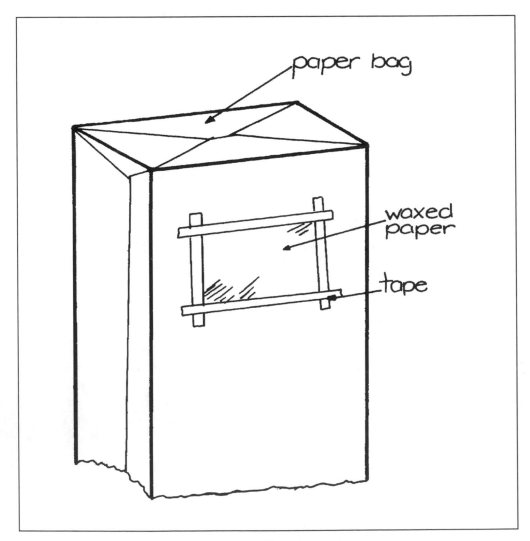

Fig. 24.2. A Sight Distortion Bag

23. The eye helps us estimate distances. Have the children each toss a cotton ball in front of them. Have the children estimate the distance from each child to the cotton ball, then measure the distance. Compare the estimate to the actual distance.

24. Recycling old eyeglasses is a project of the Lions Clubs service organizations of this country. Have the students use the Internet to request a free brochure on this activity from the Lions Club using the key words "Give the Gift of Sight North American Program."

Related Books and References

Cole, Joanna. *The Magic School Bus Explores the Senses.* New York: Scholastic, 1999.

Long, Michael E. "The Sense of Sight." *National Geographic* 182, no. 5 (November 1992): 3–41.

Chapter 25

SHADOWS AND LIGHT

Shadow
Blaise Cendrars, translated by Marcia Brown
New York: Macmillan, 1982 (Reprint: Aladdin, 1992)

Summary

This African folktale personifies the shadow as a creature of both day and night and good and evil. Shadow is a living being of great importance to the people in this tale.

Science and Content Related Concepts

Formation of shadows, shapes of shadows, light sources, movement

Content Related Words

Shadow, shaman, mute

Activities

1. Have the children make hand-shadow animals on a screen, using the slide projector as a source of light. How many different animals can they create? Do they move?

2. Place a large piece of light-colored paper on the wall and have each student stand between the light source and the paper for a profile drawing. Have the students cut out the light paper and use it as a pattern to duplicate the profile on a piece of black paper. They then mount the black profile on a backing sheet. Can students identify one another's silhouettes?

153

3. Discuss where and when shadows are found. What circumstances make it possible for a shadow to appear or disappear? Use a portable light source to make shadows around the room. Have the children define or explain "shadow."

4. Set up a sundial in the school yard on a clear, bright day. Fasten a pole to the ground in a spot where other objects will not cast a shadow on it. Indicate which direction is "north." Have a student mark the length of the shadow and the time of day with chalk every hour (see figure 25.1). Ask volunteers to continue doing this until the sun goes down. With the class, examine the lengths of the lines. Ask the students: When are shadows the shortest? The longest? How did people use this method to tell time? What are the disadvantages of this method? Will the shadows be the same at all times of the year? Are they the same in every part of the world? **Note:** On a hard-surfaced playground, stand the pole in a bucket of dirt or sand.

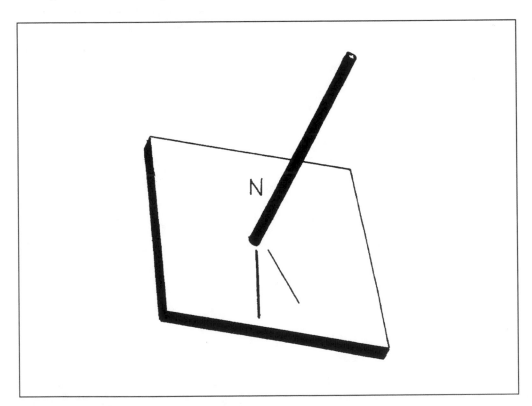

Fig. 25.1. A School Yard Sundial

5. The story of Shadow takes place in Africa. Have the students find this continent on the globe, then locate and research countries in Africa.

6. Ask the library media specialist to locate other books about Africa. Fiction books should include those by Muriel Feelings and Tom Feelings, Verna Aardema, and Leo Dillon and Diane Dillon. Nonfiction books should have a recent copyright date to ensure their timeliness.

7. Poets like Robert Louis Stevenson have written famous poems about shadows. Ask your library media specialist to help you locate other poems about shadows. Do those poems speak of the shadow in human terms as this book does? Do they contain scientific facts or concepts?

8. The shadow in this folktale is personified, or treated as if it were a person. Ask the students: Why is this so? Why was this story told by the shaman only on certain evenings? Are there times when we speak of objects in nature as if they had human qualities (for example, the man in the moon)?

9. Ask the students: What adjectives does the author use to describe the shadow? To what senses does he appeal? What mood does he set? Is this a common association with shadows?

10. Have the children write "shadow" poetry. This is a cinquain form.

   Line 1: Write a noun.

   Line 2: Write two adjectives describing the noun.

   Line 3: Write three participles (ending in "ed" or "ing") to attribute action to the noun.

   Line 4: Write a short phrase describing the topic.

   Line 5: Repeat the topic or use a synonym.

   Shadow
   Dark, scary
   Stretching, reaching, growing
   Playful and happy
   Silhouette

   Demonstrate this activity with a group before having individuals or pairs attempt it. Emphasize the role of the words and not their grammatical names (that is, "action word," not "verb").

11. This book is rich in action words that describe what the shadow does: prowls, spies, and so forth. Have the students find other verbs in the book and act them out or use them to tell stories.

12. Make a class booklet about shadows. Have each student contribute a sentence and an illustration about shadows, such as "Shadows are places to tell ghost stories." This could be accompanied by a picture of children around a campfire.

13. "The Shadow" was a famous crime fighter program during the golden age of radio. An episode of this program can be downloaded at http://www.shadowradio.org. Play an episode to the children and discuss with them why the main character was given this name. What tactics did he use in his fight against crime? How do the words and sound effects create a mood of suspense and mystery? **Note:** Downloading time is 30 minutes.

14. Have the children design and make a shadow mask like the ones worn in the story.

15. Have the children cut out two identical silhouettes of an object, one in black and one in any other color. Have them put the black one underneath but leave about $\frac{1}{2}$ inch showing on two sides. Notice the three-dimensional effect that is produced by this "shadow." Make a bulletin board scene using several cutouts. **Note:** The scene of the men going to war illustrates this.

16. Have the children make a shadow theater and figures (using the instructions below) to produce an original or adapted story. Invite others to a performance.

    Puppets: Cut black silhouette figures. These may have separate arms, legs, and head, joined to the body with brass fasteners. Attach the figures to soda straws or rulers.

    Theater: Cut a stage opening in the front of a box. Remove the back of the box and tape a piece of thin tissue or tracing paper over it. The opening on the front of the box remains uncovered. **Note:** Caution students on the use of scissors. The teacher may wish to cut the cardboard stages for the students.

    Production: One student sits behind the back of the box and shines a flashlight onto the tracing paper. Another student sits next to him or her and manipulates the puppets behind the screen. The audience will see a shadow effect in the stage opening. **Note:** The children should be lower than the table on which the box is placed so that their own shadows do not interfere with those of the puppets.

17. Invent some "shadow dancing" routines. Have two children, one behind the other, do identical parallel movements. The child in back, who is the shadow, might wear dark clothes to heighten the effect.

Related Books and References

Aardema, Verna. *Who's in Rabbit's House?* New York: Dial Books for Children, 1977.

Asch, Frank. *Bear Shadow.* New York: Scholastic, 1992.

Feelings, Muriel. *Moja Means One.* New York: Dial Books for Children, 1971.

Stevenson, Robert Louis, "My Shadow." In *A Child's Garden of Verses.* New York: Morrow Junior Books, 1998.

Chapter 26

SHAPES

The Secret Birthday Message
Eric Carle
New York: Harper & Row, 1986 (Reprint: Harper Collins, 1998)

Summary

A secret message sends Timmy hunting for distinctively shaped clues. At the end of the search he finds a very special birthday present.

Science and Content Related Concepts

Geometric shapes, diagrams, following directions

Content Related Words

Circle, square, rectangle, triangle, oval

Activities

1. Have the children make cards with a name of a shape on one card and the outline of that shape on the other card. Gather the cards from all the students and try to match the word cards with the drawing cards. Hang the matched cards together.

2. Have the children look at one wall of the classroom and name the various shapes that are seen (square storage compartments, a round clock, and so forth). Ask the students: Which shapes are most common? Are some superimposed on others, such as a round clock in a square frame? Are there some common shapes you don't find?

3. Traffic signs show a variety of shapes. Have the students name the shape and the message of the sign associated with it (see figure 26.1).

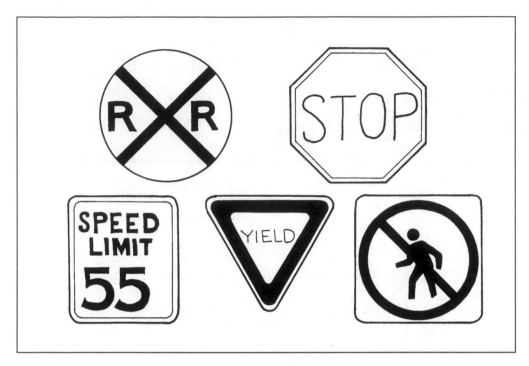

Fig. 26.1. Traffic Signs

4. Make a "Concentration" or "Memory" game. Prepare several pairs of cards that show common shapes or silhouettes. Mix them up, turn them face down, and allow a student to turn over two cards at a time. If the pair matches, the player may take them. If not, the cards are turned face down again and the next student tries to find a match. The student with the most pairs at the end wins.

5. Have the children use their bodies to form shapes. Have others guess what they are.

6. "Who Am I?" Have students describe the shapes of objects. Guess what the object is.

7. Place objects on the overhead and project their shapes onto a screen. Can students guess what they are? Use items such as a football, a carrot, and a pine cone. **Note:** Shield the sides of the projector so objects can't be seen except on the screen.

8. Blindfold some students and have them sit with their backs to the class. Hand them an object, such as a seashell. As they manipulate the item, ask them to them think of descriptive words. Record these on the board. Other class members must try to identify the article from the description.

9. Hide several large cutouts of common shapes around the room. Divide the class into small groups and give each a list of clues to help find their shape. Each group should have a floor plan of the room and mark where they find each clue. The pathway they followed can then be plotted as in the book.

10. Have the children write an adventure/mystery story using their choice of shapes as clues. Have other students try to solve the mystery. Make a booklet of the story. The shape of the cover and pages can be an outline of the main character, such as a bear, a child, or a ladybug.

11. What are the names of the shapes that make up a Tangram puzzle? (See figure 26.2.) Have the students use the pieces of a Tangram puzzle to form an object, then trace the item on construction paper, cut it out, and mount it. How do the pieces fit together to form a square?

Fig. 26.2. Tangram Puzzle

12. Have the students write a story about a specific shape or an item that represents a certain shape, such as a quarter. This can be a group story in which someone starts the adventure and passes it along for the next person to add on to it.

13. Have the children make leaf rubbings or preserve leaves between sheets of clear adhesive film or waxed paper and classify the leaves by their shapes.

14. Have the students make mosaic pictures by pasting squares of colored paper (about ½ to 1 inch in size) onto another sheet of construction paper or light cardboard. These can be done on both sides of a cutout to form mobiles or holiday hangings.

15. Modern art often contains geometric shapes as an important element. Have the students study some plates from an art book in the library media center. Ask them to identify some characteristics of modern art. Have them try to use these in a work of art. Projects can be drawn, painted, sculpted, or composed of pieces of paper cut into shapes. Tissue-paper shapes can be layered or partially superimposed on one another for exciting effects.

16. A hopscotch diagram is a series of geometric shapes (see figure 26.3). Ask the students to identify these. Can they make other arrangements or use different shapes to create their own hopscotch board?

17. Have the children put math problems on the hopscotch grid in place of the numbers; for example, number 12 can be 3 x 4 or 7 + 5.

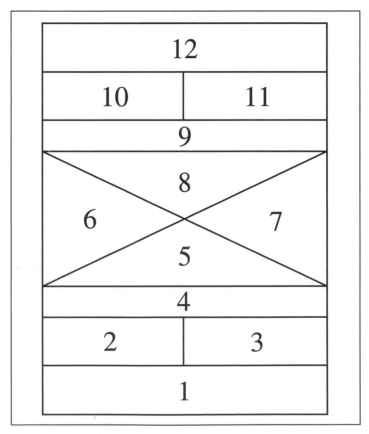

Fig. 26.3. Hopscotch Diagram

18.   Have the children study a street map of the town. How many different-shaped blocks are formed by the intersection of the streets?

Related Books and References

Driver's Instruction Manual. The manual from your state will include the major traffic signs used in this country.

Ehlert, Lois. *Color Farm.* New York: Lippincott Raven, 1990.

———. *Color Zoo.* New York: HarperCollins Juvenile Books, 1997.

Roucher, Nancy. "Experience an Abstract Mood." *Instructor* 97, no. 4 (November/December 1987): 70.

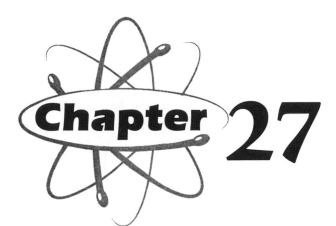

Chapter 27

MEASUREMENT

How Big Is a Foot?
Rolf Myller
New York: Atheneum, 1962 (Reprint: Turtleback, 1991)

Summary

Beds had not yet been invented, so the king decided to design one for the queen, since she had everything else. Counting paces as he walked around the queen, he estimated the bed's size to be 3-by-6-foot. Unfortunately, the finished product was much too small. The apprentice who made the bed had smaller feet than the king. A mold of the king's foot produced a standard of measurement that could be used to make a bed that was a "perfect size."

Science and Content Related Concepts

Measurement, arbitrary units of measure

Content Related Words

Mile, yard, foot, inch, kilometer, decimeter, meter, centimeter

Activities

1. When reading the book, stop after the apprentice goes to jail and see if the children can predict the ending. Write down the predictions to see how accurate they were.

2. Cut a soda straw to the length of each child's foot so that they have their own personal standard of measurement. Have the children estimate the size of common items such as a pencil, table top, and book. Measure the objects to see if they are accurate. Measure a variety of objects in the classroom, library media center, or cafeteria. Is there agreement between the children who are using their own personal soda straws as a unit of measurement?

3. Have each child lie on a large piece of paper and trace their outlines. Measure their sizes using their "soda straws." The paper cutouts can also be labeled with body part names.

4. Divide the children into teams and have each team decide on one of the soda straws as a standard measure of length. Have them find objects that are the same length as the soda straw. This works well in conjunction with a nature walk. **Note:** Soda straws can be cut into lengths representing fractions, as well.

5. Have the children make abstract art pictures in which all lines are the length of their soda straws.

6. Have the children estimate the size of an object using their index fingers as another unit of measurement. Ask them: Why does everyone have different answers? Is this unit of measurement practical?

7. Standard units of measure such as the inch, foot, yard, centimeter, and meter can be learned by estimating lengths of objects and then measuring them. Have the children work in pairs and see which pair has the greatest number of correct estimates.

8. Teach the history of the metric system. Use centimeters and meters as a unit of measure. Also teach that liquids are measured in liters; grams or kilograms are used for weight; temperature is measured in Celsius degrees. Compare the metric system to the English system that we use in the United States.

9. Have the children measure common distances in your school, using standard English measurement and the metric system. Begin with the size of a desk, the room measurements, and the distance to the cafeteria.

10. Ask the children how many different devices can be used to measure length. If there is an industrial arts/homemaking department in the school, ask them if you can borrow various measuring tools (for example, a protractor). Ask the children to find out what the specific purpose of each of these tools is.

11. Hang a measuring chart on the wall so students can see how tall they are now and speculate about how tall they will be in a few months. What height do students hope to reach? Have the children explain why they would like to be the height they chose; for example, to be tall enough to play basketball or to be able to ride on the roller coaster.

12. Borrow a metal measure from a shoe store and figure out the actual shoe size and width for each child. Do any of them have copies of their footprints in baby books? If so, how does it compare to this measurement? Ask the students what other implements can be used to measure people's sizes.

13. Track and field events are usually measured in the metric system. In the library media center, have the children check the *World Almanac* for the names of these events and the record times that have been set. Compare these figures to those of the children when they run these events.

14. Have the children measure their beds at home. Are they 3-by-6-foot? Have them measure other beds in the house. Are they smaller or larger than 3-by-6-foot?

15. Have the children make up stories about the invention of other units of measurement; for example, liquid measure equals how much the king drank in one day, distance is how far the king went on his daily stroll, time is the length of the king's dinner. Have them write these down as stories and illustrate them.

16. Have the students write a television or radio script of the story and act it out or make paper bag characters and have a puppet show.

17. Let the children walk barefoot in brightly colored water-based paint across a large roll of paper. Use the "footage" to make a large wall mural.

18. Make a scale drawing of the classroom and its contents using graph paper with 1-inch squares. Each square will equal 1 foot.

19. If the school has a mascot, ask for permission to paint big footprints of that animal on the sidewalks. Use different color paint to mark walkways from the exit door to the bus area, the playground, or fire drill safety spots. Ask the children how big they think the prints should be to be effective?

20. Have relay races to use systems of measurement; challenges may include hopping, jumping, skipping, three-legged races, and the like. This is particularly exciting if children put on dress-up clothes over their own clothes before running to the goal and back. The dress-up clothes are removed and passed to the next person in line. This adds a problem solving challenge to the physical feature of the race.

21. Have bean bag tosses. Have students estimate the length of the toss, then measure to see how close they were. Also, pick specific distances, such as 10 feet, and have them try to toss the bean bag that far. How accurate can the students be?

Related Books and References

Birch, David, and Devis Grebu. *The King's Chessboard.* New York: Puffin Books, 1993.

Briggs, Raymond. *Jim and the Beanstalk.* New York: Coward, McCann & Geoghegan, 1970 (Reprint: Paper Star Books, 1997).

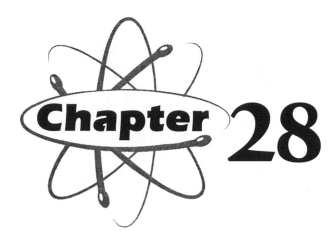

Chapter 28

ENERGY AND MOTION

Choo Choo: The Story of a Little Engine Who Ran Away
Virginia Lee Burton
Boston: Houghton Mifflin, 1937

Summary

Choo Choo, the little steam engine, was very tired of pulling a long line of passenger cars. One day she took off alone, over the hills, through the cities, and into the country, where she ran out of steam. Choo Choo was rescued by the Streamliner train and returned home, happy to be back with those who loved her.

Science and Content Related Concepts

Energy conservation (heat to mechanical), simple machines, force, momentum

Content Related Words

Speed, distance, inertia, momentum, freight, passengers

Activities

1. Choo Choo was tired of pulling heavy passenger cars. Simulate this task by having relay races. Have the children pull various weights in a wagon as they move, such as a dictionary, a cement block, a bag of sugar, or a brick. Slowly increase the weight. How does the increased weight affect the efficiency of the runner?

2. Tie a piece of rope onto a large piece of cardboard and have the children pull it up a grassy or snowy slope. Have them slide down the hill, then pull the cardboard up again with someone sitting on it. Is there a change? What happens when two children slide down together?

3. Use a wide board or other device to make an inclined plane. Have races with identical toy trucks that have been weighted with differing amounts of stones. Have the students predict the winners before the race. Use vehicles that are not the same shape or weight. What will happen? Add identical loads. Do the results change?

4. Ask the students: If you put a board in front of the moving vehicles, what happens to the vehicles and to the contents of the trucks?

5. Make two inclined planes that touch the floor opposite each other, about a yard apart. Have the students release a toy vehicle from each side and observe which reaches the floor first and which will bounce the farthest as they collide. Use toys that are not the same weight, size, or shape. Keep track of the results. Vary the angle of the ramp to see its effect. Do the results follow any pattern? (See figure 28.1.)

Fig. 28.1. Double Inclined Planes (Crashing Cars)

6. Set up two inclined planes or ramps to represent the open drawbridge that Choo Choo crossed. Have the students use wind-up cars to see if it is possible to jump the gap and land on the other side. What distance can the cars jump?

7. Have the students make a bulletin board poster or a mural showing a side view of Choo Choo. Ask them to label the simple machines that combine to make the engine; for example, the cow catcher is a wedge and the train rides on a series of wheels and axles. Other examples of compound machines in the book include the drawbridge, which is both a lever and an inclined plane, and the train derrick, which uses a pulley.

8. Bring in hand tools and non-electrical kitchen utensils to see which simple machines they exemplify and how they work. Have the children describe a tool in words well enough that someone can guess the tool by the description only.

9. Speed is measured in miles per hour (mph). Ask the children: What does this mean? Does an object need to move for a whole hour for its speed to be measured? Check how far a child can run in one minute. To get mph, multiply the distance by 60 (minutes in an hour) and divide by 5,280 (feet in a mile). Calculators will make this easier. **Note:** You may wish to measure only 15 seconds of running and multiply this by 4 to get the time in a minute.

10. Measure how far a child can walk, skip, hop, run, or jog, in 15 seconds. Put the results on bar graphs. You can use the actual distance instead of converting to mph this time. **Note:** Multiply the results by 4 to see how far a child can move in a full minute.

11. Objects usually start slowly, then go faster. This is called *acceleration.* To demonstrate this visually, poke a tiny hole in a paper cup and fill it with water. Walk along holding the cup to the side and observe the drops on the pavement. As the rate of walking increases, what happens to the distance between the drops? Vary the walking speed and see what happens.

12. Have the students make a "Speed Line" comparing the speed of various animals. They will use a large ball of twine that has been knotted every 10 or 12 inches. The distance between two knots represents 10 mph. Ask them to make cards showing the name and average speed of the following animals and attach them to the twine at the proper position.

Spider	1 mph
Chicken	9 mph
Squirrel	12 mph
Human	28 mph
Deer	30 mph
Greyhound	40 mph
Elk	45 mph
Lion	50 mph
Cheetah	70 mph

This information was taken from the *World Almanac and Book of Facts 1998* (Mahwah, NJ: World Almanac Books, 1997).

13. When water boils in an ordinary tea kettle, the attached whistle will produce noises. Ask the students: What makes this happen? How is this like Choo Choo's engine? What fuel is burned to power the train?

14. When water turns into steam it can produce motion. You can prove this by making popcorn. As the kernels are heated, the moisture inside the seed turns to steam, the heart of the seed gets bigger, and the shell bursts. To demonstrate the force of the popped kernels, spread a sheet on the floor and place a popcorn popper in the middle of it. Use about ¼ cup of kernels, but do not cover the popper. Have the students measure how far the popped corn travels.

15. When Choo Choo began to run out of steam (fuel) she did not stop immediately. Have the children imitate Choo Choo's last few minutes before stopping. Ask them to describe or pantomime other objects that run out of energy or fuel, such as a car or a music box. Ask the children what people mean when they "run out of steam."

16. Has anyone in the class ridden on a passenger or excursion train? Ask that student to describe what it was like.

17. Ask the students: Is there still a railroad going through your town? Is it a passenger train, a freight train, or both? Can you visit the station and observe trains arriving and departing? Is there an old station in the community that has been remodeled for new use?

18. To learn about American trains call Amtrak 1-800-USA RAIL for information and a time schedule. Students may also access the Amtrak Web site, http://www.amtrak.com.

19. Have the children visualize taking a train trip across the country. Consult the Amtrak time schedule to determine the departure time and city, arrival time and city, number of stops, and services available (meals, sleeping accommodations, and so forth). Ask the children what the advantages and disadvantages of train travel are compared to cars, buses, or airplanes. Create a comparison chart.

20. Ask the students: On this visualized trip, what states will be visited? How many miles does this total? If the train can average 60 miles an hour, how long is the trip? Have them make a list of items to take to help pass the time or increase the enjoyment of the journey, such as a camera, books, a tape recorder with headphones, or an atlas.

21. Have the children figure out the length of the journey for the following train trips. (Answers are in the appendix.)

> Lv New York City 9:50 A.M. Ar Montreal 7:28 P.M.
>
> Lv Washington, D.C. 5:30 A.M. Ar Philadelphia 7:35 A.M.
>
> Lv Chicago 7:20 P.M. Ar Pittsburgh 7:25 A.M.
>
> Lv Tampa 7:30 A.M. Ar Miami 5:00 P.M.
>
> Lv Chicago 8:00 P.M. Ar New Orleans 3:30 P.M.

> **Note:** Additional problems can be made using the Amtrak time schedule.

22. Have the students dramatize the story of *Choo Choo* and tape record it. Sound effects will be an important feature of the recording.

23. Compare the book *Choo Choo* to *The Little Engine That Could*. Both trains are portrayed as though they were human beings. Ask the students: What qualities or characteristics can be attributed to each of the trains? How are they different and alike?

24. Numerous books and songs have been written about the history of railroads and life on the railroads. Ask the library media specialist and music teacher to help locate some of these materials.

25. Try to find a retired railroad worker who would be willing to talk to the class about "the good old days" of the railroads.

26. Model or miniature train collecting is a popular hobby. The trains are very detailed and made to scale. Invite a collector to talk to the class, or attend a model railroad show.

Related Books and References

Crews, Donald. *Freight Train*. New York: Greenwillow, 1978.

Piper, Watty. *The Little Engine That Could*. New York: Dutton, 1998.

Siebert, Diane. *Train Song*. New York: Harper Trophy, 1993.

World Almanac and Book of Facts. Mahwah, NJ: World Almanac Books, 1997.

Chapter 29

BUOYANCY

Who Sank the Boat?
Pamela Allen
New York: Coward-McCann, 1982 (Reprint: Turtleback, 1996)

Summary

This rhyming fantasy tells the tale of a cow, a donkey, a sheep, a pig, and a mouse who attempt to go for a boat ride but end up in the water instead. The problem remains to find out who really sank the boat.

Science and Content Related Concepts

Buoyancy, balance, characteristics of matter (size and weight)

Content Related Words

Buoyancy, capsize, float, balance, bay

Activities

1. Have the students design and make an aluminum foil boat that will both float and carry a load of paper clips. How many paper clips does it take to sink each boat? Which shaped boat holds the most paper clips, and which holds the fewest? Children should record their observations using descriptive sentences, pictures, or charts. **Note:** Have them use a piece of foil 1-by-2-inch to make the boat. Small trays or plastic cartons will hold liquid to simulate the water in the bay.

2. Have the students repeat this experiment using small uniform-sized objects as boats. The individual serving-size containers that restaurants use for butter, jelly, and coffee cream are ideal for this purpose. Have children estimate how many paper clips will be needed to sink a container. Ask the children: Do the "boats" sink simultaneously if the same number of paper clips is added?

3. Have the children use coins (pennies, nickels, dimes, and quarters) to show how boats can be balanced to stay afloat. They should distribute the coins evenly in one small plastic cup but stack them to one side in another cup. Ask them: What is the result? How can the cup be balanced to stay afloat? **Note:** Have them use 6- or 8-ounce plastic cups for balancing the "boat."

4. Have the students use several sizes of coins to sink a small plastic cup. Ask them: Which order of placement allows the greatest number of objects to be placed in the boat?

5. Have the students estimate the size or volume of objects. The volume of sinkable objects such as marbles or pebbles can be measured by placing them in a glass container of water (see figure 29.1). The difference in the water level of the cup is the volume of the object. Specific measurements can be taken or general comparisons can be made.

Fig. 29.1. Displacement of Water Experiment

6. Select several items and have the children predict if they will sink or float in a dishpan of water (for example, a cork, a Styrofoam ball, a golf ball, a bottle cap, or a coin). Use different forms of the same material (for example, a block of wood, a Popsicle stick, and a pencil) and see if the result is the same. Chart the results.

7. Put an ice cube into a cup of water. What happens to it? Put another ice cube into a cup of water that has salt dissolved in it. Compare the results. Ask the students: What does this tell you about the ocean or bodies of water like the Great Salt Lake?

8. The body of water in the book is a bay. Ask the students: What is a bay? If your state has a coastline, locate the bays nearest you. If your state is inland, pick another section of the country to use for this activity.

9. The animals were not aware of boating safety rules. Have the children make up a list of rules to follow when boating or canoeing. If there is one, ask a local boating club to provide a set of regulations for comparison.

10. If a swimming pool is available, have the children practice capsizing a boat and learning to right it. Ask them what safety rules pertain when there has been a boating mishap (for example, don't leave the boat and try to swim to shore).

11. Life preservers (personal floatation devices, PFDs) should be worn in boats at all times. A catalog from the sporting goods store or a discount house will illustrate various kinds and sizes of PFDs. Ask the children to find out from the catalogs what sizes are available for children to wear and what sizes are for adults. Bring in life preservers and demonstrate how they are worn.

12. The children can learn about PFDs from the U.S. Coast Guard and Snoopy at the Office of Boating Safety at http://www.uscgboating.org/fedreq/page0711.htm. The available information covers federal regulations and safety tips about boating and PFDs.

13. Contact the American Red Cross for water safety rules to observe while swimming and boating. Discuss these rules. If there is a pool in your town where swimming lessons are given, encourage children to take them. Find out if the pool also gives lifesaving courses.

14. A dory is a small fishing boat that resembles Mr. Peffer's boat. Have the children make several dory models using the pattern in figure 29.2. Cut out the models and fold and tape them into boat shapes. Attach the dories to a stick or twig using thread or monofiliment nylon to make a mobile. **Note:** Two sticks wrapped together in the form of a cross can provide a more elaborate mobile.

15. Ask the children: What if Mr. Peffer kept a diary? Have them write an entry for the day of this fateful trip. What emotions do they think he had? Were they humorous? Was he angry?

16. Have the children write a sequel to this story telling what happens if Mr. Peffer decides to invite his friends for another ride. Ask them to illustrate the story.

17. "Row, Row, Row Your Boat" is a very well-known singing round. Ask the children to try putting new words with the melody to tell the story of the animals' boat trip. "Sailing, Sailing Over the Bounding Main" is another possible tune to use.

18. Cruises are popular vacation choices. Ask a travel agent for folders from several cruise lines. Show the children the cutaway diagram of the various decks on the ship. Ask them: What activities and services can be found on the ship? How would a boat like this suit Mr. Peffer and his friends?

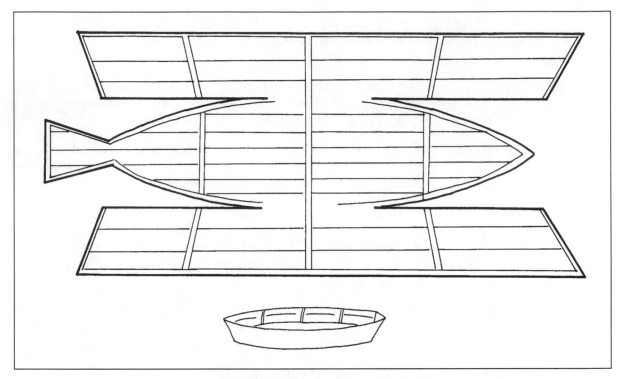

Fig. 29.2. Making a Dory Model

Related Books and References

Allen, Pamela. *Mr. Archimedes' Bath.* Sydney, Australia: Collins Publishers, 1980.

Burningham, John. *Mr. Gumpy's Outing.* Holt, Rinehart & Winston, 1970 (Reprint: Madison, WI: Turtleback® Books, 1990).

Wallace, John, and Janise Warner. "Words, Words, Words . . ." *Science and Children* 33, no. 5 (February 1996): 16–19.

Chapter 30

FORCE AND MOVEMENT

The Enormous Carrot
Vladimir Vagin
New York: Scholastic, 1998

Summary

Daisy and Floyd were amazed at the size of the carrot that they grew. But it was even more amazing when their friends came to harvest the vegetable.

Science and Content Related Concepts

Movement, push, pull, work

Content Related Words

Force, friction, momentum

Activities

1. Many items can become "stuck" where they are; that is, they cannot be moved. These include root vegetables like carrots as well as cars, wagons, sleds, and the tops of jars. Have the children discuss why this is so, and how it can be remedied.

2. Work is a push or a pull. Have the children predict the results of an experiment in which objects are pushed or pulled in a wagon; for example, will it be easier to move one child up a hill or two children on flat ground? One larger child or two small children? One tall child or one short child? For each set of children, push the wagon, then pull it. Which way requires less effort or work? What causes friction in this experiment? **Note:** Pulling the children in the wagon simulates pulling the carrot from the ground.

3. Put an object on an inclined plane and attach a rope to the object. Bring the rope over the top of the incline, attach a can or pail to it, and gradually add weights to the can (see figure 30.1). Ask the children how much weight it takes to move the object. Change the surface by covering it with waxed paper, foil, or sandpaper and compare the amount of weight needed. Attach objects of differing size to the rope and compare how many weights must be used to move it.

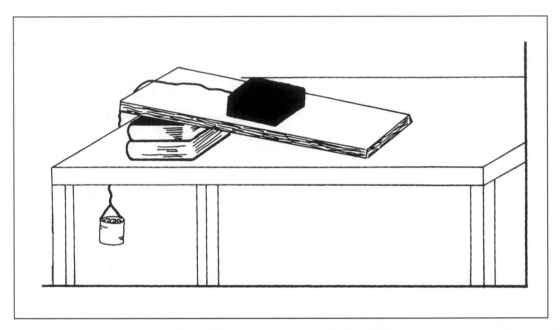

Fig. 30.1. Object Moving on an Inclined Plane

4. Ask the children to help rearrange the classroom desks and furniture. Ask them if it is easier to push the furniture, pull it, or have two people carry it?

5. Have the class cooperate in deciding how they could use the knowledge of simple machines to move a large number of books in the library media center.

6. Have tug-of-war contests. Try to make the teams evenly matched by weight. Ask the students to figure out how many children will equal one teacher. Do they think this is considered to be work? How do they think momentum affects the results? **Note:** The carrot is pulled because of the weight of the animals.

7. Ask the students: Why did the animals end up in the branches of the carrot? The answer is momentum. To simulate this simulation, place a golf ball in a small box. Slide the box slowly along the floor until it hits an object like a chair leg. The ball continues to move as the box stops.

8. The animals tried to use a lever to free the carrot. Have the children place a wooden ruler over a pencil (fulcrum), then put a stone or several washers on one end of the lever and lift the load. Have them experiment by placing the fulcrum in different positions. Ask them to determine when it is easiest to lift the weight. **Note:** Students may simulate pulling the carrot by trying to remove plastic tent pegs that have been pounded into the ground.

9.   This story is about a garden tended by the rabbits. Have the children discuss what is necessary to plant and maintain a garden (tools, seeds, and so forth). Sales flyers from garden centers are useful sources of information.

10.   Personification is a literary device that treats non-human things as if they possessed human qualities. Discuss the animals in the book and how they are depicted as human beings. Provide examples of other books in which animals are personified, such as *Berlioz the Bear* by Jan Brett. Do the children personify objects, such as stuffed animals?

11.   Ask the students why they think the author repeatedly uses the phrase "But the carrot stayed put. It wouldn't come out?" How is this effective in the story?

12.   Work is defined as physical or mental effort. Have the children write a sequel to *The Enormous Carrot* giving other examples of "work" being done.

13.   With the help of parent volunteers, organize a Carrot Feast. Carrots can be used as the main ingredient in cakes, cookies, bread, salads, and soups. Raw carrots can also be served with vegetable dip. Include other vegetables. **Note:** Have the children look up the nutritional value of carrots and other vegetables.

14.   To help prepare for the Carrot Feast, students may wish to access the Searchable Online Archive of Recipes (SOAR) at http://soar.berkeley.edu/recipes. Many carrot recipes are available there.

15.   Have the students place the top half-inch of a carrot in a dish with just enough water to cover the bottom of the vegetable. Make sure they keep the carrot wet. Foliage will grow from the carrot.

16.   A story similar to *The Enormous Carrot* is *A Coney Tale*. Have the class read this book and compare the two.

Related Books and References

Brett, Jan. *Berlioz the Bear.* New York: Putnam, 1991.

Burton, Virginia. Lee. *Choo Choo: The Story of the Little Engine Who Ran Away.* Boston: Houghton Mifflin, 1937.

———. *Mike Mulligan and His Steam Shovel.* Boston: Houghton Mifflin, 1939.

De Tagyos, Paul Ratz. *A Coney Tale.* New York: Clarion Books, 1992.

Chapter 31

CHEMICAL AND PHYSICAL CHANGE

Strega Nona's Magic Lessons
Tomie dePaola
New York: Harcourt Brace Jovanovich, 1982

Summary

Bambolona is tired of working for her father, the baker, and sets off to learn magic from Strega Nona. Big Anthony is hired to replace her, but he jealously tries to learn witchcraft, too. His efforts at both baking and magic meet with disastrous results.

Science and Content Related Concepts

Chemical change, physical change

Content Related Words

Yeast, dough, grazie, si signore, mamma mia, strega
Note: Chemical changes are usually indicated by the production of a gas, a new smell, the clouding of a solution, fire, or a change in color. In a physical change, the original object remains intact or can be retrieved, despite a change in appearance.

Activities

1. As a class demonstration, follow the directions on a yeast package mixing the yeast with water; watch the yeast "work." This activity is best done using a glass or clear plastic container so that the height of the yeast can be measured. Use variables to make comparisons:

dry yeast vs. cake yeast

yeast (either kind) with 1 tablespoon of sugar added

yeast (either kind) with 2 tablespoons of sugar added

yeast that is outdated

yeast that is outdated but has sugar added

Note: Have the children record observations and measurements in a notebook, using sketches and word descriptions. This should be done for all the experiments in this unit. Label the materials and equipment used and indicate the end result that is produced for each.

2.   Water used to dissolve yeast should be about 100 degrees Fahrenheit. Use cold water with one package and warm water with another. Ask the children to describe what happens and try to guess why?

3.   Let some of the yeast "work" in a glass container that can be stoppered. Put one end of a piece of plastic tubing through the stopper and put the other end into bromothymol blue solution (see figure 31.1). Show the class the difference in the solution. Use another container of bromothymol blue and have a student breathe into it through a straw. Compare the two. **Note:** The gas from the yeast and the student's breath both contain carbon dioxide. This causes the solution to turn yellow.

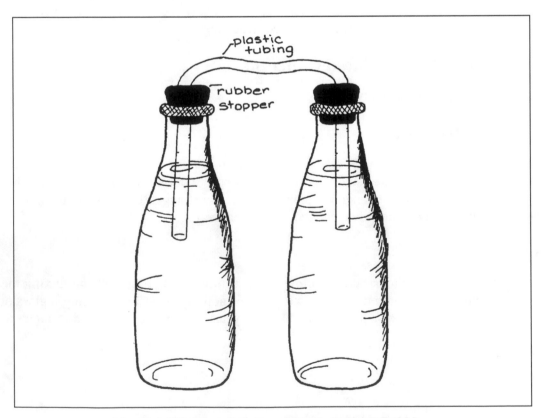

Fig. 31.1. Presence of Carbon Dioxide in Yeast Bubbles

4. Demonstrate that baking soda can produce a gas and make things rise. Take a large balloon that is easy to inflate and put 1 tablespoon of baking soda into it. Put 3 tablespoons of vinegar into a glass soda bottle. Slip the balloon opening over the bottle top and tap the soda down into the vinegar (see figure 31.2). Have the class observe what happens. Carbon dioxide is also being generated. Re-create the experiment, putting both yeast and sugar into the balloon and water into the soda bottle.

5. To demonstrate another chemical reaction, place several drops of vinegar on the copper bottom of an ordinary cooking pan. Sprinkle table salt onto the vinegar and wipe it around. Ask the students to describe what happens? Add more vinegar and salt as needed. **Note:** A very dilute acidic solution is formed chemically to clean the dirt from the copper.

6. In a well-ventilated room, clean the bottom of a copper pan or a piece of sterling silver with household ammonia. What do the students observe? Ask them to identify whether these are chemical or physical changes. **Note:** The ammonia unites with the copper or silver to clean off the oxide that had formed.

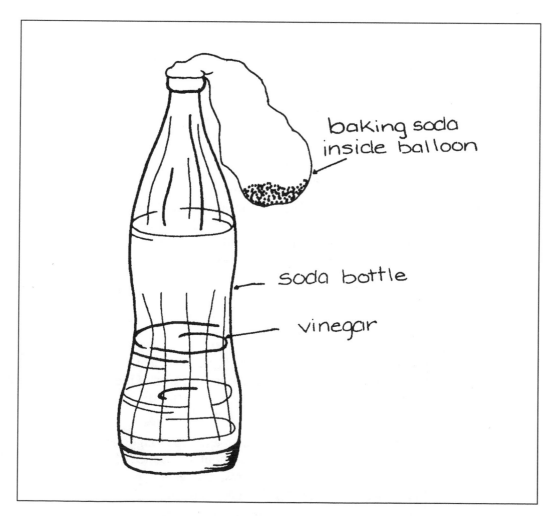

Fig. 31.2. Household Products Produce Gas to Inflate Balloon

7. Fire produces a chemical change. Strega Nona heated her potions to make them work. Light a candle and watch it burn. Ask the students which chemical changes they observe (for example, odor, smoke, color change, heat, charring of the wick).

8. Have the students find recipes for cakes and cookies in cookbooks in the library media center. They do not contain yeast but still rise. Which of the ingredients do the students think causes this to happen?

9. Objects can combine to look very different yet remain the same. Mix a spoon of salt and a spoon of pepper together. Ask the students to describe the result. Have the students run a comb through their hair or brush it against some wool, then hold the comb close to the mixture. Ask them to describe what happens. **Note:** The pepper will separate from the salt and adhere to the comb. The change is physical.

10. When Big Anthony disguised himself, it was only a physical change. In a physical change, an object can look very different but still have the same properties. Ask the children to consider, for example, a tray of water put into the freezer. Can they describe how it changes? Ask them what the result would be if the tray were left at room temperature.

11. Big Anthony tried to turn the iron pot into gold. For many centuries, people called alchemists attempted to produce gold from lesser metals. Have the children locate stories about alchemists and fairy tales or other legends about people who tried to turn ordinary items into gold in the library media center.

12. The story takes place in Calabria. Have the children locate this region on a map of Italy and look for books on this country in the library media center.

13. Perhaps Bambolona sang as she worked. Play some Italian folk songs or orchestral pieces. Many operas are Italian in origin.

14. Bambolona gets up to work before the sun rises. Ask the children: What time of day would this be where you live? Is it the same all year? When would Bambolona's shortest work days be if she works from dawn until dusk? When would be the longest? If she goes to work at 5 A.M., what time is that where you live?

15. Have a dress-up day and have the children try to fool everyone as Big Anthony did.

16. Visit a bakery or pizza parlor to see yeast dough being made. Have the children write a language experience story about the trip.

17. Ask the children how many different kinds of bread—wheat, rye, pumpernickel, and so forth— a supermarket sells? Have them compare the cost of the different breads by calculating the price per ounce. Also have them compare different types from the same bakery (for example, white bread vs. wheat bread).

18. Many breads contain preservatives to keep them fresh longer. Have the students compare breads with preservatives and those without. Put a slice of each in a closed plastic bag for several days. Ask the children to describe what happens. **Note:** The breads go through both physical and chemical changes. Explain.

19. Have the children design a wedding cake like the one Bambolona made. They may use drawing materials, colored construction paper, foil paper, and the like.

20. Have the children make Strega Nona dolls or hanging ornaments from dried apples, cornhusks, or bread dough. Books on doll making from the library media center can provide many helpful ideas. The dolls may be painted or decorated with scraps of cloth and felt.

21. Make bread dough for Strega Nona doll ornaments:

> ## Strega Nona Doll Ornaments Dough
>
> 4 cups flour   1 cup salt   1 ½ cups water
>
> Combine salt and flour in a large bowl. Add water and mix well by hand. Knead the mixture on a floured board until smooth and elastic. Break off balls and form into shapes. Moisten pieces to form dolls and place on a cookie sheet. Bake at 300 degrees F about 10 minutes or until lightly browned. Cool and dry completely before painting with tempera or acrylics. Spray varnish for a shiny finish. A paper clip can be molded onto the back of the head before baking so that a hook can be attached for hanging.

22. Have the children look up bread recipes on the Internet. How many different ones can they find for Italian bread?

Related Books and References

Consuegra, Gerard F., and Joan Hetherington. "A Change of Pace." *Science and Children* 28, no. 7 (April 1991): 13–15.

dePaola, Tomie. *Big Anthony: His Story.* New York: Putnam, 1998.

Sinal, Jean, and John Lennox. "Quick Bread: An Exercise in Microbiology." *Science Scope* 18, no. 3 (November/December 1994): 23–25.

Steig, William. *Solomon, the Rusty Nail.* New York: Farrar, Straus & Giroux, 1985.

Chapter 32

BALLOONS

The Big Balloon Race
Eleanor Coerr
New York: Harper & Row, 1981 (Reprint: Viking, 1987)

Summary

Carlotta the Great had just lifted off for a very important balloon race when she discovered her daughter, Ariel, was a stowaway. Despite the problems of extra weight, Carlotta won the race—with a little ingenious assistance from Ariel.

Science and Content Related Concepts

Balloons, buoyancy, lighter-than-air gases, heating and cooling of air, winds, directions

Content Related Words

Aeronaut (astronaut), hydrogen, cross wing, ballast, updraft, ripcord, toggles, altimeter, compass, valve

Activities

1. Using several regular round balloons, have the children blow up and tie half of the balloons. Have the remaining balloons filled with helium and tied shut. Ask the children to describe what happens when the balloons are released and guess why?

2. Attach a small cup to the string on each helium balloon and fill it with weights such as paper clips or coins until the balloons maintain a stable place in midair. Ask the students: How is it possible to have a race with the balloons. What variables are involved? Why will certain balloons win and not others?

3.   Simple methods can be used to tell wind direction. Tack a piece of ribbon or plastic sur-
     veyor's tape about a yard long on top of a pole stuck in the ground. Or, make a hanging
     windsock by cutting the leg off an old pair of pants. Secure an embroidery hoop around
     the larger opening. Hang the windsock so that it is free to move and catch the wind.

4.   Check the air currents around the school or classroom by making a pinwheel (see fig-
     ure 32.1) and seeing where it spins the fastest. Have the children use a stopwatch to de-
     termine how many times it spins in one minute. Ask them: Was the speed constant?
     What places have the strongest air currents?

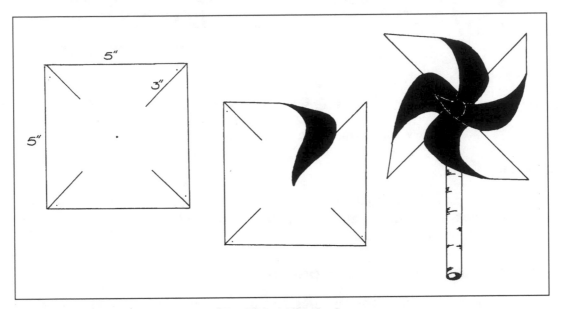

Fig. 32.1. A Pinwheel

5.   Ask the children to help determine whether warm or cool air rises? Have them measure
     the temperature of your classroom on the floor, at waist level, at the end of an out-
     stretched arm, and near the ceiling. Ask them to make a bar graph of the temperatures
     starting with the coolest (blue), and going in order to the highest (use green, yellow,
     then red). These color bands represent a thermograph used in infrared photography.
     They are also used on colored newspaper weather maps to show ranges of temperature.

6.   Teach the children to read a compass. Set the compass in an open space such as the
     playground and have them list the places they see at each of the major compass points.
     Have them identify in which directions are their homes, the sports field, the downtown
     business district, and the like. Compare their results to the compass rose on a map.

7.   Balloonists take trips of several days today. Have the students make a list of essential
     items to take. Ask them: What "luxury" items might be taken if there is room? In an
     emergency, what will be tossed overboard first? **Note:** The first round-the-world bal-
     loon trip constitutes the longest continuous journey to date.

8.   Pretend that a local television station is giving away balloon rides as part of an advertis-
     ing campaign. To win, your students must write an essay explaining why they want to
     take a balloon ride. There is a 150-word limit on the essay.

9. If possible, invite a guest to class to speak on ballooning. Have the children make a list of things they would like to know about balloons: size, material, cost, where purchased, and so forth.

10. Have the class make a life-sized outline of a modern balloon on the playground or gym floor. Mark the outline with chalk. Ask the students: How many steps is it from top to bottom and from side to side? How many people can fit into the basket for a trip?

11. Have the students use the library media center to find out how and why passenger pigeons were used at the time of the story. Ask them: Why did Carlotta take one on her flight? What would the modern day balloonist use instead of Harry?

12. Carlotta flew 2,000 feet above the earth. Ask the students: What portion of a mile is this? How high do modern balloons fly?

13. Play the type of music that may have been playing during the festivities at Carlotta's balloon launching. John Philip Sousa, "The March King," was composing band music at that time, while Stephen Foster was probably the best-known songwriter of the day. Ask the library media specialist for information on these famous composers and for tapes to play to your class.

14. Carlotta was a real person who lived from 1849 to 1932. Ask the students: How old was she at the time of the race? How many years ago did this event happen?

15. Ariel also became a famous balloonist. Ask the students: If you could write a book about her life, what title would you use? Have them design a book jacket for the book. This should include a summary of the work as well as an illustration.

16. Have the students look in a book of costumes from the library media center to see what people wore in the 1880s. Ask them to make sketches or paper dolls to show more details. Ask them how children were dressed and what hairstyles were popular.

17. The story takes place along the Mohawk River in New York State. Have the children locate this area on a map. Ask them: What mountains lie on either side of the river? Would this have an effect on ballooning?

18. Encourage the children to learn more about hot air balloon races by accessing the Web site for the Albuquerque International Balloon Fiesta at http://www.balloonfiesta.net.

19. For a short history of hot air ballooning, access http://www.balloonzone.com/index.html.

20. Ask each student to design and name his or her own balloon using construction paper, paints, or any other medium. These can be placed at various heights on a large mural to simulate the race.

21. A three-dimensional balloon can also be made from paper. Using scissors carefully, have the students cut out and assemble the basket and holder shown in figure 32.2 by pushing the tabs through the slots and taping them securely. They then need to blow up and tie the balloon and measure the distance from the basket rim, through the holder, around the top of the balloon, and back to the basket rim. Next they cut several pieces of string this length, soak them in dilute school glue, then wrap them over the balloon and them attach to the basket. After these dry the students can hang their creations.

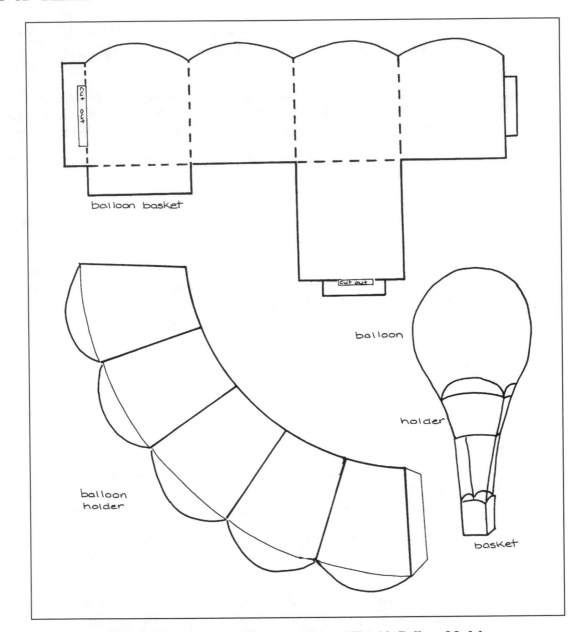

balloon basket

balloon

holder

balloon
holder

basket

Fig. 32.2. Pattern for a Three-dimensional Hot Air Balloon Model

22. Some schools have a parachute for use in physical education classes. Activities with the parachute will help children visualize some of the concepts of the book.

23. Celebrate the end of your project with a "balloon cake." Place two 8- or 9-inch cake layers about 6 inches apart on a foil-covered cardboard. Cut the bottom piece straight across the top, about two inches down, to form the top of the basket. Use colored frostings to make stripes or other designs, or use cake sprinkles and small candies to achieve the effect. Shoestring licorice forms the strings that hold the balloon to the basket. Enjoy!

Related Books and References

Brinks, Virgil L., and Robyn Brinks. "Taking the Hot Air Out of Balloons." *Science Scope* 17, no. 7 (April 1994): 22–24.

Calhoun, Mary. *Hot Air Henry.* New York: William Morrow, 1981 (Reprint: Turtleback, 1984).

Conniff, Richard. "Racing with the Wind." *National Geographic* 192, no. 3 (September 1997): 52–68.

Hillerman, Tony. "A Ballooning Interest: Albuquerque's Hot-Air Festival." *National Geographic Traveler* 2, no. 2 (Summer 1985): 142–149.

Lamorisse, Albert. *The Red Balloon.* New York: Doubleday, 1956 (Reprint: Turtleback, 1978).

Martirano, Michael J. "My Beautiful Balloons." *Science Scope* 17, no. 7 (April 1994): 16–20.

Chapter 33

AIRPLANES

The Glorious Flight
Alice Provensen and Martin Provensen
New York: Viking Penguin, 1983

Summary

Louis Bleriot was a successful inventor for the automobile industry, but the desire to fly became the driving force in his life. Despite numerous setbacks, he continued perfecting an aircraft until he became the first man to fly across the English Channel.

Science and Content Related Concepts

History of airplane flight, lighter-than-air craft, heavier-than-air craft

Content Related Words

Airship, glider, aeronaut, motor, propeller, flying machine

Activities

1. Have some students each assume the role of one of the members of the Bleriot family and write a short article for a popular magazine of the time answering one of the following questions: Father, why do you want to fly so badly? Mother, do you approve of your husband's flying or do you feel it is too dangerous? Children, how do you feel when your friends tease you about your father and his inventions?

2. Have the students locate, on a map of Europe, Cambrai, France; Dover, England; and the English Channel. Ask them: Over what body of water did Bleriot fly? In which direction did he go? The advertisement indicated "no intermediate landings." Was this possible?

3. The prize money for crossing the channel was a thousand pounds. Ask the students: How much does this equal in U.S. money today? Would money be worth more or less in 1909?

4. Ask the students: How many years ago did Bleriot start his project? How long did he work on his experimental aircraft before this flight?

5. Bleriot left France at 4:35 A.M. Ask the students: What time did he land in England? How long was the total flight? Why did the flight have to occur between sunrise and sunset?

6. Have the children write a newspaper story announcing Bleriot's achievement. Remind them to be sure the headline will grab people's attention and to include the most important details that answer the questions who? what? when? where? why? and how? Ask them how they think an English paper would report the event, or how a French newspaper would tell of the same happening?

7. Organize a paper airplane flying contest. Students can make their entries using the pattern in figure 33.1. Each participant should complete an entry form to indicate the category of entry of the plane. The class should decide the categories for judging, such as time aloft, distance covered, acrobatic display, and aesthetic design. Ask them to decide the following: Must all planes stay in the air a specific amount of time? Will there be a single try or perhaps two out of three tries? Will there be a production code (that is, no glue or tape allowed, no weights attached)? Who will be allowed to enter: students? teachers? parents? classmates from other rooms? Select judges to measure distance, time flights, and evaluate creativity of the planes.

8. Class members should be responsible for choosing the prizes that will be awarded in each category. These may be simple silhouettes of airplanes cut from colored paper, ribbons, certificates, and so forth. Computer-generated certificates are also appropriate.

9. Aviation information and materials can be acquired from the National Air and Space Museum shop at http://www.nasm.edu, or have the students try the following Web site especially for children: http://www.yellowairplane.com.

10. Have the children make a display of airplanes and rockets from various eras. These could be magazine photos or models. They should be sequenced from the oldest to present-day aircraft.

11. Have the children do research on women aviators such as Amelia Earhart and Sally Ride in the library media center.

12. Pilots must be knowledgeable about wind currents. Have the children locate information about these in an encyclopedia or other reference book. Have them locate the major wind currents of the world on a large map. Ask them: How do they affect aviation? How would Bleriot have been affected?

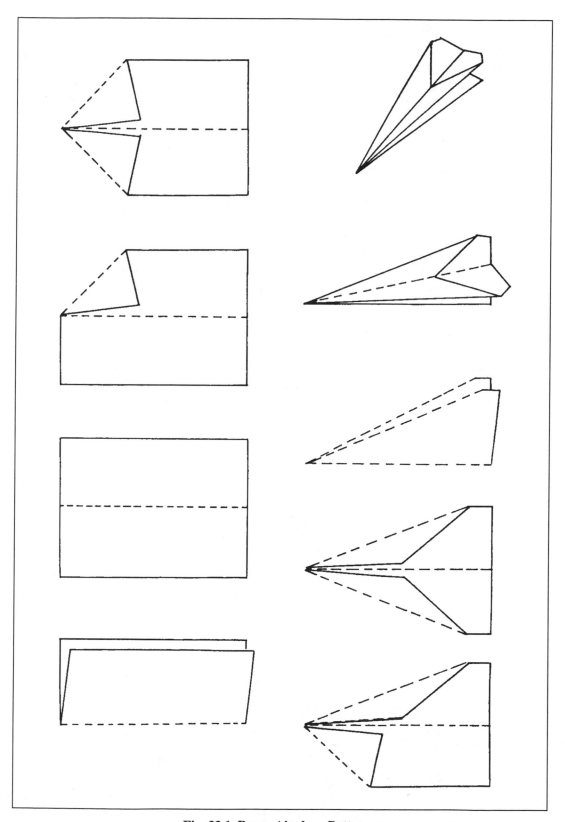

Fig. 33.1. Paper Airplane Pattern

13.   Airplanes fly because a vacuum is created against the wing. Demonstrate this with a piece of paper: 1) Hold a strip of writing paper (2-by-6-inch) between your fingers and blow against it. Ask the children to describe what happens to the paper. 2) Hold a sheet of writing paper against the palm of your hand, which should be parallel to the floor. Blow against the paper and ask the children to observe in what direction it goes. 3) Put a thumbtack in the center of a playing card and hold it beneath the hole in a thread spool (see figure 33.2). Blow into the hole at the top of the spool and let go of the playing card. Ask the children to describe what happens when you stop blowing into the spool. **Note:** These are examples of Bernoulli's principle.

14.   To demonstrate which objects move easiest in the wind, slide several 1-inch lengths of soda straw onto a length of heavy twine. Tie the twine between two stable objects. Attach several different items (paper clip, paper plate, plant leaf) to each length of the soda straw, using masking tape. Let the items "fly" along the string one at a time and point out to the students how they move and which ones move the fastest. **Note:** This can be done inside with a small fan to provide the wind.

15.   Have the students make and fly wooden gliders (see figure 33.3). Materials needed for one glider are one sheet of balsa or ash wood ($\frac{1}{32}$-by-3-by-24-inch) one piece of wood ($\frac{1}{4}$-by-16-inch), 12 to 15 inches of thin wire, sharp cutting implements, a ruler, and wood glue. The students may wish to experiment with different wing shapes and sizes to increase distance covered, time aloft, and so forth. **Note:** "Safety first" must be followed when young children are using cutting instruments of any kind.

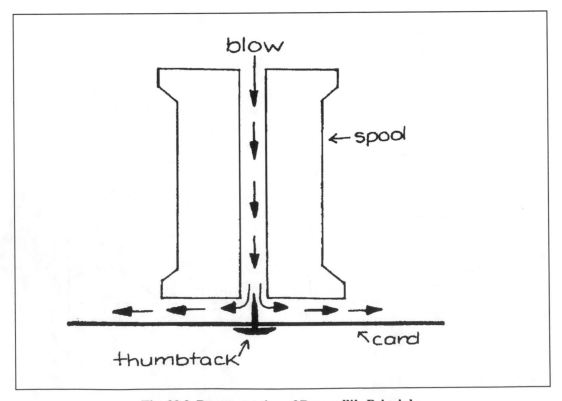

Fig. 33.2. Demonstration of Bernoulli's Principle

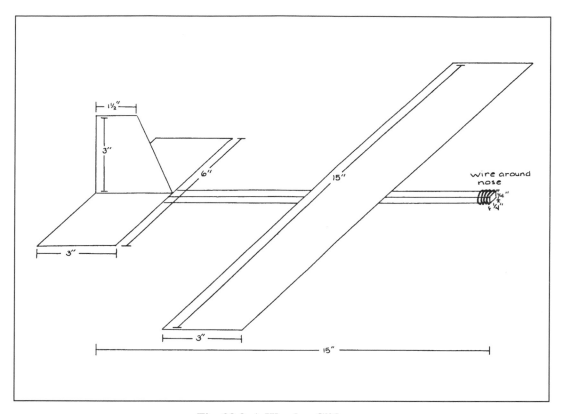

Fig. 33.3. A Wooden Glider

Related Books and References

Cole, Joanna. *The Magic School Bus Taking Flight.* New York: Scholastic, 1997.

Crews, Donald. *Flying.* New York: William Morrow, 1986.

Jackson, Paul. *Championship Paper Airplanes.* New York: Scholastic, 1999.

Kepler, Lynne. "We're Flying Now." *Science and Children* 31, no. 5 (February 1994): 44.

Morell, Virginia. "Amelia Earhart." *National Geographic* 193, no. 1 (January 1998): 112–135

Siebert, Diane. *Plane Song.* New York: HarperCollins, 1993.

Simon, Seymour. *The Paper Airplane Book.* New York: Turtleback, 1976.

Tamarkin, Cali, and Barbara Bourne. "Soaring with Science." *Science and Children* 33, no. 2 (October 1995): 20–23.

Uslabar, Ken. "Pioneers of Aviation." *Science Scope* 15, no. 5 (February 1992): 26.

Appendix

Answer Keys

Chapter 11—*Reptiles*

True/False Answers

a. All snakes are slimy..False
b. All snakes shed their skin by rubbing against rough surfaces..............True
c. All snakes live in trees, on the earth or in water. ....True
d. All snakes are helpful to the environment because they eat insects......True
e. All snakes swallow their food whole..True
f. All snakes are poisonous. ....False
g. All snakes are hatched from eggs. ....False
h. All snakes bask in the sun to absorb energy. ....True

Chapter 21—*Mussels and Arctic Life*

Mussel Word Ladder Answer Key

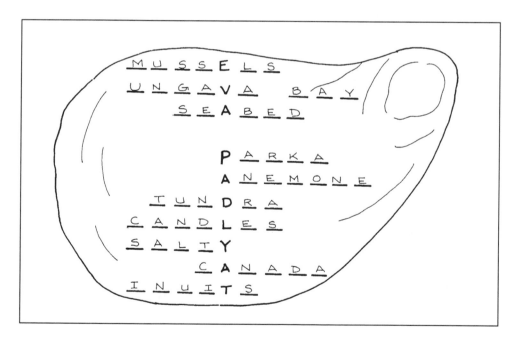

Chapter 23—*Weather and Seasons*

Snowfall Comparison Answers

(a) Children could make lots of snow figures if they lived in these cities.

Buffalo, Grand Rapids, and Pittsburgh

(b) It would probably be impossible to make a snow person in this city.

Dallas

(c) Which cities had more than 30 inches of snow in 1997?

Pittsburgh, Grand Rapids, and Buffalo

(d) Was there more snow in Pittsburgh, Pennsylvania or in Philadelphia, Pennsylvania?

Pittsburgh

(e) Alaska is the northernmost state in the United States. Does that mean that Fairbanks, Alaska, is the snowiest city?

No

(f) What else does this graph tell you about snowfall in 1997?

(Answers will vary.)

Chapter 28—*Energy and Motion*

Lv New York City 9:50 A.M. Ar Montreal 7:28 P.M

2 hours, 10 minutes

Lv Washington, D.C. 5:30 A.M. Ar Philadelphia 7:35A.M.

2 hours, 5 minutes

Lv Chicago 7:20 P.M. Ar Pittsburgh 7:25 A.M.

11 hours, 5 minutes (time zone change)

Lv Tampa 7:30 A.M. Ar Miami 5:00 P.M.

9 hours, 30 minutes

Lv Chicago 8:00 P.M. Ar New Orleans 3:30 P.M.

19 hours, 30 minutes

Index

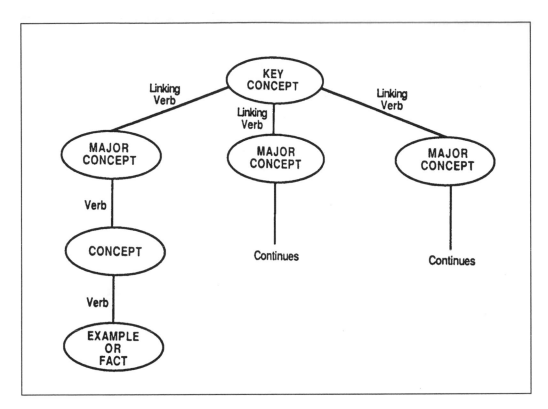

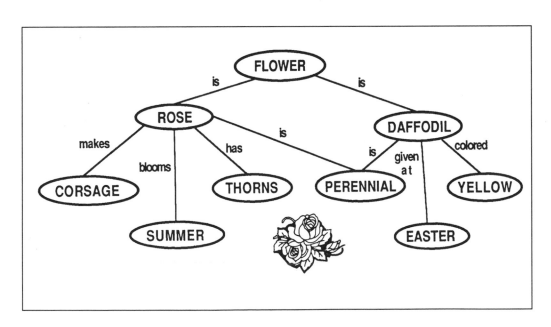

3. turn paper over   fold point C up

5. fold flap E up. Turn the figure over and do the same on the other side.

7. swing fold the other way. Straighten point out,

8. open figure slightly. push point up

9. cut on fold

10. fold tail down

Fig. 9.3. An Origami Whale

Fold over 2-inch edge of tissue paper sheet and insert 24-inch string in fold.

Fold sheet of tissue paper lengthwise.

Cut a fish shape on the open side, then glue this edge.

When dry, tighten string and tie it, forming mouth of fish. Tie string to stick.

Index